# *The*
# MISTRESS
# *of* ABHA

## WILLIAM NEWTON

### BLOOMSBURY
LONDON · BERLIN · NEW YORK · SYDNEY

BY THE SAME AUTHOR

*The Two Pound Tram*

First published in Great Britain 2010
This paperback edition published 2011

Copyright © 2010 by William Newton

Map illustration by Michael Taylor (www.equinoxpartners.co.uk)

The moral right of the author has been asserted

Bloomsbury Publishing, London, Berlin, New York and Sydney

36 Soho Square, London W1D 3QY

A CIP catalogue record for this book is available from the British Library

ISBN 978 0 7475 0980 8
10 9 8 7 6 5 4 3 2 1

Typeset by Hewer Text UK Ltd, Edinburgh
Printed in Great Britain by Clays Ltd, St Ives plc

MIX
Paper from
responsible sources
FSC
www.fsc.org  FSC® C018072

www.bloomsbury.com/williamnewton

*To Mary, my wife*

Ferdhan bin Murzuk,
slave dealer of Khurma

Mohammed ibn Ali (Mohammed the Black),
ruler of the Idrisi

Etza,
originally from Abyssinia, slave to Na'ema

Na'ema,
daughter of Red Sea sheikh, enslaved and sold at Abha

Ranya,
Na'ema's companion in slavery

Ayesha,
Tabarhla's first wife

Abdullah,
son of Tabarhla and Ayesha

Nura,
Tabarhla's third wife, Idrisi

Zahl,
Na'ema's son

Bandar,
Nura's son

Hassan ibn Aidh,
senior member of the ibn Aidh family

Faisal,
son of Abdulaziz ibn Saud

Suleiman bin Kabit,
Sheikh of Khamis Mishait

Mubarrak,
Saudi soldier assigned to Ullobi

Abu Hamesh,
leader of the Naha

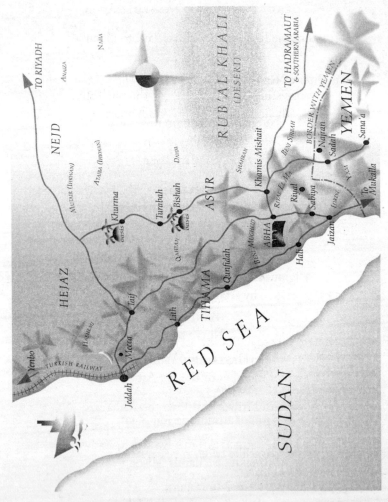

Tribal Arabia

GROUPS AND TRIBES IN THE NOVEL

THE AHL YAZID
the ruling class of Abha,
consisting of three families: the bin Tahir,
the ibn Aidh and the bin Mufarrih

BENI MUGHE'ID
the tribe of Abha

WAHHABI
Muslim sect, here more or
less synonymous with the Saudis themselves

IKHWAN
religious military group, originally founded
by Abdulaziz ibn Saud

HASHEMI
tribe of Hussein, Sheriff of Mecca, the leader of the
Arab cause in the Desert War against the Turks

IDRISI, RIYAL EL MA
powerful tribes hostile to the Ahl Yazid

SA'ER
warlike tribe, greatly feared

NAHA
tribe of nomadic outcasts

BENI ZEIDIN, BENI SHI'BAH, SHARAN, UM BINA
tribes in the neighbourhood of Abha

# Chapter 1

SIR HUGH AND Lady Parthenope Willoughby were my grand-parents. Like two great ships that had sailed the seven seas, they had come home to berth at the place where Sir Hugh had been born like Willoughbys before him, which was at Crowmarsh Battle, near the village of Benson in Oxfordshire.

For Sir Hugh it was his just reward, for as a military man he had had a distinguished career. For the most part this had been spent on the north-west frontier of India in the long endeavour to control the tribes that had risen in the aftermath of the disastrous Afghan wars earlier in the century, and supporting him in this mission was Lady Parthenope, who, in spite of all the hardships, was ever present at his side.

But India was not Sir Hugh's principal claim to fame. This came later. I find him in photographs of the time in the uniform of the Grenadier Guards, or at least wearing the insignia of that regiment. They show him in the desert, wearing khaki drill and a sun helmet. They were taken at the Battle of Omdurman or at its aftermath, in which he was clearly much involved. A substantial figure he is, in shirt, shorts, long socks and the helmet that I have mentioned, and at this moment he is supervising the unloading of a train that has brought to Cairo the British and Egyptian casualties follow-ing that great victory; it can be seen that he goes about his duties with a natural grenadier's discipline that the old pictures instantly reveal. The British casualties are mainly walking wounded, and we know that 648 others remained behind in the sand of the Sudan, hence not able to make an appearance here. It could be added that had Sir Hugh been unloading the casualties of the Mahdi, which was the other side, he would have been submerged by a mountain.

Lady Parthenope, who had been a lady long before Sir Hugh became a knight, does not appear in these photographs, and she could not have been in Egypt at the time they were taken, active though she had been throughout Sir Hugh's career. The unsurprising fact is that by then she had already retired to Crowmarsh Battle, where she was making ready the family home, not just for Sir Hugh's return, but for the festivities that were about to take place to mark the occasion of a coronation, that is, the coronation of King Edward the Seventh and his Queen, Alexandra of Denmark. This was and would long remain the most memorable event in the history of Benson, which was decked out with so much bunting and flags as could not be remembered, except at the relief of the siege of Mafeking two years before.

Seventy-six kings and queens, princes and princesses of Europe and beyond came to England to take part in the proceedings, which was twice as many as had ever attended a coronation before. On the day of the coronation they paraded in a great procession; the queens and princesses in marvellous costumes and coronets bowed to a delighted populace from their carriages whilst the royal menfolk, who could not be thus accommodated, followed on horseback or on foot. They wore uniforms of many imaginative kinds, some with polished helmets bearing huge silver birds of prey perched on top and their swords so long that the scabbards nearly touched the ground, not always worn as decorously as could be wished.

After the coronation service in Westminster Abbey had ended, all made their way to Buckingham Palace, passing through Horse Guards Parade and into the Mall, where a mighty throng assembled to cheer and witness the event.

Meanwhile, celebrations of the momentous event took place in towns all over the country and at Benson the local militia drawn from the Oxfordshire Light Infantry paraded in all its regalia. As there happened to be family connection with that regiment, naturally it was Sir Hugh, in the dress uniform of the Grenadiers, who took the salute. Lady Parthenope stood beside him, her heart swelling with pride.

The national festivities were duly recorded in a special coronation edition of the *Illustrated London News* dated 26 June 1902, and for many people, and especially the ladies of Benson, the *London Illustrated* as it was usually known was very nearly as good as witnessing the ceremony itself.

*

The Willoughbys had five children of whom only one was a son, and he was given the name of Robert de Vere Willoughby. Surrounded by a large number of family members of the opposite sex, Robert had in growing up almost everything that he could have wished. He was blessed with good looks and had the distinctive forehead of the Willoughbys together with their blue eyes and dark hair. These traits were visible in the family portraits, for generation after generation. Robert had them all; and like so many of his forebears it seemed certain that he was intended for a military career.

The martial history of the Willoughbys extended far back in history. There were Willoughbys who had fought on the Yorkist side in the Wars of the Roses, and a century before that there was a certain Godolphin Willoughby de Vere, for so the Willoughbys were then styled, who had been no less than the Hereditary Standard Bearer of England in the battles fought by the Black Prince in France. Against the odds he had survived those encounters and afterwards received from a grateful Edward III the manor and hundreds of the Cromarty Marches in the county of Oxfordshire, which of course he was expected to defend. Thereafter he obtained a licence to fortify and he built himself a suitable manor, which the Willoughbys had occupied ever since. Several hundred years after Godolphin a battle was fought in these Marches, this time between the Royalists in the cause of

King Charles and the Parliamentarians. At this battle there were naturally Willoughbys, some fighting for the king and others for Parliament. After this the Cromarty Marches, which had in the meantime become Crowmarsh, was known as Crowmarsh Battle.

But this is ancient history. At the time of which I speak Robert Willoughby had grown of age and become a soldier in turn, and he had also reached the point where he was expected to make a suitably dynastic marriage and beget more Willougbys. Robert was, if somewhat vaguely, aware of this responsibility, although not as aware as were the rest of his family and indeed all the neighbourhood. Actually, he was quite content with bachelorhood, and he regarded the countryside surrounding Benson as his fief, with the result that there must have been few maidens between Berrick Salome and Roke who had not at some time succumbed to a passing affair with the dashing lieutenant, and some bore the evidence to prove it. Robert was assisted in his conquests by having an open sports car, a Lagonda, which he drove about the countryside in such a fleet fashion that it might easily have occasioned more trouble than it actually did. It so happened that Robert knew all about cars and had a natural flare as a mechanic, so that when the Lagonda broke down, as it did in an entirely dependable way, Robert was able to fix it there and then. It is certainly the case that an association with Robert and his Lagonda made each of these maidens the talk of her rivals, and not only her rivals but also the generality of the ladies of Benson, who held views of their own concerning Robert and matrimony which they were never in the least backward in expressing.

These ladies hung together very much as a team, as they were all members of the congregation of Benson church. This was composed, in the first place, of the three families of gentry: the Willoughbys of Crowmarsh, the Littleboys of Ewelme and the Doolittles of Brightwell cum Sotwell. Next came the local farmers and their wives and the tradesmen and the labourers with theirs, most of these, naturally, in the employ of the gentry families. Of all the ladies both high and low the common interest was the weekly edition of the *Illustrated London News*, to which, as it happened, the sole subscriber in Benson was Lady Parthenope. Never was a single copy of any periodical so read and examined in every tiny detail; it was so popular that the engraved drawings in each edition were actually copied by some of the ladies, and if more of them had been able to write I dare say they would have reproduced the copy as well. In any case they made sure that one way or another each member of this inclusive society got her fair share, and most especially of the Special Coronation Edition.

There was no other meeting place for these ladies except Benson church, where of a Sunday they congregated with their menfolk, although the latter played no part in what took place there at the end of the morning service. This would have been impossible anyway, for the men sat separately on the right-hand side of the church as was the convention, whilst the others, the ladies and their children, sat on the left. This suited the ladies extremely well, for when the service had ended and the vicar and his curates had left, the men followed, so the ladies had the church to themselves and from their accustomed positions in the pews they moved to more informal ones. Their interest in the *Illustrated London News* has been mentioned, but on this particular Sunday Robert Willoughby was the main, indeed the only, subject of conversation.

It was generally expected that Robert Willoughby would marry Emma Littleboy, for it was an obvious match. Emma was certainly the prettiest girl in Benson; indeed, in the opinion of many she was the most perfect beauty that there had been in this part of Oxfordshire for as long as they could remember. Much the same could be said in a masculine sense of Robert Willoughby. As soon as he came of age he had entered the army, achieving the distinction of acceptance into a cavalry regiment, the 17th/21st Lancers, but here it has to be admitted that Sir Hugh was influential, and indeed had found the substantial sum needed to provide Robert with acceptable independent means. However, it should be added that the colonels of the 17th/21st were also impressed by Robert himself; the fact that he drove up to the regimental headquarters in an open Lagonda did not go unnoticed, nor did it when the Lagonda broke down in the middle of the drill square and was promptly fixed by Robert amidst a flurry of spanners. After this and without a very long interview Robert was offered that holy grail of prospective officers, a juncture commission. This he accepted, albeit in such a fashion that suggested that he might just as easily have turned it down.

It all worked very well for Robert, for it accorded with his passion for riding to hounds; the hunt had claimed him as of right since he had first ridden with the South Oxfordshire at the age of eleven on his own chestnut pony. By the time he was commissioned in the 17th/21st he possessed a string of hunters and in season was out hunting several times a week, even as a junior officer. The colonel of the 17th/21st placed nothing in the way of his officers' hunting, so long as their string of hunters kept to cavalry specification, for it was regarded as a form of training. The headquarters of the regiment was at Leicester and consequently Robert and his fellow officers were generally part of the field with the Pytchley or the Quorn, to which the railway company conveyed their horses in advance of the hunt. There were of course regimental matters which also claimed some of his time, and none more important than the regimental dinner nights, which were most formal affairs. At these Robert, being the junior cornet of the mess, sat at the bottom end of a long table loaded with gleaming silver, and it was his role to rise before the port was taken to propose the loyal toast, using the customary words 'Gentlemen, the King'. Unfortunately, on one memorable occasion, Robert was so drunk that he rendered the toast as 'Kinklemen the gents'. As may be imaged this caused quite a stir in the mess and it was only on account of the stern countenance of the colonel commanding that decorum was maintained. It earned Robert two days in solitary, which endeared him to his fellow cornets, and the libellous toast itself soon passed into the regimental lore.

To return to Emma Littleboy: it hardly need be said that Robert, when on leave from his regiment, pursued his courtship ardently.

He would ride out of a Sunday to Ewelme for the morning service in Ewelme church and then call at the manor, where he left his card in the silver salver on the hall table, tipping the butler as he did so. At first no actual contact was made with Emma on these occasions, although as he became a Ewelme familiar this did begin to happen. The trouble was that the visits were soon noticed by the neighbourhood and Robert began to encounter other female persons along the way to and from Ewelme, and then simple good manners made him respond, in a fraternal way, as they greeted him. And so on the occasions when Robert was able to obtain leave from his regiment at Leicester, there was quite a hurly-burly of enjoyable connections, both with the quality and with others beneath it, for Robert Willoughby was not one to waste time.

Into this rich chapter of his youthful ardour there now entered another contender, the Doolittle counterpart of the Littleboys' Emma, and her name was Lavender. Both the Littleboys and the Doolittles had been established in Oxfordshire for a considerable time, from the eighteenth century perhaps, and although they were much more recently landed than the Willoughbys they held a considerable acreage themselves. Lavender was beautiful, although nowhere near as beautiful as Emma, but she had had a splendid education at Cheltenham College for Ladies, where she had been not only a scholar but also in her last year the captain of hockey. She herself took much of the initiative and in courting Robert, certainly the ladies of the sorority of Benson church took her suit, for so it has to be called, entirely seriously. So Robert had the choice all to himself, having no rival in Benson or any other place until one reached Oxford itself. He was able to take his time, with some diversions on the side, although in the end it seemed that he was bound to settle for Emma Littleboy of Ewelme.

This had been long decided in the distaff pews at Benson church, and there they were simply waiting for the match to be formally announced. So when the senior curate, in the vicar's absence, commenced his fortnightly reading of the banns, the congregation, even though half asleep, expected to hear Robert

Willoughby's name. What the curate announced, however, was that Robert Willoughby and Lavender Doolittle were to be wed. It would be difficult to exaggerate the hush that fell over the pews in Benson church; you could certainly have heard a pin drop. Just for effect, perhaps, the young curate, who knew that for once he held the congregation in the palm of his hand, and not wanting to lose this golden moment, took it upon himself to repeat the bann a second time: Robert Willoughby and Lavender Doolittle were to wed. Quite soon after this the male part of the congregation filed out of the doorway and into the churchyard. Not so the ladies on their side, and what they said will never be known for sure, but certainly they took a very long time saying it; indeed, they were still talking outside as the curate, having hung up his cassock, was seen to mount a bicycle parked in the church precinct and pedal off.

All this, I must confess, is a matter of hearsay only, for the fact is that I did not myself witness these proceedings. I could not have done so because I was not born at the time they took place; as it happened I was not born until seven months later, that is, seven months after Robert and Lavender were married. Lavender is my much loved mother and Robert, my father, is my idol, although now a largely unseen one, for reasons which I shall explain. As may easily be imagined, my appearance on the scene, first as a bump then as a newborn and finally at the time of baptism, caused among the sorority at Benson such a commotion that paled everything that had gone before into insignificance. However, as I would have told them had I been there, here am I, Ivor Willoughby.

# Chapter 2

WHAT, IT MAY be wondered, happened to my mother's rival in love, the beautiful Emma Littleboy? She was often spoken of in Benson at the time when I was growing up, although she herself was no longer living in our neighbourhood. Many years later I discovered the answer to this question, for I chanced to meet her brother when we were both surveying the same gold mine in Costa Rica. He told me that Emma had remained unmarried and had died whilst still young and that a marble tablet to her memory is set in the wall at Ewelme church.

Of my father I have only a limited recollection. We lived at a lodge on the Willoughby estate at Crowmarsh, to which he came at weekends and at other times as his duties permitted. However, when I was seven years old this came to an end because it was the turn of his regiment to take up an empire posting; the place it went to was Egypt, and there, unfortunately for us, families were not allowed to accompany. So my father disappeared from my life when I barely knew him and after that all that I remember of him were the letters with Egyptian stamps on them. These I soon began to collect, wondering at the strange lettering they bore.

At Crowmarsh, and bereft of my father, my mother grew close to the Willoughbys senior, who generously extended their family life so that it included us both. As I grew up there I liked to think that my upbringing was the same as that of my father; I found that I liked the things that he had liked, and used his fishing rod to catch roach and perch on the same stretch of the Thames at

Wallingford as he had. When I grew old enough I too had a pony and rode with the South Oxfordshire as he had done, and by the time I was ten years old I took my emerging role as head of the family in his absence with gravity. This was partly to sustain my mother, who took my father's continued absence very hard.

In due course I was sent away to the preparatory school for Wellington College where all the Willoughbys had been educated and no doubt received a discount as officers' sons. I know now that my own education was largely due to Sir Hugh and Lady Parthenope, who funded it, as my mother was dependent on erratic remittances and on her own family at Brightwell cum Sotwell. It was altogether typical of my grandfather that he weighed in whenever there was trouble, although he never mentioned it to anyone. For the whole time that I was growing up my father remained in the East, and the Egyptian stamps gave way to others with even stranger scripts from obscure places such as Syria and Turkey and then Arabia. Alas, the letters gradually dwindled and finally they ceased altogether, and a note came from Brigadier Allenby, his commanding officer in Cairo, stating that Robert had been sent on a mission 'to the interior' and since he would be away a long time the staff office would be responsible for sending my mother his monthly pay cheque. My mother, who had grieved at Father's departure, now had to face what amounted to his disappearance. She handled this grief by simply refusing even to admit the possibility of such a disaster, clinging to her own certainty that in due course Father would return and that it was only a matter of time before this happened. The route from the East was the P&O line whose steamers plied to India via Suez, so Lavender took the practical step of visiting the company's office in Piccadilly to arrange that she received a copy of the passenger manifest for all the boats out of Port Said sailing homewards. These arrived at our house at intervals of about a month and Mother would pore over them with breathless intensity.

It took a long time to happen, but in the end there did come a day when there was indeed a Captain R. Willoughby on the manifest, and Mother was in ecstasy. The vessel's arrival was scheduled for ten days ahead, which proved to be barely enough for Mother to prepare for Father's return. I was taken to the department store in Oxford to be fitted with a new suit, whilst Mother, heavens knows, got herself into a great state, trying on all manner of clothes and dresses.

When the great day arrived she hired a Daimler to take us to Liverpool, which considering the state of the family finances must have been quite daring. But a Daimler it was, with a chauffeur besides, and in it we sallied forth to Liverpool. We reached it just as RMS *Star of Bengal* was arriving, and then had a long wait whilst mother occupied herself with a discussion with the shipping company's representative as the liner was hauled in by the tugs and berthed.

Mother was quite breathless. 'It is all arranged,' she explained. 'The purser has very generously offered to let us have his sitting room so that we can all be reunited there.' Mother's face could have beaten the Virgin Mary's for beatitude, and she made all sorts of cosmetic adjustments and alteration of her clothes and then of mine.

Finally a company official appeared, and with a certain ceremony we were escorted up the covered gangway and into the interior of the ship, which was dark and smelt of oil. After what seemed an infinite number of staircases and passageways we were finally shown in to the purser's quarter, which was comfortable, even plush, with clever little curtains over each port hole and a carpet upon the floor, and here we were bidden to wait. In a little while a door on the other side of the room opened and an elderly man and a boy were ushered in, apparently somewhat against their will, the steward announcing 'Captain and Master Willoughby'.

It was not my father.

The first move was made by Master Willoughby, who was an Indian boy only a little older than myself and quite the handsomest I ever set eyes on. He came straight towards me and I stretched out my hand to greet him, but at the last minute, and as we were about to touch, his face contorted into a scowl, and, glaring at me, he spat on the floor: on the purser's carpet. I wondered whoever he thought I was, for he seemed to take me for some sort of rival.

'I am Captain Rupert Willoughby,' said the man. 'I am a tea planter in Assam and I have come back to England to retire. I'm not in this office of my own choice and I did not expect to be treated in such a fashion.' He turned to the steward, whose face was now ashen. 'Let this charade be ended – now.' Although I was sorry for them, and embarrassed, there was something distinctly queer about the pair of them, and certainly the boy could not have been his son.

We returned in silence to Crowmarsh in a state of desolation as the December night closed in on our journey, and it was the end of the passenger manifests so far as Mother was concerned.

*

The period that followed this confusing episode was not a happy one for either of us, although I had at least my school life to occupy me. There was also my hobby, my model soldiers, which absorbed much of my time, another expression, perhaps, of the Willoughby martial habit. All my pocket money was spent on soldiers and their papier mâché battlefield, which was generally set out on the floor of our parlour since Mother only used this room when we had guests. Although the soldiers were made of lead, for me they were real soldiers with their own names, ranks and different uniforms; I especially liked uniforms. The weapons they carried were equally varied, for there were rifles, machine guns, mortars for the heavy infantry and heavy artillery for the gunners. My side, my own Imperial Guard, it could be called, were of course the British redcoats, and though heavily outnumbered these always came out on top; my stratagems certainly flattered the redcoats.

A year passed and then one day our household was abruptly galvanised when there arrived on our doorstep an unexpected visitor in the person of a certain Sergeant Dundas. He explained that he had come from Arabia on a mission to bring important documents to the Foreign Office, but he also had instructions from the commanding officer in Cairo to call upon Mother to inform her of the latest state of affairs. He told us all about the war that had started there.

The year before, a guerrilla unit with Arabic-speaking officers had been sent to foment an Arab rising against the Turks, whose empire ran down the Red Sea coast as far as Yemen. Sergeant Dundas and my father were part of this unit, which was commanded by a certain Captain Lawrence, and with the assistance of Hussein the Sheriff of Mecca, and the Hashemites, they had just succeeded in capturing the port of Jeddah. This provided the British force with a proper supply base and also for the first time a means of contact with the outside world. It was only to be expected that we should have received no letters, since before the capture of Jeddah the only link had been by messenger travelling by sea to Suez and thence to the Arab Bureau at British headquarters in Cairo. The Foreign Office, by which the campaign was managed, would do its best to keep Mother informed and in the meantime could confirm that Father was alive and well.

We hung upon Sergeant Dundas' every word. I delighted in this real war, war as a great adventure, much different from the games I played with my model soldiers, and a wave of pride surged through me at the thought that Father was sure to be one of the leaders. As for Mother, relief and happiness spread over her face, and Sergeant Dundas was quickly made welcome. He stayed until the following day and all the time he was with us he told us stories, especially about the capture of Jeddah. He explained that this was a port halfway down the Red Sea, protected by a fort built by the Turks, with plenty of small artillery in placements to contain the local Arab tribes. As a result, the guns were on the landward side, and therefore Captain Lawrence had chosen to attack Jeddah from the sea; the planning and the means to carry out the attack had been the work of Captain Willoughby. He had found a steam packet, owned by a man called Vartak, whom he had befriended. Vartak, although partly Turkish himself, hated the Turks for their brutality at Jeddah, which was his home port, and he was persuaded by the promise of sharing the loot to transport the British force of 120 men to Jeddah. The boat was well known there and so, flying the Turkish flag, it aroused no suspicion when it tied up at the quay below the fort early one morning. The British force was landed and scaled the wall of the fort unnoticed, after which they opened fire with Lewis guns on the Turkish soldiers, who were facing the other way. This was the signal for an attack on the gates by the tribesmen, and after one gate was forced in spite of fearsome casualties, the garrison ran up a white flag. No British soldiers were killed or wounded.

Great rejoicing had followed at Jeddah as the townspeople emerged from their houses and the British who had assailed the walls were noisily feted, as the air filled with cries of 'Lurens' and 'Ullobi'. What happened afterwards to the Turkish garrison was a matter that was best not gone into, but for ever after this, Captain Willoughby was known to the British and Arabs alike as 'Ullobi'.

All this had happened three months before, in August 1915, and Jeddah had now been turned into an arsenal with a vast quantity of war materials brought from Suez and India by the Royal Navy. With relish, Sergeant Dundas explained that they had acquired a lot of explosives with detonators and fuses and with these they had just blown up the railway line from Jeddah to Medina, thus preventing the Turks from reinforcing for a counter-attack. At the point when Sergeant Dundas had set out for England, Captain Willoughby – Ullobi – had been sent on a mission with another officer to raise a force from the tribes in the As'ir, the mountainous province inland from Jeddah, and had been gone for more than a month. This item of information somewhat dampened our spirits, and the glee with which we had greeted Sergeant Dundas' account evaporated at this new disclosure, especially when he explained that we could not expect to receive any further letters from Father.

It was not long after the visit of Sergeant Dundas that the newspapers, bored no doubt with reporting the fighting on the

Western Front, began to carry news of the desert campaign in Arabia and in particular of the exploits of Captain Lawrence, who was busy blowing up railway lines up and down the coast of the Red Sea. We diligently combed the papers in the hope that there would be news of Father, but, alas, there was never any mention of him. Rabegh and Yenbo fell and finally, after a great attack from the desert, Aqaba fell too, and then all the tribes of western Arabia joined the revolt. The Turks fell back but their retreat was doomed to become a rout, and finally the army of desert warriors led by the British entered Amaan. With much ceremony their Cairo commander, General Allenby, rode alongside Captain Lawrence and the leader of the Arabs, whose name was Faisal. There were plenty of cries to be heard of 'Lurens' and 'Faisal', but this time there were none of 'Ullobi'.

*

The end of the war in Arabia seemed to make it certain that Father would soon return to Crowmarsh. I found it difficult not to blame him for not communicating with us by some means for so long. I resented the fact that my mother was in just the same position as all the other war widows who filled the pews at Benson church, and yet she was not a war widow at all.

I was fifteen years old and had just come home from Wellington College for the Christmas holidays, the armistice had just been signed and rejoicing and relief were palpable in Benson as they were everywhere else. An almost miraculous deliverance it seemed to be, and then all of a sudden we had another deliverance of our own. One evening there came a knock on our door. I opened it, to behold a man whom I took to be a street Arab or a pedlar. His clothes were rags, he had wiry black hair and a straggly grizzled beard and his face was the colour of mahogany, and when he opened his mouth there came out a stream of words I could not understand, but at this point there was a wild cry from Mother behind me, and it dawned upon me that this man must be my father.

No arrival could have been more chaotic. There was Mother fussing and still screeching, there was myself in floods of tears, and there was Father attempting to withstand our combined onslaught whilst lying, quite evidently exhausted, in a heap on the floor. In the scenes that followed the evening slipped past, and no one had any chance of recovering during the remainder of that day.

But by the next morning the three of us had done so. All manner of attention had been lavished upon Father, and by the time he appeared he was dressed anew in an immaculate army uniform that Mother must have been keeping in readiness for the moment. He wore an officer's jacket with shoulder flashes of the 17th/21st Lancers, a brightly polished leather Sam Browne belt and perfectly creased trousers. Gone was the beard; his hair was now parted in the middle and pomaded with oil so that it lay flat upon his head. He had also rediscovered his native tongue.

He soon found my model soldiers in the parlour and seized upon them with a show of enthusiasm which I took to be a sort of ice-breaking, a compliment to myself, and perhaps approval that I too in my way shared our family's military bent. We settled upon the floor, surrounded by my battlefield collection, but it was not long before I realised that he wasn't paying me compliments at all; quite simply, he was as enraptured by the model soldiers as I was.

Almost the whole of that day we played games of war, and poor Mother was neglected altogether. He demonstrated how his battles had been fought – and many there were – the tactics he had used, movements to keep the initiative, feints and counter-feints to confuse the enemy when they were outflanking him; and then the great charge of the camels straight at the centre to break the Turk and scorch his guns. He showed me how to make a battle plan, one that was simple and would progress even if the commander became a casualty. He described the fog of battle and how to make rapid calculations after mistakes had been made, and how actually to take advantage of these. He played it like a game of chess.

After a time we left the model soldiers and he told me, in much more detail than Sergeant Dundas, of the capture of Jeddah and then Rabegh and Yenbo. It was Father who had been in charge of the explosives that blew up the Turkish railway because he had been trained in their use in England in the years before the war; after this I had to add a railway line to the papier-mâché battle-field. There was also much about his friend Captain Lawrence in the first year of the Arab revolt, and the difficulties they had with Hussein, Sheriff of Mecca which had led to his own mission to raise an army from tribes in the mountains; at this point he became strangely excited and I wondered what might be coming next.

'Father,' I said, 'now that the fighting is over you will be able to stay here in England.'

My father shook his head. 'I'm afraid that cannot be. A soldier's life is never his own and new events have arisen which mean that I shall have to return to Arabia. Later, when you're older, I will explain them to you.'

I was desperate. 'Father, when I'm older you may not even be alive. Please don't leave us in the dark. I want you to tell me exactly why you have to go back although the war is over.'

'In the first place, it's not for me to decide. One of the reasons I have come to England, apart from coming to see your mother and yourself, is to report to the Foreign Office, who will not even know whether I am still alive. I shall ask to return to Arabia to resume my original mission, which was to gain British influence and allies in the province of As'ir in case there is further fighting. A new threat is arising in Eastern Arabia where the Asheukh in Riyadh has become increasingly powerful, and no one knows whether he will be a friend or an enemy. It will be a help that your mother has found me a new uniform, for apart from anything else this will secure me free travel, even all the way to Cairo, where I shall go to talk to the powers that be at the Arab Bureau. After that, if all these gentlemen can agree, I shall return to Abha, which is the capital of the As'ir, for I have unfinished business there. There are things that have happened in Arabia that have not been heard of in London and I shall have to give them a full account of these, with all the gruesome details; I have no intention of inflicting

17

those upon you. Perhaps I shall do so one day when you're older, but then I doubt that I shall remember.'

I felt that Father and his world were slipping away from me. 'Father,' I said, 'I want to hear all the details, however gruesome they may be. You seriously underestimate me. I may be a schoolboy but you forget that I am also a Willoughby. One day I may be a soldier too. I have my own strength and nothing you can say is too tough for me to hear.'

He made no reply as he could see that I was quite worked up.

'I don't believe you have told me the full story and why you must return to Arabia,' I continued. 'I insist that you give me a proper answer. Mother deserves an answer too. Don't you see how she frets? Not knowing anything makes her terrified.'

'I do see', said my father. 'I do indeed see, but I can't see a way of telling you without making both of you grieve the more. It can only add to the burden of my absence that you carry already.'

'As I've said, you underestimate me, Father, just as you under-estimate Lavender, too.' It was the first time I had ever referred to Mother as Lavender but this is the way it came out.

'Then I see that I must tell you, although I shall regret doing so and you may regret it too. I absolutely forbid you to speak of this to your mother. We wanted to raise an army from one of the fiercest tribes in Arabia, called the Beni Mughe'id, because we thought they could be useful to us. Just two of us went, a lieuten-ant called Hastings and myself, with the object of making contact with the Amir of Abha, a man by the name of Zeid bin Tahir, who is one of their great warriors. We rode on camels and went by a route that passed through territories of tribes that were friendly with the Sheriff of Mecca, whose letters we carried. These tribes not only provided all our necessities but every small luxury they possessed, and everywhere we were treated as honoured guests. Each one provided us with a *mahra*, a guide, to take us to the territory of the next tribe and although there were skirmishes and we sometimes had to use our rifles, with the help of the *mahra* we always got through. But the friendliness was deceptive, for what we didn't know was that from the time we left Jeddah spies of the Turks were watching our every movement, all the way until finally we reached Abha. There we found that the city was still held by Turks, and the spies, with delight on their faces at the prospect of a reward, delivered us into their hands. It was not a nice thing to be taken prisoner by such people. They started by slicing off the head of my fellow officer. I don't think I wish to continue.'

'Father, nothing will make me flinch. Anyhow, you are here and you are alive.'

'It is remarkable that I am. Very well, I will tell you. The Turks ruled the people of Abha by brutal methods and I was just the object they needed to demonstrate them. They paraded me through the town, dragged by the chains that bound me. I didn't expect to survive and envied Hastings his quick release. I was taken to the fortress which we had seen as we had arrived, which was called Manadhir. There I was released from my chains and pitched through a hatch into a dungeon. I fell many feet on to a pile of what turned out to be bones. The Turks knew exactly what to do to their prisoners and had elaborate ways to ensure that I suffered a slow death. I was weak from my injuries, and cold; much of the time I was unconscious, but I knew that somehow I had to survive.

'I must have spent several weeks in darkness in the dungeon, but there was no way of measuring time. I realised that all the prisoners died there, for beside me were their skeletons. I prayed, which I had never done before. One day there came a light in the doorway above. There was a great commotion and I saw that instead of Turkish soldiers there were men in Arab clothes and headdress. The Beni Mughe'id had retaken their city. I was hauled out and a big man carried me in his arms to his house. He was the son of the Amir, Zeid bin Tahir, and was called Tabarhla. He made sure that everything was done for me and I slowly recovered. He saved my life.'

He paused as though searching for words. 'Did you ever hear the story of Charlemagne and Rolande and the pass at Roncesvalles?'

I shook my head.

'If you had, then you would understand the debt that I owe now. Such a debt that I can only repay by fighting the battles that Tabarhla fights.'

For some time neither of us said a word. Finally I found my tongue. 'And so what happens now, Father?'

'Whatever fate has in store. I must return to Abha. That's all.'

My heart was filled with a terrible despair. I stared at my father. I saw again the face that looked like beaten bronze. I saw not a uniform but the ragged clothes, the beard and shaggy hair. In my mind he seemed to transform before my eyes.

Next morning I rose later than usual, for my sleep was full of wild dreams and terrible imaginings. As I came down the stairs the house was strangely silent and I knew at once that my father had gone.

I went to the manor to talk to my grandfather and repeated everything that my father had told me, but to my surprise there was nothing that he did not already know.

# Chapter 3

'YOU SEE,' MY grandfather said, 'it's all to do with politics. Like the rest of us, Robert is concerned about the threat from the east. Everyone has assumed that Arabia now belongs to Sheriff Hussein, and his sons Abdulla and Feisal, but this may not be so. A tide of Wahhabism is rising in the east, or has already risen, and this is led by Abdulaziz ibn Saud, a warrior asheukh who rules in Riyadh and for sure will want to make the As'ir his own. Robert will certainly be needed, for the whole of General Allenby's success in driving out the Turks is threatened. The British have spent a great deal of money on Hussein and the capital of Arabia should certainly be Mecca, which is the very heart of the Muslim world. Hussein is its custodian and will assume the Caliphate when the Turks have gone.'

'But surely,' I said, 'one Arab leader is much the same as another. It's for the Arabs themselves to choose.'

'The problem is, which one will bring stability to a region that is vital to us because the Red Sea is our route to India. We have backed Hussein, and the whole of our influence may collapse with him if he falls. The Arabs rightly seek independence – from the Turks, from the French, from ourselves – it doesn't matter which, for we are all foreigners to them. Sooner or later they will achieve full independence and then there will be matters of trade, in particular permission to decide who drills for petroleum oil. The British influence must be preserved at all costs or it will be replaced by an American one. It's even possible that the French might enter the stakes and then any number of bad consequences could follow.

'There is also the matter of the Jewish state. With Hussein, and especially with his sons, there is at least a chance of there being a peaceful border, which we shan't have if the Wahhabis take control. I must say I often think that Arthur Balfour would have been wiser to have offered the Jews Uganda, which is what he intended until he was talked out of it by Theodor Herzl. But all that is incidental now because the Jews are there, and all we can do is exert our influence with the Hashemites by helping them to achieve an independent and friendly Arabia. We shall have to wait and see, for soon there is to be a peace conference of the victorious powers at Versailles. We must hope that the Arab voice is properly heard, which I am prepared to believe it will be, because Lawrence will look after that – *inshallah*, as they say in those parts.'

'But, Grandfather,' I said, 'it's not just what happens in Arabia, although what you've told me sounds terribly important. There's also the problem of Mother, who is very upset, and I grieve for her. Father seems to have completely gone out of our lives and being alone she frets terribly.'

'She's not alone because she is part of our family, just like a daughter, in fact. The lot of a soldier's wife is often a very difficult one and great sacrifices have to be made. When the government decides to start a war in faraway places, army planners – and as a brigadier I've been one myself – are only too aware of the hardship caused to wives, and wherever possible they are permitted to accompany their husbands; but in some places that is not possible. Sadly, as a result many a soldier returns home to find his wife or his girl has gone off. We do everything we can to keep families informed about what's happening.'

'Did Grandmother suffer in the same way when you were away fighting?'

'No doubt she did suffer in the same way, although in her case she had a habit when I was serving abroad of just turning up. Her sister knew Florence Nightingale and she got herself made an inspector of nursing in what is now called the Queen Alexandra Nursing Corps. I can tell you she was the very devil and made me the laughing stock of the regiment when it was found out. Ah, Parthenope!'

'Could Mother become an inspector too?'

'There aren't any garrisons in Arabia for her to go to. You must just do your best to comfort your mother. When you are an officer in your turn you will meet the same problems. In the meantime I can assure you how much she means to us and how concerned we are for her happiness.'

He was oddly matter of fact and the sense he made of the situation helped to soothe my grief. He made me feel proud of my father and his single-minded purpose, even if it did mean that he'd left Lavender and me alone. I saw that I should have to come to terms with this. She was so strong in her nature and I had to be like her so I could support her and we could share the burden of Father's not being there.

After my talk with Grandfather I found pictures of castles and added them to my collection, with others that looked as I imagined Arabia would. I forgot about Captain Lawrence, for now I was only interested in Abha, the city that meant so much to Father and had seized my imagination too.

I could see it just as he described it, with a great castle and blue mountains all around. As Father returned there would be flags flying on all the turrets, celebrating the great victory over the Turks. I imagined dead Turks in their funny red hats lying everywhere on the sand whilst the warrior sheikhs, perched high on huge camels, galloped about Abha, the loose ends of their turbans streaming in the wind. It had been the greatest battle they had ever fought and the city would be celebrating it for weeks and weeks. Sheep would be roasted every night in the great square, the one where the caravans that passed through Abha rested. Now in due season these would return bearing pilgrims or loaded with spices and the square would be filled with a great throng once more. The Amir would be there, riding with his escort of great sheikhs with Arabic names I could not pronounce, and hidden in the harems of the palaces and no doubt watching would be the concubines, with golden bangles on their arms and rings in their noses. I imagined the stories of adventure and victories which would be told at the nightly feasting, with Father the best of all the storytellers. Abha invincible, a byword throughout Arabia, together with its tribe with the funny name. One day I would go there too, spend my life there if necessary and find my father. It was now my destiny just as it was his; I swore this with a solemn oath.

*

I returned to Wellington, and as the years passed made my way up the school until I reached the Classical Sixth. Exams came and went and I suppose that my results were just good enough for me to keep in the same class as the scholars, although I was less clever than they were. At length the time came when I had to decide what to do when I left. What I wanted to do was to go to Oxford to read languages, and I lay awake at night trying to make up my mind which college to choose. I was about to discuss the matter with my teacher when the headmaster summoned me to his study; he informed me that, with the other school leavers apart from the scholars, he had entered my name for the Royal Military Academy at Sandhurst.

I objected. 'If I go into the army it will be the army that decides what I shall do, and that wouldn't suit me at all. The person who decides what I shall do is me.'

He shrugged. 'All your family have entered the Army.'

'They may have, but I may be an exception. There is much that I must learn and to do so I want to go Oxford. I was wondering if you could put me down for the scholarship at Balliol College?'

'You would have about as much chance of getting into Balliol as a candle in a storm. You would be blown away.'

'I am not easily . . .'

He cut me off. 'I'll put you down for the entrance examination to Pembroke College.' He rose from his chair and held out his hand. 'Good luck; you'll need it.'

So I sat the Pembroke examination and in due course was invited for interview. Several of us were ushered into the chapel to await our turn, or perhaps to pray, but the marvel of that chapel soon dispelled any thoughts I might have had that I was being short-changed in not going to Balliol. The admissions tutor was an elderly don whose name, which was on the door of his set, I quickly recognised to be that of the author of a commentary on Tacitus.

'I see that you wish to read Greats,' he began. 'That is the course we prefer all students to take.' In the conversation that followed I thought it would be clever if I brought in Tacitus.

'And why do you wish to study Tacitus?' he asked, still leafing through my papers on the desk before him.

'Because he coined the name "Arabia Felix".'

He looked up, fixing me with one eye, the good one, whilst the other drifted in another direction. 'And where does he mention Arabia Felix?'

'That I'm afraid I don't recall, but I assure you that he does so in one of the books.'

'Interesting.' He slowly stroked his chin. 'Very interesting.' He reached to the shelves behind his desk and took out a book of Tacitus, although I couldn't see which one it was. He turned the pages slowly and my heart began to sink: I realised that he must be going to test me in translating the Latin. I cursed my folly at mentioning Tacitus, the most difficult Latin author I could have chosen. I saw the rejection letter on our doormat as clear as daylight.

Nothing happened. He remained locked in concentration, turning the pages of the Tacitus in silence whilst I simply sat there. Ten minutes must have passed and still he kept reading abstractedly. I felt more and more like an interloper – here was I intruding on a great scholar immersed in his life's work. Finally I decided that the polite thing to do would be to stand up in order to remind him that I was still there and risk calling down on my head whatever inquisition he had planned for me. I got up from my chair and stood waiting, but still nothing happened so I moved towards the door. At this his only reaction was to wave his arm in my general direction, still without looking up. I reached the door, opened it and tiptoed out, closing it behind me as quietly as I could, all the time in fear that I might be hauled back to translate Tacitus.

Some days later I was seized by terrible fear for I remembered that it was not Tacitus at all who had described Arabia Felix. It was Suetonius or someone else altogether. I was a fraud; furthermore I only planned to take Greats in my first term, or whatever was the minimum, for I intended to switch to oriental languages as soon as the opportunity arose. I was sure that I would be rejected anyway. However, to my surprise I received a letter offering me a place at Pembroke, and better still they had awarded me an Exhibition.

*

At Oxford I was soon able to transfer to the school of my choice, with the result that over the next three years I received a proper grounding in classical Arabic and in the history of the Near and Middle East. I was somewhat burdened by having also to learn Farsi and Urdu, and my efforts in these languages caused much mirth to my grandfather, who happened to be fluent in both. At the end I emerged with an upper second, which was better than expectation, but to decide what to do with it was another matter and raised all sorts of difficult questions.

Naturally, I had long been driven by the conviction that I must go to Arabia to search for my father, but this was not a concrete plan; it was just a youthful dream, and present reality made me acutely aware of this. Now I was not in a dream world any more and was faced with the urgent need of finding a means to make a living, so in the end I decided to become a schoolmaster, or at least to seek a temporary post while I thought about my future. I scoured the pages of the *Times Educational Supplement* and came across a post at a preparatory boarding school at Ripley in Surrey. I applied and was engaged, taking the place of the classics master, who was away on sick leave. I settled down to teaching Latin and

Greek, and since he had also been the master in charge of cricket that duty fell to me also. I blessed my good fortune, for Ripley Court was a fine Queen Anne mansion that its owners, a Mr and Mrs Pierce, had turned into a school. Experienced professionals these two were, who charmed the parents as they deposited their sons and then ruled them by means of terror; their bedroom was just down the corridor from the dormitories, conveniently close for dispensing instant correction when needed.

I spent two years at Ripley, taking lodgings at the Talbot Arms at the bottom of the High Street, and was happy enough to persuade myself that this was to be my choice of career: I would become a headmaster. But it was only a passing phase and I could not so easily escape my avowed destiny, but in my time at Ripley I was able to save the greater part of my salary so that when I left I could return to the study of Arabic. I was advised that the best way to learn colloquial Arabic of the sort I would need was to take the examination of the Diplomatic Service, which ran a course for Middle East specialists. This was managed by the well-known orientalist C. E. Monaghan, who taught at King's College in the Strand.

I reckoned that this would offer what I needed if I was going to look for a job in the Middle East, and so it proved, for at the end of the year Professor Monaghan found me a position at the Locust Research Bureau in Cairo. It was a heart-stopping moment when I realised that my greatest ambition was to be fulfilled, yet the problem that daunted me was how to break the news to Lavender. I would be deserting her exactly as my father had done. In trepidation I gave her the news, but as it turned out she was just as keen on the venture as I was myself. Actually, she always had great reserves of psychological strength, and whilst I was growing up she had acquired new interests. She had developed a passion for golf and nowadays most of her days were spent at the club where, quite predictably, she had become ladies' captain.

*

The Locust Bureau in Cairo was not an impressive outfit. It was managed by an elderly official borrowed from the Indian Civil Service, whose accompanying secretary might, like himself, have seen better days. He supervised three field operatives whose job it was to search for the breeding grounds, from which the plagues of locusts originated, the idea being that once identified these could be bombed. As yet no one had found a single breeding ground, and I was warned that it was quite possible that I might be one of a long line who had journeyed in this field of research but failed to arrive. I would receive £200 a year, with allowances for travel, and would be based at Jeddah, where I could collect my salary each month and mail my reports to the Bureau. Arabia itself had by now been pacified, and by degrees unified, by Abdulaziz ibn Saud, and consequently it was possible to travel throughout much of the country, for which purpose a formal letter drafted by the authorities in Riyadh would be waiting for me at Jeddah. I was warned to avoid crossing the border into Yemen even if locust swarms were reported there, since that country was in a state of perennial war and was unfriendly to all.

The prospect of more or less unlimited travel by whatever means I chose naturally appealed to me. My area for study was to be the As'ir in south western Arabia, together with its plain on the Red Sea coast, called the Tihama. Much of the As'ir was mountainous and at its centre was the city called Abha. My mentor had visited it and clearly it had left a lasting impression upon him: the air was like crystal and appeared to be blue, and there was a great castle lived in by an amir. I was to start my work in the Tihama because this was the place where my predecessor had stopped; as it happened he could not have progressed further because he had died of malaria at this point. I was told that I would find his locust sightings marked on his maps, which had been salvaged and brought back to Jeddah, the port at which I would disembark. I was also provided with a note to the local quartermaster who was to provide me with British Army tropical issue, which comprised many useful essentials, including a large supply of quinine and other medicines.

Finally I was directed to make myself known to a unit next door to the Locust Bureau which was a section run by the Royal Navy. This had been established at the time of the Desert War for the purpose of making a hydrographic survey of the Red Sea ports, and it also produced a reference book for the benefit of naval captains paying courtesy visits, which gave the names of the local tribes and their sheikhs. At the Hydrography Unit I was sized up, given more detailed advice than I had received from the Locust Bureau and invited to send regular reports on anything that I might think relevant, aside from locusts. In return I could call on the unit for support when I was in coastal areas.

Such were the meagre beginnings of my mission to Arabia, the land of locusts. My head was filled with dreams of high adventure, for I had achieved my ambition and Arabia beckoned like a bride. It was January of the year 1930 and I was twenty-six.

*

My odyssey began at the P & O office in Knightsbridge. The Pacific and Orient line sailed from Liverpool to India and gave a service on which the ruling of that country largely depended, their liners bearing all the means for governing, and the civil and military officers and their families who travelled to and fro once or twice a year. The P & O had routine ports of call for refuelling and one of these was Port Said in Egypt at the head of the Suez Canal, from which it would be easy for me to reach Arabia.

The prospect of the voyage was a source of great excitement to me, for it was the first time I had left England to explore the outside world. When the great day arrived I boarded at Liverpool, settled into my third-class cabin and soon started to encounter my fellow passengers; these included an impressive supply of alluring ladies on their way to join husbands in India or find husbands to be. Altogether, this was too good to be true, and the voyage passed at lightning speed, much of my time being spent in the first-class section and especially in its cabins. Love was never far away and the prospect of India struck deeply into my imagination which tested my self-imposed mission of destiny very nearly to destruction.

However, prior experience is a form of armour, and no Circe was going to stand between me and my true destiny: my only bride-to-be was, and remained, Arabia. I recalled my last year at Oxford and the May balls, at which I had fallen deeply in love and found myself loved back. For nights I had lain awake gripped by indecision, and all too easily I might have been persuaded to stay in England and 'settle down'. My girlfriend seized upon this prospect as though it was a given, although she was far too clever to put it in this way; yet she covertly but insistently wove her web.

It was easy now to see the triteness of it all. I knew in my heart I would have to leave her or my life's purpose would crumble and turn to dust. Arabia had to win. I hated myself, all the more so when she screamed and became violent and even threatened to hit me. Now it was she who would be leaving me, she declared. After that we had made love all night – what the French call 'love in a storm'.

I couldn't, ever in my life, go through another scene like that. The pain for both of us still haunted me, yet it had shown my weakness. Before, I had thought of love as something that could be postponed for a convenient time in the future. Now I knew just how difficult that could be, for in truth I had wanted exactly the same thing as she had. My fate had hung in the balance and she had very nearly claimed me, and the whole of my rightful destiny, my Arabia. I thought of her sometimes. She had married a rival in love, a Foreign Office man. I vowed to forgo anything serious after that.

# Chapter 4

THE MEANS BY which I reached Arabia from Cairo are indistinct in my memory. However, I do recall that I went by sea to Aqaba and then made my way to Jeddah by the railway that had once been blown up by Lawrence of Arabia, the name by which he was known even in these parts. I stayed at Jeddah while setting up my base, and then travelled south by a dilapidated bus through the Tihama, the coastal plain, to a place called Qunfidah, which was the point where Bridgewater, my predecessor, had left off. He must have had a pretty dismal end, I concluded, for the country around was for the most part empty of man or beast and there was little left of the local vegetation on account of the locusts. To make matters worse and in spite of the quinine tablets, I soon went down with malaria myself.

As I recovered, it became clear that the interior of the Tihama was a death trap. The towns and villages by the sea were swept by sea breezes but inland the mosquito was king. The fertile plain went for the most part uncultivated, and the tending of any crops there were was done by black Africans, a race evidently able to resist malaria. Here only the weakest tribes remained, the others having migrated over time to the less fertile but malaria-free foothills. I promptly decided to take myself in that direction too, since Bridgewater had recorded the Tihama, whereas in the mountains I could do useful research and perhaps advance my quest for Abha.

By this time I had a clear picture of the region: inland from the Tihama and the narrow plains of the Red Sea were mountains stretching north and south the length of Arabia like a great spine, with their highest peaks in Yemen. Descending from it on each side were wadis that carried the winter rains, westward to the fertile coastal plain and eastward to the barren sands of central Arabia, which stretched for nearly a thousand miles to the Persian Gulf. Here the water ran to waste although it nourished wells and occasional oases. This was the inhospitable region where were the hardiest tribes, who existed mainly by stealing or killing their neighbours, constrained only by a code of rules that kept the violence within bounds. At its centre were the barren sands of the Nejd, and here lay Riyadh, the city of the Saudi tribe ruled by Abdulaziz ibn Saud, now called the King of Hejaz and the Sultan of Nejd. To the south was the Rub al Khali, the vast empty sands which were the wonder of the intrepid travellers who ventured to cross them and wrote the books that revealed their wonders to the world.

*

Before I left Qunfidah I sought out a local horse dealer and amongst his stock I found an Arab mare that I liked the look of. She appeared to be bloodstock and as soon as I mounted her I knew that I had a bargain. She was about fifteen hands in our terms, a chestnut, perhaps five or six years old, and her name was Dukhaala. I equipped both of us from the dealer and since I felt uncomfortable in my tropical issue I acquired Arab clothes; then, carrying only bare necessities, I rode eastward and out of the Tihama. After two days I reached Bedouin country and a small town called Suba, where I paused to take stock of my new situation. By now I had discovered that in Arabia very little goes a long way but there are two articles that all travellers must carry, which are gifts and stories; and so at Suba I purchased a large supply of trinkets. There can be no race on earth as friendly and hospitable as the Bedu and it was the custom that any stranger could approach a house, or tent, if it was an encampment, and be sure to receive hospitality. In times past the stranger would also have been protected, by their lives if need be, so sacred was the role of guest. I found that if my arrival was to be effective it had to accord with certain conventions, and a long time had to be spent dismounting and attending to the horse in a bravura display of modesty. The prospective host, having had time to decide the social standing of his guest and thus of his likely cost, would then advance with a salutation which always ended with the same words: 'O guest, your visit brings honour to our house. It is truly ourselves who are your guests and you are the master whilst you are here.' Such was the generosity of the Bedu, some of the poorest people on earth.

By observing small conventions such as this I found that I quickly adapted to Bedouin ways and used their hospitality freely, delighted by their kindness and simplicity. There was always the ritual of presents: I found that even the smallest articles, such as matchboxes, were received with delight, and I filled a saddlebag with such things, as a gift was required for each member of the household. The stories at first struck me as more problematic, but then I discovered that in Crowmarsh Battle I had a gold mine; every detail of it was savoured and had to be many times repeated. I explained that Crowmarsh lay somewhere to the north, in the direction of Damascus perhaps, or even a little beyond that. It was green – which did not fit anywhere they knew, and it was wet with too much water – to all it seemed a very paradise. Then there were the Willoughbys to explain.

In this fashion I continued my journey of exploration, riding through foothills consisting of thorn bushes and limestone crags, which at this time of the year were covered with tiny flowers. The tracks were well worn and quite easy to follow and I blessed the excellent maps left by my predecessor Bridgewater, who had evidently at some time made the same journey. I found that provided the going was good Dukhaala could cover forty or fifty miles a day, so after four days' riding I reached a village called Hamarat, where I found a lodging house, although I had to share a room with several others. At this point I had reached the mountains, and so I put the word about that I needed a *mahra* to guide me through the mountain tracks leading eastward to the centre of the province of As'ir. It was not long before I discovered Ashraf, who came complete with a camel.

It was from Ashraf that I found out how much I had to learn about Arabian travel and the customs of the Bedu. I discovered that a *mahra* was a great deal more than a mere guide, for not only must he know the tribes but his person must be known to them; he must also know the wells and have access to them. Each tribe has its own *dirah* or territory, and he has to know its boundaries and those of the adjacent *dirahs*, and whether they are friendly or hostile or owe blood money. By tradition he is honour-bound to protect the traveller by any means – which in practice means parleying – and as soon as one *mirah* reaches the boundary of his *dirah* he must find a *mahra* of the next tribe to whom he can hand over the traveller.

It was through Ashraf that I gained my first proper understanding of the geography of Arabia. He dismissed the Tihama with a shrug: he had never been there and declared that those that did were soon killed by its plagues. His homeland was on the far side of the mountains, adjoining the central sands. Here there were the wadis through which we would ride, assuming that they were dry, for these were the best routes for horse or camel and resembled thoroughfares. Although Ashraf had always lived among mountain peoples he also knew much about the central Nejd, and told me about its way of life and its famous tribes, especially the Saudi and their city of Riyadh, which he had once visited. As I mentioned earlier, Riyadh was the city of the asheukh, Abdulaziz ibn Saud, who had conquered As'ir and more recently Mecca and Medina, and now called himself King of Hejaz. In the Nejd lived the hardiest tribes, the wonder of the Europeans who had crossed these sands for a thousand miles to reach the Persian Gulf, and written about its warriors, who fought to live and lived to fight.

I soon discovered that Ashraf was indispensable, for he took it upon himself to provide our commons, which he cooked on small fires of thorn and scrub. In order to eat, we constantly made forays after gazelle, desert hare and other animals, Ashraf armed with an ancient Turkish rifle with which he never missed. I thought that this might also prove useful if we ran into trouble, but on the occasions when we saw other Bedu in the distance, Ashraf would go forward alone to greet them, and after lengthy discussion we were allowed to proceed unmolested. As to what passed between the parties, I soon discovered that it was always the same – the news.

Ashraf was a middle-aged man with a slight stoop, and he affected an indolent manner. At times he would pretend to be asleep, although when something caught his attention he was very wide awake. He was evidently quite happy in his solitary *mahra's* life in spite of its isolation, and five times a day knelt to pray on a small carpet that was stowed somewhere on his camel. It was my first close contact with a Bedu, and when finally we parted I paid him above his due and we both swore eternal brotherhood. I shall not forget Ashraf.

\*

My excitement was now rising, and finally, after a week of climbing endless ridges on the steep western side of the mountains, we could make out Abha in the distance. It was the magic moment I had waited for – the sight of the city that had consumed my imagination for almost as far back as I could remember. I would see the Manadhir, the great castle of white stone in the blue air, triple-turreted like a Crusader castle, as my father had described it; not that Crusaders were ever in Arabia. Would there still be an amir, and would I be able to get an audience and make discoveries about my father? The great caravanserai would still be there, although not with caravans any more, and also the merchants' houses, with their balconies on one side and Abha's mosque with its round tower and muezzins on the other. Beside the mosque would be the palaces of the Ahl Yazid, the three great families that ruled Abha: the bin Tahir, that of Tabarhla, my father's best friend;

the ibn Aidh, always the troublemakers; and the bin Mufarrih, who constantly foiled their plans. All this would lie revealed, and after, I had seen it I would meet with Abha's citizens, the tribe called the Beni Mughe'id, peaceable nowadays since the coming of Abdulaziz ibn Saud, I assumed.

I knew from what Professor Monaghan had said that much of the old style of life would have changed since the Saudi conquest ten years before, but the traditions and the history must have survived, and I was sure I would easily recognise most of what my father had described. The citizens would talk about my father, and I would write down their stories – especially about Zeid, the old Amir, he who had driven out the Turks but now no longer alive; and of course, Tabarhla. I supposed that Father must be at least a sheikh by now. Tomorrow, would I see him plain? That would be too much to hope for. When I did so I would send word to Mother. My mind was full to bursting with these heady thoughts as the wonderful vista opened before my eyes.

It still took a long time to reach Abha. As we descended, the city appeared to lie in a valley, although from the eastern side, as I discovered later, it seemed to rise from the mountains themselves. It consisted of several hundred lime-washed stone *qasrs* of a single storey, and on the far side I could see the Manadhir on a bluff of rock that guarded the city's eastern approach, vast, inscrutable and just as I had imagined it. We made our way and entered by the western gate, which was open and unguarded. Ashraf seemed to know the city and he soon fixed up lodgings for me near the centre of the town, from which I could see the caravanserai. After attending to my needs he found good stabling for Dukhaala, whom I would not be riding for a while.

After settling in and sleeping for a couple of hours, I set about my first duty, which was to present myself with my Saudi credentials to the city governor, whose house had a green Wahhabi flag over the entrance. The governor himself proved to be elderly, doubtless a war veteran now in a retirement post. His hair and beard were black, carefully barbered and doubtless dyed, which gave him a rather acerbic air. I explained that as my papers showed, my mission from the Locust Bureau in Cairo was to survey the area of As'ir to discover if locusts bred there. As he looked at my passport I realised he would see that I was English, which I thought might ease matters, but here I was mistaken. He looked up sharply.

'Anglees, are you indeed? The Anglees have given us a lot of trouble. They supported our enemy the Hashemite Hussein who calls himself Sheriff of Mecca. They paid him a lot of money, several hundred pounds each year, I believe.'

'But that was so that he could help fight the Turks with Colonel Lawrence and win independence for Arabia.'

He swept the comment aside. 'You think that was what the Anglees wanted? I will tell you differently. What they wanted was to make the whole of western Arabia their own protectorate, like Palestine, Jordan and Iraq. We had to fight the Hashemi to get them out of Mecca, then what did the Anglees do? They found thrones for Hussein's sons in Maan and Baghdad. That was what independence for Arabia meant to Mistair Lurens and Mistair George.'

It was not a promising start so I tried to change the direction of the conversation. 'You may be interested to know that Mr Lloyd George is not our Prime Minister any more. We have a different one, Mr MacDonald.'

'MacDoonal,' he repeated slowly, shaking his head. 'I have not heard of MacDoonal.'

'Ullobi,' I suggested. 'Was there not an Englishman called Ullobi at Abha, who fought for the Beni Mughe'id?'

'Ullobi', he said absently. 'Ah yes, Ullobi.' I thought it had registered but then I realised that the name meant nothing to him. 'The Beni Mughe'id, you say. I should think they mostly went off to Riyadh after our asheukh conquered Abha.' He gave a sinister laugh.

'But surely,' I said, 'Zeid, the Amir, was he not one of the greatest warriors when you were fighting the Turks?'

'I do not remember him. I believe he died in the plague, the great influenza.'

'What about Tabarhla, his son? He must have become Amir.'

'There are no amirs at Abha any more. There are only sheikhs of the tribes. The Wahhabi conquest was completed long ago and at Abha the sheikhs no longer cause us trouble. Our problem now is a different one altogether and I will tell what it is so that you may learn and be warned. It is the Ikhwan.'

'Is that another tribe?'

'It is not a tribe at all. If it were we would simply break their necks. They are fanatics who would try to change our Wahhabi faith. They claim that they alone are the true followers of the Prophet – an absurd idea – and wherever they go they tyrannise the people on whom they descend. Their *ulemas* trap them with religious arguments and punish them. You cannot argue with the Ikhwan. Nowadays we kill them wherever we find them, but they are, how do you say, a hydra and if you cut off one head another grows. One day we will rid Arabia of them, but since you are Anglees I advise you to have no dealings with the Ikhwan. Avoid their white turbans if you value your life.' He made a dismissive gesture, whether towards the Ikhwan or myself was not clear, then turned and walked away, leaving the official who stood behind to stamp my passport with impressive seals.

In any case I had heard enough. He had shattered my treasured images, dismissed them as though they were foreigners' dreams, and for good measure confronted me with a new menace instead. It was unnerving to discover that such as he had described might be encountered in these parts and I was beginning to think that, what with the malaria in the plains and the Ikhwan in the hills, Arabia was a more dangerous place than I had imagined. But when I thought it over, what the governor had said was not at all surprising, for he was a Saudi, an outsider, and what could he know about the real Abha? For the true story it was obvious I would have to ask its citizens. I believed that it should not be difficult to find some who remembered the old days and knew my father and might even know where he was. I left my lodgings and wandered into the old caravanserai. Here whole families were crowding the balconies to watch the activities of the market and for the first time I noticed that the womenfolk wore head scarves which left their faces uncovered, unlike the Bedouin; the customs of Abha were evidently liberal. Eerie calls to prayer, marking the time of day, came from the round tower of Abha's mosque on one side of the square.

I went into the market to look for someone who might help me in my search for information and in the end settled upon an elderly coffee merchant who was sitting in the open front of his shop, surrounded by sacks of coffee bearing strange markings. I pretended to examine these but soon decided that this was disingenuous and that it would be better to tell him what I wanted.

'I am trying to find a relation of mine,' I began. 'He was here at Abha some years ago before the Wahhabis came, and was a friend of the Amir. I thought you look as if you might know about that time.'

'I wish I could help you,' he replied. 'But I am just as much an outsider here as you are yourself.'

My belief that I had mastered the As'iri dialect suffered a mortal blow.

'I come from Mukalla,' he continued, 'which is the port where they land the coffee from Africa and India. Except for the Arabian moccha, that is where most of the coffee you are looking at comes from. Mukalla is at the end of the Red Sea and we bring it to Abha through Yemen.'

'But isn't there a war going on in Yemen and does that mean you have to pass through fighting areas?'

'It does, but we are used to doing so.' He shrugged. 'It is a matter of knowing the Yam.' He touched his nose. 'Riyals.'

'Do you make this journey alone?'

'My son does. Two or three times a year he brings me a fresh supply. Come with me and I will make Mukalla coffee for you, then one way or another we will try to find out what it is you wish to know.'

He led the way to the rear, where there was a *majlis* with benches heaped with cushions. The coffee was already brewed, and he poured some into two china cups and handed one to me. Whilst doing so, he called in a dialect which I could not understand to a young lad, who at once dived out into the souk. He then wanted to know by what means I had reached Abha and I told him about the journey from Hamarat, at which he expressed surprise: the road I should have come by was the one from the east. Abha, it seemed, was at the end of the trail, the last city you reached before the high mountains.

'After Abha you only meet with the devil,' he averred.

At this point I became aware that the *majlis*, and indeed the shop in front, had begun to fill with market folk, all of whom examined me as if I was a curiosity. I realised that they must be other stall-holders from the market and were somewhat younger than the coffee merchant himself. He put the problem to them.

'My friend is from the north and wishes to know about the old Amir and the sheikhs. He is looking for someone who knew them.'

At this their faces lit up, and all started to talk at once, delighted at the chance to relate stories of their beloved city to a stranger. They spoke of the Ahl Yazid but clearly their favourite was Zeid, and of him they lovingly recounted every detail: his laughter, his wives and concubines, his showmanship, especially when his battles went wrong as they generally did. Abha's enemies, it seemed, were numerous and there had been many battles with a tribe called the Idrisi. They recited their names, but what struck me about this colourful version of Abha's history was that it all seemed to have taken place a very long time ago. No one had actually fought in these battles, nor had their fathers, and everything they related had been handed down. Evidently the old Abha was quite separate from the present one, a different chapter of history altogether.

'Tell me where I can find the Ahl Yazid,' I said. 'It sounds as if they might know the person I am looking for.'

'They have gone away and we don't seem to see them any more. None of them stayed after the Saudis came, when some had to go to Riyadh. They used to live in the big houses around the caravanserai but now only the rich merchants live there.'

I was mortified. Abha without its sheikhs, whom I had dreamed about all my life – I simply couldn't believe they had just disappeared. Furthermore, it didn't seem to bother the citizens in the least. 'It sounds to me as though they must have been driven away by the Saudis, and so far as Abha is concerned, the Saudis have acted like conquerors,' I said.

'That is not true, it is quite the opposite,' one answered. 'The Saudis are responsible for our current prosperity and our whole way of life. There are no wars any more and whatever their politics may be is a matter for the city governor.'

There were murmurs of agreement, but then someone else took up the story, which now took a new and unexpected turn. Abha, it seemed, had once possessed a '*raisateiba*': *raisateiba* means literally a woman warrior. I could scarcely believe what I was hearing.

'You mean this person actually fought in battle?'

'She was a sheikha, although she had once been a slave. She dressed as a youth and learned to shoot and fight with a sword. The Beni Mughe'id loved her; it was as though she was their mascot. She fought with them and they protected her. They were the only ones who knew she was really a sheikha not a sheikh.'

'What was the name of this *raisateiba*?'

There was a confused murmuring but no one answered. Suddenly they seemed to become uncertain.

'Please,' I said. 'I wish to know her name. It is important to me.' Still they hesitated but then finally someone answered, 'Sheikha Na'ema.'

It seemed to release them, and once the name was out there was no holding them back. 'Na'ema, Na'ema,' they chanted. Then came another strange piece of intelligence: 'She brought back the virgin's chariot.'

'The virgin's chariot!' I was incredulous.

'The *markab*. It hadn't been used for a hundred years. It is the chariot drawn by the warriors which carries a virgin into battle. They drag it into the middle of the fighting and her screams make them fight harder. Then sometimes she bares her breasts and that makes them madder still. She is safe, for no one will harm her because she is a woman. It would be shameful. All women are inviolate, that is the ancient law.'

At this reminder of their colourful past and favourite piece of history the entire house began to shout '*Markab, markab*', until it seemed to echo in the caravanserai beyond. The coffee merchant and I settled down to wait for the clamour to die down and when it did I thought I saw an opening. 'Ullobi,' I said. 'Wasn't there some-one called Ullobi here at Abha who fought with Sheikh Tabarhla?'

A blank silence followed. So far from it prompting that part of Abha's history I most wanted to hear, it seemed that the mention of Ullobi abruptly cut it short, and even though I tried to turn the conversation back to the *markab* it was in vain, for it was as though a spell had been broken. The stall-holders began to drift away; but now there was an interruption, for a crazed old woman entered, waving her stick.

'Na'ema,' she screamed. '*Na'ema ya gahba, ya bint al haram Na'ema.*'

She was gently led away still screaming.

'Take no notice of her,' said the coffee seller. 'She is just a mad old woman called Nura, who wanders about the city. They say that she was once a sheikha.'

Whoever she was, she evidently did not like Sheikha Na'ema very much, whom she was accusing of being a harlot.

By the time she finished the place had emptied and my hopes of finding out more were dashed. I returned to my lodging and tried to make sense of what I had heard. I had learned about everyone except my father and I could not tell if they even understood who I was talking about, yet somehow I sensed that they knew more than they were prepared to tell. It was impossible to imagine what the reason for this could be. As I pondered, I wondered whether there was not something strangely detached about these people of Abha. They loved to talk about the city and its battles but these belonged to another generation and did not seem to involve them personally in any way at all. Abha's present citizens seemed to be voyeurs of their past – it was as though they were looking at their own Bayeux Tapestry. Perhaps, I concluded, it was all because of the Wahhabis. They seemed to have finished off tribal history. They had done something terrible, they had brought peace, and also something else, I realised, as I recalled my father's descriptions: they had brought prosperity. The citizens' clothes were clean and finely cut, not like those of tribesmen any more.

The next day I went to the most crowded place I could find and there I shouted 'Ullobi' at everyone I met. Each time the man in the mosque called the faithful to prayer I shouted with him 'Ullobi ... Ullobi.' No one took the slightest notice. I became angry with them. 'OK,' I screamed. 'So you won't say anything about my father but I'll have you know that I am a Willoughby too. If you're not going to tell me anything, that's fine by me, but it will not stop me from knocking your stupid Arab heads together until I find out about Ullobi, whom I'll have you know is my father. And I care.'

They must have wondered if I had been touched by the sun but they couldn't have understood a word since my speech was in English.

The final disappearance of everything that Arabia had previously meant to me arrived when I found in the market an ancient tin of sardines bearing the label of a firm at Grimsby. Suddenly the Arabia Felix that had existed in my imagination dissolved before my eyes – ancient Abha seduced by tins of sardines. I began to realise that I would never find what I sought at Abha however long I lingered. A question was forming in my mind which was certainly not the one I started with: was this to be the end of my search or was it the beginning of a much larger one, and if that were so, where in Arabia should I go to pursue it? I had to face the unwelcome possibility that Abha was just a place that had been washed up by the tide of history and left to dry out. Somewhere,

somewhere else, there must be people who knew my father; I had to find them and I knew that the first thing I had to do was to leave Abha. I looked up to the great castle of Manadhir which brooded over the city like an ancient guardian, ominous and full of dark secrets. I wondered whether the day would come when I would return to share them.

# Chapter 5

As I JOURNEYED I brooded, and as I brooded I became increasingly sceptical and unhappy with my lot. Which is to say with myself. Perhaps I had been trading in illusions: about myself, my purposes and even about my father, too, or the historical persona I had ascribed to him. Perhaps I had not understood him at all. Certainly he must have played his part as a warrior here, there could be no doubt about that, in spite of the citizens' ignorance of him, but had I turned him into a sort of romantic ideal? I idolised my father, as a son does, but this was a father I had known only for a few days when I was a mere schoolboy and dreamed romantic dreams. Perhaps he really was the Shakespearian character that I had conceived him to be, Abha's Antony or Pompey, but then perhaps he was not; just a loyal, hardworking soldier who was Tabarhla's friend and loved Abha more than anywhere else. Then there was myself to be scrutinised. If I dared to look in the mirror – had I possessed one – I might have seen a person immature, too impressionable, a little ridiculous even; there had never been a factor in my life that allowed me to see my father in a realistic light. I wondered why I had not taken advantage of that great store of common sense and history that was my grandfather at Crowmarsh. All my childhood he would have been at my disposal for the asking, but perhaps it was that I did not want to ask because I preferred the myth I was busy inventing, stuck in a groove of childhood fantasy.

With such thoughts besieging my mind I faced a bleak and barren road into the future: this also happened to be a fair description of the road on which I actually travelled. It led to Khamis Mishait, a town not far distant from Abha, which I had chosen solely because I remembered my father had spoken of it, and I had decided that there might be something I could discover there. The way was downhill, and whether for this reason or because we had exchanged Abha for the open road Dukhaala was frisky, and we covered the journey before midday. Soon I could see Khamis Mishait in the distance, and with the season advancing it would be a relief to find shelter from the midday heat. As I approached, there was a junction where several roads met, and from a distance I could make out three horsemen standing there, apparently uncertain which road to take. They wore ordinary Bedouin clothes but had unfamiliar turbans made of white cotton. One was mounted on a huge grey that had all the appearance of being a stallion, which was unusual in these parts since stallions are not usually ridden.

One of the customs of Arabia is the casual meeting of fellow travellers, for apart from relieving the boredom of the journey there is always the chance to gain useful information on the route ahead; and so I rode towards them, and at a distance at which I could be heard I shouted the customary greeting, 'Peace be upon you.' I continued, expecting to receive the usual response, '*Aleikum es salaam*,' 'Upon you be peace,' but instead there was silence. Dukhaala's ears dropped until they lay flat on her neck. Then came the cry '*Nasrani*,' one of the Arabic words for infidel, and the next moment a torrent of the vilest words in the Arabic language accompanied by a rifle shot. I realised too late that these men must be those same Ikhwan that I had been warned about.

Desperately, I looked around me for an avenue of escape: the best seemed to be in the direction of the sun, so I wheeled the mare about and we headed straight towards it. Terrible swearing filled my ears, and then I heard a word that made me stiffen with fear: the word was 'Ullobi'.

Without any encouragement from me, Dukhaala set off at a gallop. I released her halter rope and balanced over her neck, riding as though it had been a point-to-point in Oxfordshire, then to my horror I realised that the Ikhwan were coming after me. I had a lead of perhaps forty or fifty yards and Dukhaala was extremely sure-footed, but there were three of them and the grey stallion had looked formidable from the moment that I saw him. I was concentrating so hard on the obstacles in front and in giving Dukhaala her head that I did not dare to look behind. We galloped for several miles and the Ikhwan showed no sign of tiring or holding back; then I began to be aware that they were closing the gap. I realised that the stallion was scenting my mare and for the first time I was terrified. My mind raced, searching for some wild stratagem, and when I did look behind all I saw were the white turbans and the stallion in front, full of menace.

As has been said, the prospect of imminent death wonderfully concentrates the mind, and in the throes of terror and desperation I recalled something my father had told me. He had been on a course for advanced cavalry training at Shrivenham in England, and at one point the sergeant instructor had demonstrated how to handle an escape in just such a situation as my own. Near the conclusion of the course the sergeant rehearsed a pursuit, galloping ahead of three corporals of the staff who acted as the pursuers. As they closed at the very last moment, the sergeant had produced three small bags of sawdust, raised himself in his stirrups, and in a feat of horsemanship turned so that he faced almost squarely backwards. Then he tossed the bags of sawdust one after the other so that they landed on the heads of the horses behind, causing them to swerve and slew sideways, and although they were expecting this to happen the corporals had great difficulty staying in their saddles.

I had no bags of sawdust, but the purpose of that was to avoid injury to the horses, so any object would suffice. But I only had one chance. Ahead of me lay a ridge, and I realised that if I could reach it that would give me a slight advantage and a larger and slower target to aim at. I reached the ridge, at which point my lead had shrunk to no more than a few yards, seized the water flask that I carried slung over one shoulder, and waited until the stallion came over the brow of the ridge. It presented me with a target so large it would have been difficult to miss. I raised myself as high as I dared, turned about, which without stirrups was excruciatingly difficult, and launched my water-bottle at the stallion's head.

A colossal commotion followed, which I only heard, for I was far too busy trying to regain my balance to look back. When I did manage to do so all I could see were men and horses in a writhing, roaring heap. Still in a state of terror, I fled.

We must have gone for thirty miles or more across empty sands, silent but for the sound of Dukhaala's hooves, and although there could have been no further pursuit, fear drove me onward regardless. Wherever it was that we eventually reached must have been a long way to the south, but after my escape I neither knew nor cared where it was. We had reached mountains that were wilder and higher than any I had ridden and the track became narrower and steeper. I had hoped that there might be a Bedouin settlement where we could shelter, but the landscape was bare, empty of human beings altogether.

Finally we stopped out of exhaustion, and then as darkness fell it grew cold and I began to fret at having come to such an inhospitable place. Dukhaala herself seemed unconcerned either by the day's events or by the lack of fodder, and as soon as I released her she rolled and then settled on the ground. I was wearing garments which were quite light, the Arab ones I had adopted long since in order to be inconspicuous. On top I wore a *thaub*, a sort of ill-fitting coat made of coarsely woven goat hair, and in this I slept warmly, as it happened, since I lay between the legs of my mare.

When morning came I knew that I had to find food and water for both of us. We started soon after dawn and climbed until we reached the top of the mountain, where there was a pass that led into a different landscape, formed like a plateau and extending southward in mile after mile of rock-strewn scrub. Eventually we came to a settlement which in such a wilderness seemed an unexpectedly large one, a town built like Abha in a hollow of the mountains with houses that were made of mud bricks and not stone. I thought it best to seek out the governor since all cities in Arabia, whether large or small, have a governor, and as I had long since discovered it is important to make yourself known to him at the start lest you be mistaken for an outcast or a spy. Soon a small retinue of children gathered to greet the unexpected stranger and with their help I found the house of the governor, although I was surprised that there was no customary green flag outside, or indeed flag of any sort.

I presented myself and produced my Saudi letter of introduction to an official who turned out to be the governor himself, who examined it as if it were something of an unexpected novelty. Several minutes passed whilst he studied it, front and back and the various Saudi stamps on it. When he had finished, he looked up. 'I must ask you for what reason you have come to Yemen?'

I gasped at the word 'Yemen'. It was blindingly obvious that the route I had taken would lead me into Yemen, and I could scarcely believe that I could have been so stupid as not to realise it. Yemen, as everyone knew, was the long-time enemy of the hated Saudis.

'I must tell you,' he continued, without waiting for me to answer, 'you are not welcome here. No person from Riyadh is welcome here. We wished to make peace with the Saudi and we signed a treaty with ibn Saud himself at Taif, but he makes war on us as before.'

Plainly, I had trapped myself. I could see where the conversation was leading and whilst perfectly polite he was clearly an official who had more than local authority. Somehow I was going to have to talk my way out of such a dangerous situation; obviously I had arrived in Yemen by mistake, but I thought my best chance was to make out otherwise.

'I am here as the representative of my country and bear gifts for your Imam,' I said, in as lofty a manner as I could manage.

'We do not accept gifts from the Saudi.'

'They do not come from the Saudi. These are gifts from the King and Queen of England.'

'Vik reah!' He was better informed than I had imagined, even if a little out of date.

'Queen Victoria indeed,' I replied. I produced Bridgewater's maps, which I carried in a satchel for easy access. 'I am commanded to present these maps to The Excellency Imam Yahya with her royal compliments. I rely upon you to assist me in my passage to Sana so that I may fulfil my mission.' I laid the maps on the table before him with a sweep of the arm. 'These show the tribes along the border of Yemen, their *dirahs* and their current alliances, which will enable you to judge their intention in case of war. Our Queen is proud of the ancient friendship that exists between our two countries and believes that in the natural order of events the Imam will become ruler of all Arabia, therefore she wishes to aid him in his purpose. She has ordered me to present to the Imam Yahya the very latest maps prepared by her Royal Navy.'

'This is very strange, because we do not know England and have never had any contact with that country.' He hesitated. 'I shall need time to think the matter over and seek further advice. Meanwhile I shall hold you prisoner.'

I protested. 'You cannot imprison me, an envoy of the Queen . . .'

He interrupted me. 'It is solely for your own safety. There are no foreigners in Yemen and the reason for that is that they are killed, for this is the religion of the tribesman. Therefore the only way that I may protect you is to make you a prisoner. You will be properly treated, your horse likewise.'

With these words he turned on his heel and left me with his subordinate. I found myself escorted to another house at the rear, and the iron gate of the courtyard clanked shut behind me. After a while they brought me some dates and camel's milk. My fate clearly hung on Bridgewater's maps, which I calculated would not be forwarded to Imam Yahya or anyone else. In the further reaches of Arabia a map of any sort is a rarity and has the same novelty that a 'Brownie' camera, for instance, has for us. I took comfort from the look of surprise on the man's face when I laid the maps before him, which was a sight to see.

Next morning I was returned to the governor's office to await my fate. At least it was clear that he had thoroughly examined the maps. 'I do not understand,' he began, 'exactly how it is that you have arrived in Sadaah on this mission since we have no contact with England, although Queen Vik reah is known to us. In any case you may not proceed to Sana. I must tell you that your maps do not show us anything which we did not know already, although they seem to confirm that the Idrisi at Sabiya are forming alliances with other tribes for the purpose of making war. Doubtless they plan to attack our northern border if we do not attack them first. We know that they have bullied the local tribes before and now it is evident that they control the Riyal el M'a, just as they manipulate all the tribes. "You do the fighting and we're right behind you".' He laughed delightedly at his joke. 'The Idrisi are foul perverts who preach a heathen doctrine and carry out practices which are loathsome in our country. Our Imam has decided that they shall be driven out of Arabia all together. With regard to yourself, although you may not proceed to San'a we have decided to pardon you for entering Yemen without our permission.'

'I will report your words to our Queen,' I said stiffly.

'Now that the matter is closed I shall consider the question of how you may return to Jeddah, from which we perceive from your papers you have come. I must tell you, as *nasrani*, a foreigner and an infidel, you are in greater peril than you realise. I have arranged for you to be escorted to Hali, which is the nearest Red Sea port beyond our northern border, and no doubt at some time there will arrive a steamboat that will convey you to Jeddah. As soon as the escort is prepared for the journey you will leave.' He stroked his chin, as Arab people have a habit of doing when they are pleased with a speech that makes a fine show of their hospitality. I judged that it was the nearest I would get to a welcome and returned a modest bow, concealing my relief – and also my gratitude to Bridgewater.

*

It took just three days to reach Hali, a journey which for me might have been just an escape from Yemen but which proved to be much more than that; indeed, it was a heart-warming experience. The escort consisted of members of a tribe from the fringes of the city of Sadaah, young and mostly under twenty, who carried their rifles ostentatiously and rode camels. They were extremely adept at scavenging for our needs and once I had adjusted to their dialect they proved excellent companions, evidently regarding it as an adventure and a diversion from serious fighting, wherever that may have been.

However, the journey was important to me for a different reason, for during it I made a decision which was to radically alter my way of life. In the past I had set myself clear objectives and then striven for them, but in Arabia, as I had discovered, no one ever strove for anything; they believed that all direction came from God and everything would happen as He chose. Perhaps it was not surprising that all my efforts thus far had ended in abject failure: I had nearly got myself murdered, and after that might have had to spend the rest of my life as a prisoner of the Yam. I realised that there was something fundamentally wrong with my whole philosophy. It was certainly not that of travellers of the past, who had been patient and had adapted their ways to those of the Arabs; they had chosen no more than a general direction and then allowed their travels to be shaped by events. They never strove as remorselessly as I had done, and yet they always seemed to find what it was they were seeking in the end. Everything would happen in accordance with the laws of probability, and so long as they kept faith and were patient, solutions would present themselves, just as they did for the Arabs, who were directed by God.

I had to unlearn my whole Western way of life. I knew that this surrender would be painful and protracted, but at Hali I was determined to make a fresh start.

*

It was a prosperous little port, a point of embarkation for the pilgrim traffic, and since the *haj* had just ended there were many pilgrims waiting, like myself, for boats to take them home. The port itself was not much more than a simple mooring place where steamboats of shallow draught could tie up at a long wooden jetty beneath a small castle. Considering the fact that there were many miles of sand and no trees at all, the wooden construction seemed remarkable, until I realised that it must have been built by the Turks for their intended conquest of Yemen. What was also remarkable was that the whole of the shore bordering the town, which seemed to lie on the sea as much as it did on the land, was lined by sharpened wooden poles driven into the seabed some fifty yards from the shore. These were invisible at high tide and half uncovered at low, the tides of the Red Sea being much smaller than elsewhere. It was difficult to imagine the purpose of such a barrier since it could scarcely have been built to repel the sea, nor would the Turks have had any reason to construct such an obstacle. Perhaps it had been there before they came and was to repel something else – intruders such as pirates from Somalia? I lodged it in my mind as something I would one day look into when I knew that country better, since at some time I needed to visit the other side of the Red Sea, where I was beginning to suspect I would find the breeding grounds of the locusts. Did Somalia export something else besides locusts, such as pirate dhows? In that case Hali, rich and right on the sea, was a perfect and wide-open quarry.

I found lodgings in the town and settled down to wait for a boat, which was not irksome at all for the season was advancing and with impending spring the Red Sea coast was very agreeable. However, the month of February can deceive a newcomer and at this moment I had no experience of what was to follow during the dry season, when my present way of life would be changed out of recognition. But for now the wells of Hali ran in abundance and the townsfolk were friendly, contented after a season which had been prosperous, as was shown by the steamboats sailing southward, packed with pilgrims.

The sands of the seashore were limitless and deserted, and I rode Dukhaala each day mile after mile along the tide's edge, and grazed her on the lush vegetation behind, until her condition was so improved I wondered that she had ridden so well before. As a matter of fact, Dukhaala was causing me some concern for I had become so used to her, so dependent upon her, in fact, that the prospect of having to part with her was becoming painful. That our adventures together, and our misadventures, should end when Dukhaala was exchanged for a handful of riyals seemed contrary to the natural order of things. The local horse dealer was keen to make the deal, and was quite prepared to pay me a sum that would show me a profit, which I certainly had need of at this moment, so I steeled myself to spend the next morning on the sands and afterwards bid her farewell.

When that moment arrived, I rode into the dealer's yard, where I hoped the matter would be swiftly concluded. However, the plan I had formed had not reckoned with Dukhaala herself, for once we were in the dealer's yard it was plain that she knew exactly what was going to happen, as indeed I might have guessed for I had long known that she could read my mind. She stood stock-still, raised her head and stared at me, and I found myself gazing at two enormous dilating almond eyes – 'Dukhaala' means 'almond-eyed'. I froze; I told the dealer that his price was too low and in doing so realised that what I was really saying was that I would refuse any price he might offer.

Somehow, I had to change the arrangement altogether. I mumbled an apology and as the dealer's face lengthened I jumped on to Dukhaala's back and rode away. I resolved that somehow I would contrive to take her with me, and having made this decision I awaited the arrival of a northbound boat with a lighter heart. As I looked at the horizon each day I thought of the story of Vartak, the Turkish sea captain that Father had told me about, with whose help they had liberated Jeddah. Vartak, I decided, was just the person I needed now.

# Chapter 6

WEEKS PASSED, AND one day there did arrive a steamer bound northward. It was a small enough boat but my hopes that it might be Vartak were dashed when I saw it had two funnels, for as I knew from what Father had told me that his boat had only one. It tied up at the quay and remained there for the whole day, taking on fuel and supplies. Its name, the *Alhambra*, seemed familiar, and I wondered whether I had encountered a vessel of that name somewhere else. For me it looked like a good prospect since the aft deck where the passengers and cargo were carried was empty except for two Bedouin shepherds with their goats, which were hobbled and tied to the guard rails. There were also a lot of chickens in wicker baskets, no doubt destined for the markets of Jaizan or Jeddah.

When they had finished loading stores, a small kiosk opened at the landward end of the gangway where a steward took fares and issued tickets. He also carefully recorded the names of the passengers in a ledger, a task with which I had to help him, since Willoughby, even in Arabic, proved to be beyond him. So I wrote my name myself, first in Arabic letters and then in English, adding Dukhaala and making a light-hearted gesture towards her which made him laugh. To my relief we were allowed to board, although matters became more complicated when we reached the aft deck where the first mate was supervising the loading. At the sight of Dukhaala he raised both hands in a gesture that boded ill, but for this I was prepared and before he could say anything I pressed into his hand my last riyal. At this he relented and let me tie Dukhaala's halter to the rail and put a loose hobble on her forefeet, to which she was quite used. I persuaded myself that my plan had succeeded and in due course made a place beside her for my straw palliasse. To my relief, my cargo was evidently deemed acceptable, and after that no one seemed to take much notice of us, least of all the pilgrim families who had boarded at the same time, as they were taken up with their eating arrangements. Eventually, having raised steam, and to a blast from the horn, we set forth on a sea as dark and smooth as the surface of a pond.

Dukhaala did not seem to be concerned by her boat trip and after a while settled herself on the deck, at which I did the same. Some hours later I was just nodding off to sleep when the ship's rudimentary intercom, which was not much more than a loud-hailer, came to life. At first it was difficult to make out what was being announced but then I heard the name Willoughby and my heart sank. I realised that the first mate must have reported that I was travelling with a horse and that the ship's captain had prob-ably taken exception to it; our situation suddenly began to look bleak. I glanced at the distant shore line and tried to reckon our chances of reaching it: I decided that they were poor. I got up to go and report myself. 'If they want to pitch Dukhaala into the sea then I'll go with her,' I said aloud. 'We'll ride the waves together as we've ridden other waves before.' I reached the ship's bridge and found the captain in a smart naval cap above his overalls, with the first mate standing beside him.

'I am so sorry,' I stammered. 'I have to get the mare to Jeddah and I'm not allowed to let her out of my sight, she is blood-stock.' I named the most famous breed in Arabia – *al hamdani*. 'I'm quite prepared to pay for her passage, although on this particular trip I have no more riyals so it will have to be by scrubbing your decks.'

'I don't understand what you are talking about,' replied the captain, speaking in very passable English. 'I called you to come because I happened to see that your name was Willoughby. A long time ago I had a great friend of that name, a Captain Willoughby who was known as Ullobi, and I thought you might know him.'

'Praise God,' I said. 'Am I imagining things or is this real? Can it be possible that you are Ahmet Vartak?'

The extraordinary encounter soon led to an exchange of our histories, which assumed Dickensian proportions. It continued in the captain's cabin over a dinner which was accompanied by several bottles of Turkish vodka, and our respective tales grew larger as the evening progressed. It was my first real encounter with my father in Arabia, and to my embarrassment it ended with Vartak vacating his own bunk and insisting that I should sleep there whilst he himself slept on the floor.

It was clear that Vartak and my father had shared extraordinary experiences, which he was bursting to tell me about, and as the story emerged I realised that never before had Vartak found so willing an audience as myself. He had encyclopaedic knowledge of the Red Sea coast, having spent his whole life sailing it, and also knew much about the As'ir at the time my father was active there; but his abiding obsession was with the *Alhambra* itself, to which he always returned and which was the subject of his great story. Given his vivid way of putting things, this proved to be a captivating odyssey and provided me with an entirely new perspective of my father.

'One day we were coming into port at Yenbo,' Vartak began, 'when there was an almighty bang and I knew at once that she had broken her propeller shaft. Next thing I saw was that the screw had ripped through her stern timbers and it looked like we was going to sink. I went below and there was busted machinery all over the engine room and it was a miracle no one was hurt. Somehow we got her into Yenbo, where we was lucky the dry dock was empty. Next day I took my engineer, and in the next few weeks we went through every shipyard right up to Aqaba itself, searching, but there was nothing that would fit the *Alhambra* because she weren't a Red Sea vessel. She'd been built on Tyneside in England. So we went back to Yenbo and looked to see if there was anything that we could do, but there wasn't and truly it looked like she was a goner. My engineer took himself off to look for work on another boat but I couldn't do that. I couldn't just leave the *Alhambra*. I hung about at Yenbo, feeling worse and worse. Suddenly, praise be to God, your papa turned up, which he used to do from time to time when he wanted me to ship him and his men somewhere for fighting. I told him what happened and he got excited and wanted to see for himself, so I showed him the engine room and all the mess. A strange look came over his face and suddenly he was like a kid that's been given a new toy.

'Now I knew that your papa was handy with explosives but I never knew he was an engineer. "Bring me some tools," he said and there and then blow me if he didn't start taking the whole assembly apart, which was several hours of work. I couldn't see the point of it myself because there were no new shafts to be had, that I knew, but I just went along with it and after a while started helping him. We got it all to bits, as far as the engine itself, where we found that the drive itself was intact, undamaged, and your papa started smiling and laughing and swore he could fix it.

'He wanted everything packed into boxes that we could load on to camels or donkeys. "We're going to Jeddah," he said. "What for?" I said. "Because we're going to find a new shaft in the old British arsenal. I've known the place for years because it was where I used to get my explosives from, and there's lots of other stuff there. The quartermaster who worked for Captain Lawrence is a friend of mine."

'So off we went to Jeddah and by now he'd explained more about the place. There was a whole section for Royal Navy spares and he was sure we'd find a shaft that fit the *Alhambra*. We got there and blow me if the corporal on guard at the gates didn't blooming well salute him as if he was the general himself. He made me wait in the quartermaster's office while he went and saw what he could find. It was about three hours before he came back and then his face was as long as could be. "You can't believe it," he said, "this place was stacked with naval stuff and now there's none at all. That can only mean one thing, it means the navy has got here first and stolen the lot. We're going to have to make do with the tank spares." "Tank spares!" I said. "Oh, I know there were never any tanks here in the desert war, there were never any tanks in Arabia at all. What must have happened is some clerk made a mistake and instead of sending the spares to the Western Front he sent them here instead." So we went into the town and found a doss-house and I'll tell you we neither of us remembered much of what happened because I'd brought some vodka with us and after that we didn't notice what a hovel we was in.

'Next day we went back and he sorted out everything what we needed. He found two tank drive shafts with their assemblies. He said he was going to need two to get the length. He even found a complete field workshop with a generator and had the depot staff pack it all up in regulation teak chests. I hired a couple of drivers with camels and back we went with all the stuff to Yenbo. He'd thought of everything, and I said to myself, Vartak, what you have to do is to be the apprentice, give him what he wants and wait on him hand and foot, because I could see that a miracle could be goin' to happen.

'We got to Yenbo, which I knew pretty well, and I found a place where your papa could set up the workshop and get the generator going. We started from scratch and in a few days he had built a test rig where we put the two drive shafts together, the same as they would be in the boat, to see what parts had to be made. Then he made me fetch all the busted stuff from the *Alhambra* right back as far as the engine itself. In a week we'd set up the assembly and he found out what was going to be needed and started the lathing. He got fidgety because he'd calculated the stresses, and it was a question of whether the shafts from Jeddah were going to be strong enough. "Anyway, we just have to hope," he said, and then he had to find a way of matching it all to the *Alhambra*'s engine. All the time he was machinin' and doin' it again and again for days on end.

'Finally he was satisfied, put oil into all the bearings and sealed them and started the testing rig on lowest revs. He said we'd run it for an hour and then dismantle it and check the parts. Next day we ran the rig for twelve hours before he dismantled it and I began to think, Vartak, you could be in the shipping business again. I said, "Willoughby, if you get my ship to sea I'll sail you anywhere you ask for half a year." "Done," he said, "only you don't know what you're letting yourself in for." "Then you pay for the oil," I said, "by the way."

'About two weeks later he was ready and we dismantled the rig and took everything onboard. There, it was much more difficult than he had expected and it was a long time before he could make it fit the *Alhambra*'s engine, and we had to go back to the workshop time and again. Meanwhile, I got a team of shipwrights to work on the hull and it was lucky that were in a dry dock that was empty. As it was a timber hull with copper plating, the carpenters were doing the same as what they were used to with the big dhows, and they certainly took a lot of trouble. I think by now the whole of Yenbo was looking at the *Alhambra* and the work Captain Willoughby was doing, which was a wonder to them. Eventually we got to the point where we could do a sea trial, and I'll tell you when they let the water in and I saw my *Alhambra* floating again I had tears in my eyes. "Come on," he said, "you haven't seen anything yet, and you watch out she doesn't sink or all my work will be wasted."

'He wasn't taking any chances with the screw and he only let me turn the engine over slow whilst he oiled and oiled. We sailed round the harbour until he was satisfied and finally he said we'd try it in the open sea. The problem was the screw going fast then slow when the swell struck her, and he studied all the parts like a doctor would.

'It turned out to be a good thing that all Yenbo was watching us, for one day who should turn up at the quay but my old engineer. He couldn't believe his eyes when he saw the *Alhambra* steaming round the harbour. We had a right reunion, I can tell you, and then of course he was raring to come back. So he met Captain Willoughby and in no time they were at it together down in the engine room, which was handy because my engineer knew how she would behave at sea.

'We did trials for the next week and all that time the new shaft held and there were no problems that they couldn't sort out between them. Then we took our first pay load, which was a dry cargo for Jeddah, and when we got there that night we were so high we all go off to the what's yer fancy house.

'By this time I was wondering what would happen next, and I didn't have to wait long to find out. "You'll have to excuse me," your papa said. "Since I'm in Jeddah I'm going to collect my pay arrears, because I'm still in the army as far as the British know, and after that I'm going back to Abha." "Wait a minute," I said. "What happens if she breaks down again?", for my heart was bleedin' at the thought of him going. "She won't," he said. "I've had her on full revs and everything held perfectly," and blow me, the next minute he'd gone off. So me and my engineer, we got back into the business, but all my life I'd never forget who it was that got us out of the mess we were in.'

*

'Vartak,' I said, 'tell me one thing about the *Alhambra*. It has two funnels, but my father told me about it and I remember he said she only had one funnel.'

'She does have one funnel and your memory is right,' he laughed. 'She still has, but we disguise ourselves when we're in foreign waters, like when we're working up from Yemen. In Arabia there's always fighting somewhere and everyone wants to know what side you're on, so it's safer to keep them guessing. We were once shot at down there and several times there was trouble, so if there's a green-and-yellow flag on the stern and two funnels we're taken for a Yemeni boat. The second funnel is made of old oil drums and we take it down as we come north and put up a green flag, though maybe we was a bit late the time you noticed it. There's something else I have to be careful about, which is my being Turkish. That don't matter in Yemen where there weren't any Turks, but up north at Aqaba, where there was a Turkish occupation, it's another matter. If they knew I was a Turk they'd have my ears off, so down here I'm Vartak and up there I'm Ahmet from Syria. You've always got to keep looking behind you in this business.

'Another thing we have is pirates and that's what this cupboard full of rifles is for. They're handy if they try and board us. "Pirates astern" is the order the crew loves best, though only me or Masalik the mate is allowed to give the order and then the rifles are passed round. Often they keep comin' even when the odds are stacked against them, and I'll never know if the Somalis are brave or just stupid, but they soon find out what they've taken on. I've never seen Masalik miss a Somali once he's got him in his sights.

'As I was saying, it half broke my heart to see your papa go. I didn't see him for a while and several pilgrim seasons passed before he turned up again. Then I got word that he wanted to meet me in Jeddah because he was after another load of stuff from the arsenal. That made me wonder what was in his mind and if he was going to take me up on my promise to sail him where he wanted to go, so after I got his message I didn't take on any more passengers for awhile. We met up in the quartermaster's office same as last time, as he'd arranged.

'"Hello, Vartak," he said breezily. "What we've come here for is guns." "What," I said, "like Lewis guns?" "No," he said, "big guns." "What for?" I said, because I was getting suspicious. "Why, to put them on your boat, of course," he said. "To ship them somewhere?" I said. "Not ship them anywhere," he was bold as brass and laughing, "to fire them from your boat." I tried to interrupt because I thought he was talking no sense but he'd got it all worked out. "We're going to attack Jaizan," he said. I gulped because that's the Idrisi and I knew he had scores to settle with them.

'So after his explainin' we went into the stores and looked at the field guns he'd discovered. They were all in pieces, still packed in their cases for shipping, and never been assembled. With them were boxes of shells and fuses, lots of them, which he opened and showed me, what looked to me like three-inch ones or bigger. It dawned on me that what he was after was to turn my *Alhambra* into a battleship so he could go and blow up Jaizan. "Have you gone crazy?" I said. "My ship's not your HMS Hood, it can't support guns like that, think of the recoil." "It will," he said, "after we've made a few alterations." So we loaded the cases and a lot of explosives he had found and sailed back to Yenbo, where the first thing he did was to get the workshop goin' again.

'We put one of the guns together, and a beauty it was when we had finished. Now I could see why he was so keen, but they were never made to be used on board a ship. I went along with him and we put one of the guns aboard and tied it with ropes to the moorin' bollards. I'd never had much to do with guns myself and I don't think your papa had either, for that matter, so I saw it was going to be learning time for both of us. We went to sea and he put a shell into the breach, lit the fuse and fired. It nearly deafened us and it was lucky he was not in the way because the barrel reared up, pointing to the sky, all its moorings broken as though they were made of string. The gun was smoking hot and the ropes were smoking too. "Wait," I said. "Don't touch it till I get the asbestos gloves from the engine room."

'After that we went back to Yenbo and your papa wasn't saying much at all. I said that we had to build a proper emplacement in the stern with steels bolted to the bulkheads. It had to be anchored with chains and have proper anchorages welded to the steels. Like this, we talked it over for the rest of the day and decided while we were about it to raise the gunnels so there would be a bit of protection if someone fired back.

'After that we made the emplacement, and while he was working I read the instruction manual for the first time and found we had to prime the barrel before firing – which was why it got so hot and it's a wonder it didn't set us on fire. Then I worried about the extra weight and how it would affect her sailing, but when we started a trial I saw it was no problem at all. We fired a shell and the gun held firm and there was a white splash where it landed most of half a mile away. "Hold it there," I said, "and wait now till we've got a proper target," because I could see that the *Alhambra* was goin' to be a warship all right and there was no point in him getting carried away and wasting good shells. So he got his men and explosives and off we went to Jaizan.

'The old Turkish fort was built for a garrison of a hundred or so and your papa had already decided which end he was going to start on. "Get in close," he said, "and lay off shore about two hundred yard." "What about their rifles?" I said. "That's what we raised the gunnels for," he said. "There aren't any gunnels on the bridge," I said. "In that case I suppose you'll feel safer at four hundred then," so I could see he was callin' me a coward. "I have to think of the *Alhambra* and the crew," I said. "Don't worry," he said, "I'm going to blast the fort so hard there won't be any answering back," and nor was there. I'll tell you, once your papa got the range that Jaizan fortress might have been a sandcastle, and the Idrisi came out like ants when their heap's been trodden on. They swarmed on top of the walls and his *ghazzu* picked them off whilst he went on shellin' till there were no more comin' out. "All right," he said, "now's the time we'll sail into the harbour and see what the opposition's like. If it's not too bad we'll land." Myself, I wasn't so keen on this at all because if there was trouble we'd be stuck, so I was hesitating. "Don't you mind, I'll make sure you're safe," he said, waving the new service revolver he found at the arsenal. See, he was getting at me again.

'So I decided I would chance it and we sailed into the harbour, which to my surprise was as quiet as if it was a holiday. Your papa was boiling with excitement and there was blood lust in his eyes and nothing I said was going to stop him. "Land the gun and any shells that are left and the explosives," he said, "because I've got work to do. I'll come back and see you at Jeddah when I've sorted this thing out. The *ghazzu* are only boys and I've got to look after them. Then we'll take the gun back to Abha. I'll pay for the oil next time we meet like we agreed."

'With that, he hopped ashore and that was the last I saw of him. I stood off Jaizan for a bit and there were some almighty explosions. The cranes and landing quays all fell into the sea, so I thought I might as well go back to Jeddah whilst the *Alhambra* was still in one piece. After that, Jaizan went quiet as the grave, and I can see there isn't going to be much pilgrim business there for a while.'

As Vartak finished, my brain was flooded by the pictures he painted of my father, and what this episode must have been like. But I was left confused. 'How do you know he wasn't killed after that?'

'Man like that doesn't get himself killed that easy. Been in too many scrapes before. It's my belief it's just a matter of time before he shows up again.'

'When did all this happen, Vartak?'

'A few years ago now, maybe ten, it's hard to remember.'

'Well, I can't just leave the story there, I still want to know what happened. There must be someone who knows and I must go and find them.'

'By now I should think everyone in the As'ir knows what happened. Your papa must be part of history in those parts.'

'That's not how it seemed to be when I went to Abha. They hadn't heard of him or if they had they wouldn't say.'

Vartak looked surprised. 'Then you should ask them in Khurma.'

'Why Khurma?'

'Because they know everything in Khurma. It is the place for news, because it's at the centre of Arabia. It's where the Hejaz meets the As'ir and the Nejd, where west meets east, and all the travellers pass through Khurma. It's also where the past meets the present, and times are changing – this is always the way in Arabia, I've seen it over and over. First there's Turks, then Idrisi, then Hashemites and the Sheriff of Mecca. Everything changes anew now the Wahhabis arrive, and I've got to get new flags again. But it's only on the surface it changes; underneath, everything in Arabia stays the way it always was for ordinary people like me. So long as there's Mecca there'll be pilgrims and so long as there's pilgrims I'll have my business and my home.' Vartak's Turkish cigar wafted about us and I thought what an adaptable man he was, the best I had met in these parts.

'Are you married, Vartak?'

'Yes, I am. Not in the old Turkish way for I have only one wife. We live at Lith with our six children. One day my son will sail the *Alhambra* after me, and I have sent him to Cairo University to study shipping and navigation so that he may know better than I do. Anyway, to go back to what we were talking about. I have just thought of something else. There's another reason for you to go to Khurma, where I said. There's a man lives there who knows what goes on everywhere in Arabia, a slave dealer I often used to carry on my ship, coming back from the market at Mukalla. We became friends, although I had to be pretty careful around Jeddah because what he carried was really contraband. He goes everywhere because his caravans travel all over Arabia. He only deals in the best quality, so he knows everyone from the Asheukh downwards. His name is Ferdhan bin Murzuk, and if anyone can tell you what happened to your father he will be the one to ask.'

# Chapter 7

IT WAS NOT until after we moored at Jeddah that I had time to reflect on what Vartak had told me. For the first time I had gained some real understanding of my father. I could imagine what his life was like, how he thought and the way he drove himself. Very hard; just as it had seemed on his visit to England. Perhaps this was just because he was a Willoughby. My grandfather had told me so many stories about the fighting Willoughbys, whose paintings hung on the walls at Crowmarsh, and indeed of his own exploits on the north-west frontier of India, recorded in the book of sepia photographs. Or could it be that Father was trying to escape from something in England? From domesticity, perhaps, even from marriage. I began to wonder if I had inherited the Willoughby trait and was a fighting Willoughby myself underneath. I'd fight all right if I had to protect my family or in a war, but this blood lust thing some of the Willoughbys had, I didn't have that and I suppose I'd known it all along. I wasn't escaping from anything, just searching.

Meanwhile, I had to supervise the landing of Dukhaala, who seemed to have survived the voyage quite happily in my absence, having being cared for by a deck-hand assigned by Vartak for this sole purpose, as she was such a valuable *hamdani*. I have to confess to a pang of guilt that she whom I was not prepared to allow out of my sight should have been forgotten and neglected by myself throughout a voyage that had lasted several days. However, she did not appear to hold it against me and I found lodging for both of us in Jeddah whilst I wrote up my reports for the Locust and Naval

Bureaux and then sent an account of what I had learned about Father to Lavender, as this was the first time I had the means of doing so. She had been very brave when I left and had made me swear to tell her the truth of everything, however painful.

This done, I took Vartak's advice and we set out for Khurma. By this time I had adopted the easy-going habit of hurrying slowly in the best tradition of Arabian travel and now returned to my previous routine of stopping at Bedouin settlements along the route. After a week I reached Khurma, a perfect oasis in the middle of Arabia with a dense fringe of palm trees that was visible for miles across the silver mirage reflected by the sand. It was a welcome relief from the desert, one that I sensed my one-man caravan shared with centuries of travellers upon countless similar arrivals at this oasis. I knew at once that I had reached the very heart of Arabia.

The hour was just before midday as I had planned, in order that I should have sufficient time to search for the *qasr* of Ferdhan bin Murzuk. However, this took no time at all for the first person I asked pointed to his house, and probably every other citizen in Khurma would have done the same. It was the only large house in the oasis and lay in a compound of its own, half hidden behind high stone walls. I rode through the open entrance and into a courtyard, where I dismounted, and then as custom required, contrived to busy myself with Dukhaala's *risan* until a servant approached. After explaining what I wanted I was conducted to an inner courtyard, where the lady of the house stood waiting, heavily veiled in the custom of these parts; this indicated that Ferdhan himself was not at home. After we had exchanged formalities, I ventured the reason for my visit in a suitably fulsome speech which I had prepared for the occasion:

'O honoured lady.' I paused for effect. 'By God's grace I have journeyed to Khurma, to bear to the person of Ferdhan bin Murzuk a greeting from the sea captain of Lith, whose name is Ahmet Vartak.'

This certainly had the effect I intended of breaking the ice, indeed rather more than that. I had been fairly sure that Vartak would be remembered because he was not the sort of man that anyone would forget, but now, at the mention of his name, her whole manner changed. She at once led me into the house, which was like a palace, to a reception *majlis*, where she beckoned me to a chair and sat down facing me. Then she made her own speech of welcome with a perfect economy of words whose quaint formality and elegant elaboration of the hand of the Almighty in the matter made my own effort seem homely by comparison. However, no formality could disguise her excitement for she repeated the name of Vartak several times, gazing heavenwards as she did so, and raising her arms so that I even wondered if they might be going to descend about my neck in an embrace.

A slave was despatched to convey the news of my arrival to Ferdhan, and then as custom everywhere dictates, the coffee ritual began, after which I was besieged by a barrage of questions and was made to relate every detail of my voyage with Vartak and the *Alhambra*. As I finished, it prompted the good lady to begin a story of her own involving Vartak and her husband, which Vartak had not told me. Evidently the three had shared a drama which had begun at Sabiya, where one of Ferdhan's caravans had been ambushed by the Idrisi and Ferdhan himself had been put into prison. After a month of anguished waiting a ransom demand reached Khurma by one of the camel drivers, who was released for the purpose of conveying it. Great consternation ensued and the outcome was that Vartak, out of his friendship with Ferdhan and doubtless in one of his chameleonic disguises, had been the agent for conveying the ransom to Mohammed the Black. The result was Ferdhan's release and a species of sainthood for Vartak ever afterwards. I could only bask in the after-glow of this honourable deed since I now received my own portion of the lady's gratitude, being awarded the status of guest of honour. At this point Ferdhan himself appeared, his entrance creating a perceptible stir through the household, and my mission having been explained to him, every detail of my story had to be repeated for his benefit.

I soon found myself sharing the general sense of awe at his arrival, which was celebrated with due ceremony fitting to the grandeur of El Donaiis – which as I learned was the name of this palace. Ferdhan had his own style of *noblesse oblige*, quite different from that of the tribal sheikhs, although like these he had presence, aided by good looks and a very erect carriage that made him appear taller than he actually was. He was perfectly groomed, his beard carefully trimmed, and he wore an expensive *abbah* of fine white camel's hair and a *kefiyah* with head ropes. The whole impression he gave was certainly grand. Evidently he was also a stickler for correctness, apparent in the way his every need was at once attended to by the diligent slaves, and at the times for prayer everything in the house had to stop as soon as it was called. He was also particular in the matter of hospitality, for one of his first acts upon arrival was to order a sheep to be slaughtered and a feast prepared in my honour. This was long before he knew who I was or that I had come from Vartak, and would probably have always been his custom on receiving any guest.

In due course I was allotted a slave, who prepared my quarter and attended to my needs. His services turned out to include preparing a bath, an ancient affair filled by buckets, into which I sank as soon as I was allowed to retire and refresh myself. I found myself in a room overlooking an elegant stone court which, as it was now past sunset, was lit everywhere by oil lamps. It was my initiation into the world of El Donaiis, and when the meal was ended and I went to bed, I lay awake listening to the sawing of the cicadas and the mating calls of the owls. It was a stark contrast with the Bedouin settlements where I generally spent my nights.

*

The following morning I made my way to Ferdhan's quarter, where he lived apart from the rest of the household. I found him listening to an ancient gramophone with a trumpet loudspeaker, which to my amazement was playing Beethoven's Emperor Concerto. As

I entered he lifted the head off the record, wound up the machine, then with a pen-knife he sharpened a new thorn, which acted as the stylus, and started playing the record again.

He greeted me brightly. 'I thought that this might make you feel at home. It is my favourite music, although it is a pity that it is so short; whoever wrote it should have made it much longer.' I realised that he had only a single record, which like others of the time recorded no more than five minutes, and that the rest of the work was missing, a matter he had evidently not appreciated.

'Indeed, it is very beautiful,' I said. 'Actually, I came to talk to you about Abha, because Vartak told me that you sometimes go there, and you know the sheikhs. They might have information about my father, who has been in Arabia a long time and was at Abha when we last heard of him. He was a friend of Tabarhla, the son of the Amir, and I am trying to find someone who can tell me what has happened to him. He is known there as Ullobi.'

'Let us take a walk,' said Ferdhan. 'I will show you El Donaiis and I will tell you what I know concerning your father. Some time in the past I heard that there was a *nasara* at Abha and that he had become a famous figure there. Since I had never encountered a *nasara* I decided to make a trip to Abha, where I often went, and so I met your father. This was before the Saudis came and took most of the sheikhs to Riyadh. Abha was ruled by an amir, Zeid bin Tahir, with the sheikhs of the Ahl Yazid, the ruling clan. Tabarhla was the eldest son of Zeid, who was a spiteful old man, and both of them had a great love for Ullobi. Until I met him I didn't know what to expect, but I can tell you he may have been a *nasara* but I would never have known it. He dressed like a Bedu sheikh and from his accent I would never have guessed he was anything else. I could see that he was very popular and he had a great sense of fun.

'On the first evening of my visit we all sat down together, and when we had finished eating they told me Ullobi needed my help because he was looking for a wife. Certainly, I said, he could have the pick of any number of wives if he would say exactly what he wanted. Then Ullobi spoke.

'"Unfortunately it's not quite so easy. The problem is that I have a wife already and being a *nasara* I'm not allowed to take another."

'"By the rule made by the Prophet himself you can have four wives," I said.

'"Not in my religion you can't," he replied. "You may have only one at a time".'

'I became angry. I said that this was ridiculous; such an arrangement was unnatural and would put honest brokers like me out of business. Tabarhla and the others were sitting there with long faces, contemplating Ullobi's predicament, but then someone started grinning and with that everyone burst into laughter. It was only then that I realised Ullobi had been speaking in jest. After that, they all turned on him and swore by God that he was lying and had more wives, or whatever he chose to call them, than anyone else. The joke lasted the rest of the night and the two of us became good friends.'

We had entered the courtyard that lay beneath my window in the tower, and it looked different in the light of day. I knew that the Khurma oasis was famous because it had water in plenty, and here, that most precious commodity flowed in wasteful abundance. I could now see that in the court which I had looked down upon there was a great fountain with four lions at its corners which cascaded water into a great pool. Beyond it was a stone cloister with narrow columns and Moorish arches forming arcades which were sculpted in all manner of geometric designs. We entered another court and after that a whole series of them, some with pools or fountains, others with mulberry, juniper and fig trees, havens for the thrushes and bulbuls whose song filled every corner of El Donaiis. Each court had a loggia decorated with tiles glazed in different colours, which covered the walls and the benches beneath.

We sat down to enjoy the scenery. 'I recall Abha with pleasure', said Ferdhan. 'I will tell you a story of my first visit there some years ago. I had heard in the souks that the Amir was looking for a concubine, so I spread the word that amongst my load I had two white slaves. No doubt they had been stolen from some coastal village for they spoke Arabic. I discovered that the Amir's son, Tabarhla, also wanted a concubine, and I managed to play the two off against each other. I set up my stage in the old caravanserai and showed what I was carrying, but very discreetly, and soon these two were bidding against each other, father and son, and neither would give in. The price went up and up because the Amir wanted both of them. In the end they settled for one each, but the money I received for these two paid for my entire trip – their cost at the slave market in Mukalla, the caravan journey to Khurma to get them ready and then the journey to Abha to sell them. The rest of the cargo was pure profit. I was carrying plenty of slaves and the other sheikhs of the Ahl Yazid bought them all because no one wanted to be left out. It was just as well because it kept everyone happy, which is the important matter in my business. I can tell you those two white virgins had been so groomed by my wife and the girls that they did me proud. I heard it said that one of them was even taken in marriage later and became a sheikha.'

There was something in Ferdhan's story that sounded familiar. 'It's curious,' I said. 'I think this is the same as what I heard in the market there. I talked to a coffee merchant and some of his friends who told me about a sheikha called Na'ema who had been a slave. They loved her because she had revived the custom of the battle chariot that held a virgin, called the *markab*, and was even said to have fought herself. But when I pressed them they seemed reluctant to talk about her. Why do you suppose that was?'

'I dare say there was some good reason. If this sheikha actually fought they might have feared that word of it would reach the Ikhwan.'

'Why would that matter?'

'Because it is nowhere written in the Qur'an or shariah that women may bear arms, so the Ikhwan would have sworn that it was against the holy writ and could have killed her or had her publicly whipped, sheikha or not, if they found out.'

'I don't understand how the Ikhwan are allowed to do such things. It's worse than the religious bigotry which we had in Europe many centuries ago. Who are these Ikhwan, anyhow?'

'To help you understand the Ikhwan I must tell you the history of the Saudi tribe. There was an imam called Abdul Wahhab who lived over a hundred years ago, who preached his own strict version of the Muslim faith, and this came to be called Wahhabism. The sheikhs of the Saudi were also the religious leaders of the tribe, and as followers of Abdul Wahhab they preached his doctrines and do so to this day. Now in the last ten years the Saudi have defeated most of the larger tribes, including the Hashemites, and so have gained control of Mecca and Wahhabism has spread. It is the genius of ibn Saud that he found a way to win power by making settlements for his warriors. They came to be called the Ikhwan, and they provided his army. He told them that they were the servants of God and their mission was to make all the tribes of Arabia follow the Wahhabi faith, and this allowed them to kill those of other faiths, and especially infidels. Each sheikh he conquered was made to swear an oath of allegiance, and then for good measure ibn Saud would marry the daughter of the senior sheikh, having divorced one of his wives beforehand to create the nominal vacancy in the customary manner. After that the sheikh would be reinstated and ibn Saud would move on to the next tribe. But if any sheikh went back on his oath the full might of the Ikhwan descended upon him and his tribe.

'Now the Ikhwan are out of control, and have even crossed the border into what you British call Mesopotamia to terrorise the country. However, the British have woken up and are now assisting ibn Saud. They have aircraft and will drop bombs on the Ikhwan, which will be ibn Saud's only way of regaining control. Much blood will be spilt, but now you can see why he is careful to be diplomatic with the British.' It was clear from the length of this speech that the matter lay close to Ferdhan's heart, and probably to his commercial interest as well.

'What you have told me is borne out by my own experience,' I said. 'At the time I left Abha the Ikhwan tried to murder me and I was lucky to escape their clutches.'

'As a *nasara* you were indeed lucky. Your best hope would have been to throw money at them at the start, which is your ransom paid in advance. I too have suffered at the hands of the Ikhwan. One of the slaves I carried managed to obtain and smoke a cigarette, and they caught him. They cut off his hand. This made him unsaleable, and I had carried him all the way from Mukalla. The Ikhwan are a great threat to our trade, but it has to be said that they are also the custodians of our ancient faith. Your own experience must have been a shock, but Abha has always been full of surprises. I will tell you something that happened on my first caravan there, the one I mentioned. There was an Abyssinian slave called Etza with the two white virgins, and she claimed she could foretell the future by reading the stars. One day she came to me as the camels were being loaded and swore by God that an hour after the midday prayer we would be attacked by bandits. I took no notice, but the men did, and sure enough we were caught in an ambush and at just the time she said. We got out of it somehow but we wouldn't have if the men hadn't had their rifles at the ready as a result of the warning. In caravans you can become superstitious about such things. If this slave still reads the stars she will be well known at Ayinah, and if you go there you should look for her because she might know about your father. Such people seem to know everything. But now let us go and look for Omai, who is responsible for all we are looking at.'

We had entered another court, still in the process of construction, where we found some masons and Omai, an African, who as Ferdhan explained had once been a slave. If so he was now a master, Napoleonic even, for he dominated not only the other masons but apparently Ferdhan as well. He was standing in the centre of a courtyard laid with flat stones, around which were the lodges where the masons lived and worked, and on the pavement he was drawing with a stick of charcoal the outlines of the stones that would form an arch, each precisely shaped and numbered. He perfectly conjured up the image of a medieval mason setting out his cathedral stone by stone. What touched me was the relationship between mason and master. As Ferdhan explained: 'Many times I have offered Omai his freedom but he always prefers to remain at El Donaiis, which perhaps is not surprising since it is really his home as much as it is mine. Therefore in place of freedom I have given him a house and a wife, one that he has chosen himself from my best caravan. Now he has children and when they are grown his sons will learn his craft just as he once did, although no one knows where that was, not even Omai himself. In this way stone cutting will go on and El Donaiis will continue to grow.'

Omai was at his side as Ferdhan spoke, and seeing them standing there it was hard to say which was the servant and which the true master, so even was the relationship between them.

We reached the house and entered it by a separate wing that I had not noticed previously, where the tools of Ferdhan's trade were to be seen. This, he explained, was the slavery, where the slaves were groomed and trained, although none of these were on view. As we entered, a cluster of young women, doubtless the unmarried daughters of the house, flitted away like moths, leaving us on our own to marvel at what must have been the most up-to-date beauty parlour in Arabia. Paints, dyes, brushes, jars, ointments, cosmetics of every kind lay everywhere, bowls for washing the hair in camel's urine and even European scissors for dressing it. At the sides were bales of cottons and silks for making the slaves' garments, all of which, Ferdhan was at pains to tell me, were not included in the sale but were brought back home.

The slavery, it was clear, was his pride and joy. 'One of the reasons I am the most famous dealer in Arabia is that all the slaves that pass through my house are kindly treated. They are attended by the women of the household, with my daughters and my wife, who is the mistress of the slavery. You would scarcely believe the transformation that takes place when the slaves have been properly fed and come here, where all manner of attention is lavished on them. Even the plainer ones become pretty when they are taught to present themselves well, and so fetch good prices, whilst the best are sought for beyond any in Arabia. I can tell you, when it is going my slavery is a sight to behold.'

This I could easily believe, although I had some difficulty concealing my horror at witnessing at such close quarters the practicalities of this barbaric trade. Yet if one accepted Arabia at all one had to steel oneself to such a commonplace matter.

'But what about the slaves, what do they make of it all?'

'They forget they are going to be sold or are even slaves at all. They are promised they will soon have rich, powerful husbands and that some may even become sheikhas. You would see for yourself, if some of them were here, how happy they are, but at the moment we are waiting for a new caravan to arrive. It is the happiness that makes them bloom and, even if the promises we make are false, it is this that will guarantee they look happy and confident and become concubines of the richest men.'

We left the slavery and went into a paddock where camels were grazing, a stock of forty or fifty beasts now with mountainous humps from the lush spring growth. At one side were the *dhallas*, the huge butterfly-shaped constructions made from hazel rods and bamboo in which the slaves were transported, generally in pairs, with one sitting on either side and a serving slave sitting on the floor between them. They looked awkward and incongruous although refined for their purpose over centuries of use, and no more uncomfortable in practice, I dare say, than many a berth of my own.

We returned to Ferdhan's quarter, where before long he was playing his ancient gramophone again. I was curious to find out if he knew about the attack on the port of Jaizan by Vartak and the *Alhambra*, and what happened to Father's field gun after that. Evidently he had heard all about it.

'He got back to Abha, and I can tell you that it didn't stop there. The Idrisi took a long time to recover from the loss of their port, although Mohammed the Black went on warring with the local tribes. If he took prisoners he had them publicly circumcised by a butcher in the main square of Sabiya, a horrible practice the Idrisi brought with them from North Africa, where they came from. I don't care to pass that way these days and there are no caravans of pilgrims for Vartak at Jaizan.

'The last time I went to Abha, Tabarhla had become Amir and Ullobi had helped him. As a result of his raid on Jaizan he had become immensely popular, and if for any reason Tabarhla was away, Ullobi was left in charge at the daily *majlis* and settled all the quarrels himself. He had a great reputation for fairness and the Beni Mughe'id accepted his judgements without question, for they saw him as one of their tribe. Even the sheikhs of the Ahl Yazid didn't object, as they didn't have to contend with each other for this position. However, times were not easy for Abha. They were increasingly having trouble with another tribe, the Riyal el M'a from Riyal, who had become daring and had started fancying their chances of taking Abha for themselves. They had got hold of the guns and bullets which the Turks had left there, which was serious for the people of Abha because they didn't have many rifles or ammunition. It was Ullobi's idea that he should attack Riyal first, before the Riyal el M'a arrived at Abha, but the difficulty was that the element of surprise was missing, for by now the Riyal el M'a knew all about Ullobi and his exploits from their spies.

'What came of it I do not know, as I have not been to Abha since then, because not long after this ibn Saud and the Wahhabis arrived. They say that Abha was taken by them without a battle and afterwards ibn Saud placed a governor there. Tabarhla and some of the sheikhs were said to have been taken to Riyadh, and it was some time before they were released.' It was the first time that this had been mentioned although I knew from what Professor Monaghan had told us that the Saudis had conquered Abha in 1921.

'In that case,' I said, 'do you think they could have taken my father to Riyadh? Perhaps I should go there and find out.'

Ferdhan considered this. 'It is possible that they might have taken him, but when they found out your father was British ibn Saud would not have dared to keep him there. As I said, he had a lot of help from the British, and even if Ullobi had been taken to Riyadh he would have already been released by the time a sheikh called Hassan ibn Aidh killed the governor and ibn Saud sent his son Feisal to sort it out. Faisal recaptured Abha, and captured ibn Aidh and took him back to Riyadh for the second time. After this, the rest of the Ahl Yazid, afraid that the new Saudi governor might send them all to Riyadh, left Abha and went to Ayinah, in the mountains, where they had their summer quarters. I expect they are there to this day. It is time that I paid them a visit. But the problem nowadays is finding the slaves. The Zanzibar traffic has been ruined by the pirates that prey on the dhows, and the market at Mukalla is a shadow of what it used to be. The prices paid now are ridiculous, enough to put honest traders like me out of the business because the sheikhs don't have the money to pay fancy prices. If I know them well enough I give credit but I have been let down. I can tell you, sometimes I'm gloomy about the whole future of slaving. I worry that the market could fail altogether, and then where would Arabia be? For me it is terrible that such an honourable trade and with a history over so many centuries should all go to waste. In any case, how would everyone manage without slaves? As I have said it saddens me greatly, but I have to move with the times and now I have started dealing in something else instead. When I go back to Ayinah I shall take something the sheikhs can afford, for I must tell you they are extremely greedy and their greed needs to be satisfied, if not by one thing then by another.'

As he spoke he produced a tiny chest; he unlocked it and took out a handful of the largest pearls I had ever seen. The chest itself, made from teak or some exotic wood, was bound with a filigree of fine brass-work, broken and battered by long use. It was evidently a treasured possession which had been handed down by generations of pearl dealers and said much about Ferdhan's love and respect for old traditions. 'As expensive as slaves, but you save on the transport and they don't die; also they are easy to handle and if you get into a tight spot you can always swallow them. I buy from the pearl dealers in Kuwait and Bahrain and from the boat captains, even from the divers themselves, who steal them. I sell them to the sheikhs who used to buy my slaves and this is what I shall take when next I go to Abha and Ayinah, or, if it's on my route, to Riyadh.'

'Concerning Riyadh, in spite of what you said earlier I believe that I should go there. The Amir must hold an open *majlis* each day.'

'Abdulaziz ibn Saud is no longer called Amir. He made himself Sultan of Arabia and now is proclaimed King of Nejd. However, I foresee there may be difficulty in seeing him. If your mind is made up I will give you a letter to the court chamberlain. He arranges the disposal of my slaves and since I usually make him a gift of one or two, he may regard me as due for a favour and assist you in your effort. On the other hand, gratitude in such matters is sometimes fleeting and he may not. By the way, there was something else I meant to tell you about your father that was connected with the chamberlain, though I don't suppose it's important. He used to send a messenger to Khurma with packets for Sheikh Tabarhla, letters or something that he wanted me to take to Riyadh when I went there. I used to go often at that time because there was a market for pearls there and it was much nearer than Kuwait. I would give them to the chamberlain, who knew Tabarhla quite well. He'd stayed at Riyadh longer than the other sheikhs, for some reason, and they all liked him there. I never found out what the packets were but your father trusted me and I was happy to do it for him. After a while they stopped coming and I never found out what it was all about.

'In any case, I would suggest that you visit Ayinah. If Tabarhla isn't there one of the Ahl Yazid will have taken his place. Besides, when you're there I believe you should try to find Etza, the Abyssinian slave I told you about. People like that seem to know everything that's going on and whichever sheikh is in charge may be using her services. If you find Etza I would be grateful if you can give to her this mark of my gratitude.' Ferdhan opened the little chest and selected an enormous pearl. 'She can exchange it for riyals in case of need and it might even help her to see a bright future for yourself.'

It was a fine example of Ferdhan's style: always ready to give honour where due, and master of his trade that he was, he never forgot a debt or a friend.

# Chapter 8

I LEFT KHURMA and set off on the road which would take me through the province of Nejd, a vast expanse of barren land, whose emptiness seemed to match that in my own heart, leading to Riyadh. Nevertheless, it was during this journey that I had an insight. The more I pondered Ferdhan's words, and before that, what Vartak had said, the more I sensed that they were sceptical of my conviction that I would find my father. The truth was beginning to break through: my father was so well known that if he had been alive everyone would know where he was. I began to see that I had been in a state of denial, my confidence based on assumption only, that I was pursuing an illusion which was no more than a psychological defence that I had constructed for myself over the years: the pursuit of an imagined father who had been absent for most of my life. The stories of Ferdhan and Vartak seemed at the time to offer me hope, but now I began to realise that they were no more than the afterglow that gathers about a memory.

So it was during this journey that my conviction that I would find my father alive began to fade. This did not lessen my purpose because whatever may have happened I needed to know the truth, and if all else failed I had to find the earth that made his final bed. My conversion, like that of St Paul of Tarsus, came about on a pilgrim road, in this case the one that leads to Mecca. I realised that it was pointless for me to continue to Riyadh.

We had reached a crossroads. Where the two roads met there was one that led southward to Bishah and the As'ir, and I knew that I should take it, go to Ayinah and there search for Etza the

Abyssinian slave. This would mean returning to Abha and this I discussed with my *mahra*, who so far from being put out by my change of plan rejoiced in it, for we had reached the border of the *dirah* of the Qahtan, which was his tribe, where he would have had to hand me over to another *mahra*. However, if we went to Bishah we would remain within the Qahtan and he would be entitled to extra riyals, no doubt to be decided after a long and enjoyable debate. I had learned much about such matters from Ferdhan, and now took care to use his methods in negotiating the *mahra*'s tariff, which usually entailed spending a whole day in bargaining and was really a test of perseverance. This did not matter for it accorded with the wisdom of the Arab proverb that reminds you that haste is of the devil, delay of the merciful.

The route the *mahra* chose took us to Turabah, where we climbed the dry bed of the wadi as far as Bishah, which had abundant water from wells and waterholes fed by the winter flow and was a place I had long hoped to visit, though not for locusts. At Bishah I paused to take stock, for we had been many days on the road and the journey had been hard for Dukhaala, who needed to recover condition. Fortunately there was sufficient pasture of *nassi* grass where I could graze her, and I decided to break my journey and take lodgings for a week.

I was interested in Bishah because much history had been made there. It was the site of a battle fought by ibn Saud ten years earlier which had decided the fate of the As'ir, and afterwards that of the Hejaz and Mecca. Long before this, its water had made it precious, and it lay upon the ancient incense road where for more than 3,000 years there had passed mighty caravans laden with myrrh and frankincense from the Hadramaut in southern Arabia. This was the land of plenty, real or imagined, called Arabia Felix, famous throughout history and described by Pliny and Strabo. In ancient times it was the land of the Sabaeans and Himyarites, who left their enduring monuments there; it was also the world of the Old Testament and the fabled demesne of the Queen of Sheba.

At length I departed from Bishah and after a week reached Abha and finally the village of Ayinah, fifteen miles beyond it in the mountains and so elevated that one could sense the thinness of the air.

*

As in most other things, Ferdhan was correct in believing that the Ahl Yazid had forsaken Abha and gone to Ayinah. Here in their villas they lived more or less screened from the world and from the Saudi governor at Abha, all the Ahl Yazid, that is, except the ibn Aidh, of whom none were to be seen at all although their villa was open and the household servants remained. Ayinah itself was a small community of *qasrs*, each with some pasture. It was evidently self-sufficient, for although high in the mountains, there was a well nearby at a place called Zamzim, from which donkeys carried water in never-ending succession.

Ferdhan was also correct in guessing that Etza lived at Ayinah, although as I quickly found out, no longer in a state of slavery by any means. Her large house was at the top of the village beneath the steep limestone cliffs and had walls freshly painted with yellow ochre. The large upper floor was hidden from view by trellis work, which gave it a gracious air and hinted at modest prosperity. The door was opened by a tall man who eyed me suspiciously and returned my greeting in a manner that was brusque to the point of rudeness. I explained that I had come from Khurma at the direction of Ferdhan bin Murzuk, and I had the bright idea of proffering Ferdhan's pearl, which I took from my pocket and gave him. He seized it, examined it carefully and then placed it between his teeth. The pearl apparently passed this test and his manner somewhat improved; but at this moment Etza herself appeared and the man, who turned out to be her husband, was dismissed with a gesture and skipped up the stairs on long legs like a grasshopper. In his place a crowd of children of all ages now gathered about her.

I studied Etza carefully, marvelling that an Abyssinian slave had managed so to rise in the world. She wore an indigo gown like most of the women of these parts, and was without face covering. She was tall and statuesque, with the high cheekbones of her race, and she wore a diffident smile. She was now in middle age, but the thought occurred to me that had she not been black, and with the valuable gift of foretelling the future, she would probably have suffered the fate of being taken as a concubine herself. The children who had gathered around were unusually quiet, and judging by their number and diverse appearance were evidently not her own. Now, at a word of command from her, they all returned upstairs with such obedience that it was difficult to imagine whose children they were.

'I had better explain who I am and why I have come,' I began.

Etza cut me short. 'There is no need. I can see quite well who you are: you are the son of Ullobi. I have known all year that a *nasara* would come.' Her voice was sharp and authoritative. It occurred to me that Ferdhan must somehow have sent her a message, yet that could only have been very recently. Perhaps the people at Abha had told her about me.

'I saw when you arrived in Arabia,' she continued, 'and later when you seemed to cross it like a comet from west to east. You seemed to be in a great hurry as though you were escaping or something was driving you.'

'I have been searching for my father,' I said. 'I hoped that you might know about him and can help me to find him.'

She made no answer and for a minute her gaze wandered; then the diffident smile returned to her face. 'Please be comfortable, for you must be tired after your journey. I'll fetch some refreshment.' I heard her speak to someone in the room behind, and shortly a servant or slave entered, bearing a tray of cardamoms and tiny bowls containing honey with small sticks to dip into it.

Etza sat on the floor on a cushion. 'Now tell me first what I can do for you. Do you have accommodation here at Ayinah? It's a very small place.' I admitted that I did not. She got up and left the room again to give another instruction, then returned. 'I have arranged it. Now enjoy your honey, which is made from the flowers of the '*ilb* trees. I believe it to be the best in Arabia although the season is brief and the bees have to work extremely hard before they die.'

This struck me as an apt description of Arabia as a whole. The honey was indeed excellent and as I finished it I was emboldened to try again. 'To return to my father . . .'

Etza cut me short. 'We live in a world which is a different world from your own. I must tell you that warriors do not grow old in Arabia, it is only the women who do that. God in his wisdom wills it so and the warriors do but honour him.'

There was a silence and the ominous words were left hanging in the air. They had to mean what I thought they did. 'You mean . . . you are telling me that my father is dead.'

She did not answer. No answer was needed, for deep within me I realised that I already knew it; that my hope had died somewhere on the long road from Khurma when I had lost the conviction that I would find him alive. Now, amidst the welter of anguish, I felt a strange sense of relief, that of finally knowing. It was a tender mercy to have at last found someone who might lay to rest my demons. I blessed Ferdhan for his wisdom in sending me to Ayinah.

Etza remained impassive. 'It was a long time ago. I will tell you what I know about Ullobi but it must be later, after I have had time to remember. It may be that we shall have much conversation, but now you must go and find the accommodation I have arranged for you.'

She summoned a slave, who entered and took possession of me whilst Etza herself silently slipped away, a matter which I only realised after she had left.

The slave was called Ali. Together we fetched Dukhaala, whom he took by the bridle, and we descended the hill to the settlement, a collection of a dozen or so small *qasrs* clustered about the grander villas of the Ahl Yazid. Somewhat to my surprise, it was to one of these that Ali led me, that of the ibn Aidh, where, as he explained, in the absence of the family the place was empty except for the slaves. These fell about me as we arrived, relieved perhaps at finding some object for their attention, and treated me as though I had been one of their sheikhs. I was received with much deference and ceremony, and unlike most hospitality that I had received in Arabia, I was fed in solitary splendour, my only companion being the domestic cat.

This suited me quite well, for at this moment I wanted my own company and time to consider what Etza had told me and its terrible new certainty. Even though I had sensed that my father was dead the reality of it still came as a shattering blow and seemed at first to threaten the whole purpose of my being in Arabia. But then I realised that mine was no longer a simple quest; it would not be fulfilled until I had found everyone who had known my father, for only then I would know the truth and have a complete understanding of him, like a picture I could always look at. So far there had been only glimpses of fragments of his life, and I needed much more than that. The truth was that my quest was as urgent as ever, for his life had been so full of meaning, as well as colour, that I knew that I would not rest until I had found answers to all my questions; indeed, had found something else, for here, as I was beginning to sense, lay the key to my own understanding of my own driven self. For the moment all my hopes hung upon Etza.

*

The next day I was introduced to the workings of Etza's unusual household. Children swarmed everywhere; I counted at least twenty, and I am sure there were more that I did not see. It was apparent that they were Etza's only in the sense that she had collected them, for they proved to be the waifs and strays of Abha, its orphans or more probably its foundlings, hastily hidden from the Wahhabi *ulemas*. Nevertheless, they were in every sense a family, and moreover, so far from being the recipients of charity, they were, I found, part of an ingenious and carefully organised business. This was conducted on the spacious upper floor, an area common to all the larger houses, roofed over simply and open on all sides, although screened by lattice. Such an area is normally the preserve of the women of the household but here it was in effect a factory where the children worked. What they were making was a single article of women's clothing which for most of the time goes unseen, being hidden behind their voluminous outer garments. It is that part of a dress which is its tapering central panel, effectively a sort of frontispiece. Each one is different, which offers great scope for artistry, so that making them is a craft of its own, for all are embellished with beads or pearls or fine needlework. They are the subject of much showing off and endless debate within the harems, as it is held that they define the status of the wearer, and every woman possesses her own collection of them. They are called *hazzam*.

The designs were created by Etza, who no doubt drew her inspiration from Abyssinian tradition, but the organising genius of the business was her husband with the long legs, Mabruk, who was a jeweller by trade and had found a way to market them. He had developed a network of merchants and middlemen, as a result of which the Ayinah *hazzam* was sold in all the souks of Arabia east or west. Thus the children's handiwork, of which they were plainly proud, provided for all the needs of this large and doubtless further to be extended family.

I was still marvelling at the ingenuity of the enterprise when finally I found myself alone with Etza, who at that moment was toying with Ferdhan's pearl. She seemed downcast, which made me wonder if our conversation the previous day had affected her, as it had affected me. I began to fear that perhaps my arrival might not be entirely welcome. Perhaps I had not found much favour in what she had gleaned from the stars, so perhaps Ferdhan's hope that what she saw might favour me was mistaken.

To lighten the atmosphere, I began to talk about the safely impersonal subject of the ibn Aidh, about whom I was curious.

'The household treated me as though I were a visiting sheikh,' I said. 'It was rather more than I expected.'

'That is what they would do, for I told them that you were to be respected since you were the son of Ullobi.'

'They were so attentive that I wondered whether I replaced something they had been used to but had lost.'

'They would naturally be attentive, for they miss their masters and mistresses. I too would mourn for old days if my life was as empty as theirs.'

'My father had a great liking for all the Ahl Yazid and told me about them. What made the family leave?'

'Sheikh Abdulla ibn Aidh was taken to Riyadh with the rest when the Saudis came. They were well treated and finally they were released. But another of the family, Hassan ibn Aidh, started a rebellion and killed the Saudi governor. There was a battle, and Feisal, ibn Saud's second son, captured Hassan and took him back to Riyadh. To everyone's surprise, Abdulaziz ibn Saud pardoned him although no doubt he will spend the rest of his life in Riyadh. But this whole event terrified the rest of the ibn Aidh, and the whole family fled from Ayinah, fearing the long arm of the Saudis, so the villa is empty except for the slaves, who are doubtless bewildered. Even the bin Tahir and bin Mufarrih prefer to be out of the way these days.

'Some of this I heard at Abha,' I said. 'I became friendly with a coffee merchant in Abha, and his friends started to tell me some of this story. They also described a sheikha who fought in battle like a man. They got very excited about her and said she had revived the old tradition of the *markab*, the chariot with a maiden dragged into the middle of the fighting to encourage the warriors.'

My words had an electrifying effect upon Etza. At once, her whole manner changed, she became animated and her eyes shone. Evidently I was the first person in years to mention the warrior sheikha and the *markab*. Her voice rose a pitch. 'It is Sheikha Na'ema they speak of,' she cried. 'Na'ema was my whole life, my everything. It was I who made her what she was. I protected her by listening to what was happening in the harems and finding out who was plotting against her. When she learned to fight I healed her wounds. In the end the people loved her so much they would have had her as their ruler if they could, and would have followed her anywhere. I despair because now all this is forgotten. The story of Sheikha Na'ema is the greatest of all the sagas but the people don't care about these things any more. Nowadays there are no battles and they forget the old traditions; they only want a life of idleness and ease.'

Etza seemed quite reborn. She began to relive the past, which evidently meant so much to her, and the drama of Sheikha Na'ema and the part she played in the history of Abha came pouring forth in a vivid torrent of words. Her recall was astonishing, and I knew for certain that at last I had found Abha's muse.

However Etza was a creature of impulse and so obsessed was she with her mistress that at first she would talk of nothing else. She began to relive the past as though it was a living drama, telling the story in the present tense so that events unfolded as if they were happening and the listener seemed to become the witness of history as it was being made. Charmingly, she invariably referred to herself as Etza in the third person which, since she always seemed to be at the centre of the action, gave the story a sense of continuity. Events when she was not actually present she filled in by other means to complete the picture. I was to discover that Etza had an extraordinary nose for what was happening around her and very little if anything escaped her. I concluded that this was also the Abyssinian tradition, and the way stories were told there.

In general, it was left to me to work out the proper sequence of events for her outpourings were often somewhat random, yet she remembered conversations with such accuracy – even word for word in their entirety – that this made it possible for me to fill the gaps in the story. So fascinating was the gallery of characters that was brought to life before me that I was quite ready to receive Abha's history on Etza's terms. I soon realised that I must contrive to write it down as a history, for if I could make sense of Etza's avalanche of words it was surely the story that I had come to Arabia to hear. Its importance could not have been higher and I easily persuaded myself that the result would be a new chapter of 'Arabia Felix'.

We slipped naturally into a pattern. Each morning, as soon as the children had been set to work, Etza would recount her story until midday, when she left off to pray; and then there would be another session when the work was finished upstairs and a meal, which the whole household ate together, had been taken. In the evening I would retire to the villa of the ibn Aidh and write down everything whilst it was fresh in my mind.

In this routine the days went quickly by, the seasons came and went, and all this time Etza's outpouring continued. The pieces of the jigsaw puzzle that was the story of Abha gradually fell into place and I never tired of it or of being its amanuensis. I was so drawn into the drama that sometimes it played tricks on my mind and certain of the characters seemed to assume a life of their own. Their ghosts would appear unbidden, as though determined to have their say, and like actors upon a stage would speak their lines, bow and then dissolve. They became my friends. Perhaps this was no more than a trick of my imagination but to me they seemed real, their words to be recorded as the precious echoes of time lost.

# Chapter 9

As I have said, Etza had a flair for discovering everything that happened, sometimes sooner, sometimes later, even if she was not actually present at the event she described, and so it is at the castle where the story begins.

Halfway down the Red Sea's eastern shoreline and close to the southern limit of Arabia it stood, not a large and important castle but rather an elaborate *qasr* built of stone with a roof fortified with castellations, and it was very close to the sea. Here lived the sheikh, the ruler of his tribe, whose family consisted of a wife, seven sons, some grown to manhood, and one daughter of fourteen years whose name was Naomi, which in Arabic is Na'ema.

The moorings beside the castle were used by the town as a port where boats of shallow draught could anchor and discharge their loads. The boats also transported the goods which the small town traded, the means by which it survived, for in this part of the Red Sea coast the soil is meagre and supports only limited crops and husbandry. The town was unusual in its isolation and as a result the tribe did not have to concern itself in conflicts with other tribes as most did. In this respect it was fortunate, and perhaps almost unique.

Nevertheless their bucolic and peaceful existence was threatened because from the sea also came enemies, and hence the townsfolk always carried arms. Throughout history the Red Sea had been a prey to pirates, and with small tides and shallow waters it was easy for these pirates to come ashore to plunder; some came from Arabia itself but the worst came from the Horn of Africa and from Somalia in particular. Against such as these the defences of the town were always being strengthened, but even so they were not always sufficient to meet this threat, as events were to show.

The seashore was where most of the little town's activities took place. It was where the mares that belonged to the sheikh were exercised, part of a cherished stable of thoroughbreds known as *hamdani*, one of the breeds of *al khamsat al rasul*, the five of the Prophet. These were ridden by the sheikh's offspring, including his fourteen-year-old daughter, all of whom had received a thorough training in horsemanship from an early age. Each day they could be seen racing on the hard sand at the tide's edge, eagerly watched by the townsfolk, who placed bets, contrary to the precepts of the Quran. There were also fish to be caught. In spring and autumn great shoals of *battan*, *saft* and *shim* were driven by their predators into the shallows, and they were harvested in vast drag nets that stretched almost to the horizon. Salt pans had been constructed behind the shore and here the womenfolk sorted the catch. Salted fish formed the principal diet of the tribe and was also the basis for its prosperity, carried in boats of shallow draught and of many shapes and sizes to markets on both sides of the Red Sea, as it had been since biblical times.

The drama with which Etza's story began involved a small party of pirates such as I have mentioned. These had been eyeing the town prospectively, and each time they had sailed past it the better it had seemed, so by now they knew its habits and daily routine and had made their plans. Their craft was a *zaraqah* that had a single mast bearing a lateen sail, and a conveniently shallow draught, allowing it to get close to the shore, which was reached by its long protruding bow.

The castle belonging to the sheikh was built on a promontory extending to the sea's edge, where at high tide it seemed to rise from the waters itself, and here, out of view beneath the walls, the *zaraqah* anchored and three of the pirates climbed out and hid themselves. At first light, slaves from the castle appeared, unsuspecting, and one by one these were seized and strangled. After a while, members of the sheikh's family emerged, the seven sons and finally the sheikh himself. A skirmish ensued, but there could be only one outcome for the pirates were armed and the sheikh and his sons were not, and so before long they met the same fate as the slaves; all of the family, that is, except for the daughter of the house, and she was seized. None of this should have come as a surprise since it had happened countless times in history at this same place. The name of this town is not known, for Na'ema, the fourteen-year-old survivor, was so traumatised by the experience that this and all other details of her early life were erased from her memory.

One slave only was a poor haul after all the trouble they had gone to, but the pirates quickly re-embarked with their booty and the *zaraqah* went on its way. Meanwhile, the maiden entering slavery was cast into the covered stern to join the rest of the cargo, five others like herself and some negresses. The *zaraqah* now set course south-west and thus against the prevailing wind; its destination was further south and on the other side of the Red Sea where lies the Horn of Africa. So the human cargo it carried faced many days of misery, and the maidens' terror increased when one of the deck-hands descended with a bodkin and sailor's tar twine for the purpose of infibulation to ensure against interference and loss of virginity.

However, the voyage was interrupted. A much larger dhow, known as a *muhailah*, with two masts and carrying a heavy weight of canvas, was sailing in the same direction, and as soon as it spotted the *zaraqah* it trimmed its course and overhauled it. The master of the vessel guessed what the pirates had been up to and the boats were soon grappled together and the *zaraqah* boarded. It was routine, and everyone concerned knew the plot, for confrontations such as this were a common event in the Red Sea; the outcome was always the same, which for the pirates meant the bottom of the sea. And so the matter was quickly settled: the Somalis were despatched overboard, no doubt to the surprise of the porpoises in the wake of the boat, the cargo was transferred and the *zaraqah* abandoned to drift at the behest of the wind and the sea. Thus the maidens exchanged one quarter for another, albeit a rather larger one, and their slave master for a new one.

The great *muhailah* now resumed its course, sailing for its home port, which was Mukalla. This lay at the southern tip of Arabia at the lowermost limit of the Red Sea and hence on the sea lanes to Zanzibar, which made it the natural port for trade with East Africa. This trade was mainly in slaves, and Mukalla had the largest slave market in southern Arabia; from here slaves were taken by caravans to all corners of Arabia and beyond. Thus endowed by its geography, Mukalla was a prosperous place. It was finely set beneath terraces of rock leading upwards like a giant staircase to the mountains behind, which at evening, the time the *muhailah* arrived, appeared to be made of amethyst. The port was proficient at handling arrivals such as this and the slaves were swiftly transferred to the quarter of the market used to house them.

For Ferdhan bin Murzak the slave dealer – for it was he and no other – who in due course acquired the *muhailah*'s cargo, things could not have turned out better since he did not even have to bid for it at auction. It happened that agents of the Sheriff of Mecca had just arrived at Mukalla for the purpose of tracking down new arrivals and supposedly suppressing the trade. Slaves were contraband, to be seized before they were hidden in the northbound caravans and had crossed the border into As'ir; they would be taken to Mecca and given their liberty, or so the story went. It was only natural that the Sultan of Mukalla in his well-appointed palace wanted beyond anything to protect his slave market, and so he instructed the city governor to clear it of slaves as promptly as possible. Ferdhan's arrival was just what was needed and the sea captain was forced to sell his cargo at the derisory price that was offered. Ferdhan was delighted at his good fortune and the disappointment on the face of the sea captain, making a mental note that the next time he visited Mukalla he must bring cloth and incense for the city governor, a nervous man whose face twitched as he spoke and who was ever looking over his shoulder for imaginary spies.

The deal having been concluded, Ferdhan had to agree to remove the cargo at once, which was far from convenient since he had to reload the camels before they had been fed and rested. They noisily protested; however, he was soon on his way.

I need hardly say that the appearance in Etza's story of the very same Ferdhan bin Murzuk whom I had come to know so well came as a great pleasure to me. Neither did I need to be told, because I had already guessed, that one of the negresses in the cargo of slaves would prove to be Etza herself. Thus she witnessed all that follows, although exactly how she became privy to the domestic secrets of Ferdhan's family and the conversation that took place at his home-coming remains a mystery. However, I was soon to discover that Etza and mysteries followed each other like Castor and Pollux, and I soon ceased to try to unravel them myself; the simplest way was to take what she said as gospel truth and ask no questions.

*

Ferdhan's caravan took a month to near the end of its journey, and now everything was forgotten at the prospect of arriving at Khurma, the oasis in the centre of Arabia where he lived. All day a sandstorm had raged. The camels with their great *dhallas*, like monstrous butterflies, which carried Ferdhan's merchandise, shuffled ponderously, making irritatingly little progress, and would easily have settled on their haunches if the drivers had let up with their camel sticks and exhortations.

Now as they descended the slopes of the Sumaan the oasis came into view for the first time. Khurma had no city walls and the first that you saw of it was its green fringe, although in the present conditions the palm trees were the same colour as the sand. It would have looked on this occasion very different from the Khurma I knew myself, for in these times it was a small place and of little importance.

'Ba'irh, ba'irh', shouted the drivers, and although the camels kept their heads down they scented home and their pace quickened. At length the caravan entered the western portal and went onward into narrow streets that were bustling with activity in spite of the storm. It wound its way through the crowd until it reached the *hautah* of Ferdhan, which was usually a verdant place although that was not apparent now.

'*Qaraint ainak ya ammi*', said a voice at the gate, and Ferdhan recognised Mabrak, his personal slave, at that moment covered in sand. He dismounted, handed Mabrak the halter rope and gestured towards the *dhallas*.

Many eyes had watched his arrival through the alabaster windows of the upper floor, and as soon as he entered the doorway his ten-year-old son was pushed forward to greet him first. Ferdhan raised him and kissed him on both cheeks, remarking on their ruddiness. At once they were joined by Gymsha his wife and his two daughters, who were hiding shyly behind their mother's housecoat. As Ferdhan greeted them they all began to speak at once, and the clamour increased when Mabrak appeared with armfuls of gifts from the caravan, lengths of cloth, colourful *dishdashas* for his wife and daughters and a miniature dagger with a studded handle and silver sheath for Ahmad his son.

A slave came forward with a towel and a bowl of water with rose petals floating on it. Fordhan washed his face and then his hands and arms, savouring the water's coolness. It was exactly as he had known it would be, like all his other homecomings, for as always Gymsha had prepared everything.

Presently he ate, voraciously, for he had scarcely eaten for days; all the time Gymsha stood beside him, directing the slaves. He tried to talk between stuffing the balls of mutton and rice into his mouth but Gymsha cut him short. '*Tadfalu*,' she said. 'Eat till you are filled. The news will wait.' It was just like Gymsha, he thought, so disciplined. He had to admire her self-control, for he knew that she was only concealing her mountainous curiosity. In this as in all things she was practical, and he had long known he could never conduct his affairs without her.

97

Half an hour later, the ceremonies of the meal concluded, he withdrew to the *diwan* where a pipe of opium had been prepared for him. Only when they were alone did Gymsha betray her eagerness, and her eyes were bright with anticipation.

'First tell me how many.'

'Twelve, and we shall be rich.'

'In fair condition?'

'I'm afraid the journey was long and the circumstances were against it.' Ferdhan measured his words to heighten the drama.

'If they are half-dead then how shall we be rich?'

'You will see. They will gladden your eyes, which you will think deceive you.'

She looked at him questioningly. 'Tell me quickly.'

'Six . . . white . . . virgins . . .'

'White?'

'Six white virgins,' repeated Ferdhan, savouring every word.

'It is not possible. You made sure?'

'Of course I made sure.'

'How much?'

'The six, and six blacks, one hundred and fifty riyals.'

'It is not possible.'

'I told you that you would not believe it. When we left Mukalla they were as comely as you could wish. You will see for yourself when they are recovered.'

'How many days was the journey?'

'Over a month. We had a little trouble as we were leaving Yemen but we had our rifles loaded and fired shots before they got too close.'

'Only the Turks have white slaves,' said Gymsha, turning over the matter in her mind.

'Nor are we likely to have any again, which is why they will fetch so much.'

'Wherever did they come from?'

'Who knows? They speak Arabic. I made the purchase from a sea captain at Mukalla. It seems that he took them when he intercepted a Somali pirate ship. They must have been stolen from somewhere on the coast or they would have died from fever by now.'

'Sold by their own people in all probability,' said Gymsha, with a gesture of contempt. 'Those coastal people are no more than a bunch of pirates themselves.' Having been born and brought up in Jeddah, Gymsha regarded herself as an authority on all matters relating to the Red Sea coast.

'Anyway, we don't have to worry where they came from, that's the concern of others.' Ferdhan looked at his wife intently and leaned forward so that his black beard jutted towards her. 'Ours is to get them back into shape, then consider where to get their proper price.'

'They would sell for a good one in Jeddah.'

'I prefer to find somewhere new.'

His wife nodded, knowing that Ferdhan would have spent much of his homeward journey considering the matter. He paused for a moment as if savouring his solution. 'The mountain sheikhs of As'ir, they'll buy them; probably the first white virgins they've ever been offered.'

He got up and walked over to Gymsha and clasped her hands in his. 'Properly worked on, they'll fetch a fortune. Take as long as you like, only they must be quite perfect.' He smiled, savouring the prospect, for he was still blessed with youthful arrogance. 'Each like a pearl in a freshly opened oyster.'

Gymsha beamed in turn. 'By the time I have finished they will be pearls fit for kings,' she said quietly. She was nothing if not a woman happy with her role in life.

# Chapter 10

FERDHAN HAD NOT yet at this time ascended to what might be called middle-class respectability, but he was on his way. He had spent all his life on the move, and now it was scarcely a week before he was back on the road to convey some of the black slaves to customers in the Nejd, for as usual it was the black slaves who recovered first. He pretended that their delivery was overdue, although no one really believed this for Ferdhan's departures were as predictable as the phases of the moon. As soon as he had left, the household resumed its rituals and the grooming of the slaves. The six white virgins were not in reality white but merely pale-skinned from having been screened from the sun, and otherwise had normal Arab countenances. Since they were so precious they were quartered with Gymsha and her family and were treated in much the same way as her daughters and allocated slaves of their own, who soon began a rivalry in the grooming and toiletry. It was Gymsha's own concern to provide the clothes, and she had bales of brightly coloured silks and cottons to make an array of garments – *sirwals* and *thaubs* from the finest cotton, *dishdashas*, coloured *sibums* and cloaks, and for modesty a great variety of *milfas* and *burqahs* with almond-shaped eye slits decorated with stitchwork. Lastly, she bought sandals imported from Mecca in the market.

Every moment that was not occupied either by prayer or eating was given over to toiletry. Black henna was applied to the soles and palms, red to make patterns on faces and fingertips, always in four applications. This decoration was traditional but there was also invention, for one of the slaves was accomplished in the art of tattooing and the girls in her charge were decked out with lines, dots and patterns. Lips were reddened with *darum* and teeth cleaned with the bark of a certain tree. Hairdressing was almost a separate department of the house, where bowls of camel's urine were always at hand for washing the hair and *dahen* oil for dressing it when dry. Then, with combs made of wood, it was divided into plaits, two on either side at the front and six at the back, each starting at the top of the head. It was a source of much pleasure to all, and often at the end of the day dancing would take place and the mostly carefully plaited hair was allowed to fall loose again. As appetites returned, complexions improved and eyes once more became lustrous, whilst the girls' spirits were revived by word put about by Gymsha that each of them would presently be married to a young and handsome sheikh. Thus by degrees they found their voices and exchanged elaborate daydreams of the futures that awaited them, assuming that their present enslavement was but temporary.

The gaiety of the household was somewhat dampened upon Ferdhan's return. The moment he arrived the atmosphere altered, the principle of commerce replaced the pursuit of beauty and peace gave way to anxiety. His smile, with its dazzle of ivory teeth, was like a weather-vane pointing adversely. He ordered two of the girls to be prepared for travel, leaving the choice to Gymsha, who was always somewhat saddened by the prospect of these departures.

From the money obtained from the sale just completed Ferdhan had re-equipped the caravan. Mountain camels had been acquired to replace those from the plains, together with new *dhallas* curtained with woven camel's hair. He was determined that from now on, when his cargo came to be scrutinised, it would be seen in a properly expensive setting. It took but a short time to load the camels and the household abruptly found its members reduced by three, since the slave attending the two virgins went with them. Afterwards, it was some time before Ferdhan was out of the virgins' thoughts and they were disquieted once more when the same thing happened a few weeks later.

This second reduction left just two white virgins, whose names were Ranya and Na'ema, and their Abyssinian slave, Etza herself, humbler in this setting than I would easily have guessed. Several of the Africans had been disposed of in the market by Gymsha who balanced the modest price she received against the cost of feeding them, and was relieved to have the riyals to meet her recent expenses. With her customary frugality she had retained their clothes.

She had long decided to keep Ranya and Na'ema to the last because she judged that these two had the most potential, equal in quality yet each distinctive. Ranya was the more mature and was coming into bloom, her large jet eyes enhanced by kohl and her full saffron-red lips as sensuous as one could have wished. Her body proclaimed itself: she walked with poise and frankness and the eye was arrested by her perfectly shaped breasts. Such *nuhaid-ain* as these, Gymsha remarked, would secure her price wherever she came to be placed.

The attractions of Na'ema were different, which is why she had paired them. Na'ema was younger; her quality was in her promise and in her soft intelligent eyes. She was as tall and slender as a youth, well proportioned, with underlying strength. Her figure would become rounded in time and the sweetness of her face could only improve, for all her features had fine bone structure. There was a certain sensuality about her nose that made it look as if it had been lightly pressed by the touch of a finger the moment it had been made. Altogether it was an unforgettable face.

Now that the two were left on their own they spent hours plaiting and oiling each other's hair and comparing the length. This would continue until Etza, who spoke fluent Arabic, appeared with fresh instructions and the process of beautification started anew. Etza was one of the best slaves that Gymsha had ever had and she was deeply sorry that she would have to part with her. In a few weeks she had become indispensable, seeming to have a solution to every problem in the household; she could settle an argument as deftly as her nimble fingers sewed a garment and when it came to bargaining in the market she outshone even Gymsha herself. In practice she seemed to have become part of the family and privy to all its secrets. Gymsha would dearly have liked to keep her but Ferdhan, she knew, had already decided, and it would not have occurred to her even to raise the matter.

*

But now there was an interruption. Two days after Ferdhan's second departure an event occurred, and if Khurma and its oasis had changed little since the time of the Prophet, history must have decided that it had slept for long enough. Now its calm was abruptly shattered; the trouble followed the arrival of tribesmen from the Nejd who set up their camp within the city limits and claimed *dahkil* or sanctuary. At first they were tolerated and there was no sign that they would bring trouble, but presently the newcomers began to ignore the conventions that governed the behaviour of guests and strutted about as if they were conquerors. Their *ulemas* cast gratuitous insults at the Khurmans and it was a short step from insult to violence. One fracas after another took place, and the womenfolk remained shuttered in their houses and caught in the middle. It was Etza who was sent, amid conflicting demands for urgency and caution, to find out what was happening.

She talked to a spice seller and then to a slave woman she knew who lived in the street where the worst troubles were, learning something from each and hearing for herself the insults exchanged. The newcomers were arrogant and conspicuous, and were plainly hardened fighters.

'Hashemites,' they shouted contemptuously. 'Meccans, Turk lovers.'

'Wahhabis go back to the stench of Riyadh,' the Khurmans growled back.

Etza left in a hurry and went to the Hashemite mosque, where she sought out one of the *ulemas*. She knelt and started to recite the opening words of prayer, expecting that he would take up the familiar sequence, but to her surprise this priest spoke in a different dialect and when she was able to make it out she realised that he was one of the newcomers himself. He was calling upon God to avenge and even to kill. It was far removed from anything she had ever heard from a *ulema* before and she felt urged to protest, 'God is great and vengeance is His alone. He is merciful.'

The priest looked at her with undisguised contempt. 'God is great and merciful indeed but he has called upon us to purify the faith. The God of Abdul Wahhab has spoken and we obey him. Those that question His word shall perish,' the *ulema* waved his arms, 'by the sword.' Etza shrank back, fearing what this strange priest might say next. She tried to leave but he went on shouting at her. 'Slay the devil in your midst, purify yourselves before it is too late.'

Etza returned and warned Gymsha that the town was in peril, for an avenging army had descended upon it, but Gymsha replied, 'For years Khurma has been defended by the Sheriff of Mecca. We are too strong to be threatened by a small band of fanatics, who will not dare to attack us for fear of the Sheriff.' Yet even as she spoke, the sounds outside were ominous, and there was nothing to be done but to await Ferdhan's return.

When he came, he showed no surprise at all. 'I heard about it even before I left. The Wahhabis are trying to form an Ikhwan settlement for the Saudi Amir in Riyadh, whose name is spoken all around, Abdulaziz ibn Saud. It will blow over, you will see and next year they will find somewhere else to squabble over. Wahhabism will never take root here even if a settlement does remain; it is not for the easy-going Khurmans and Meccans and anyway, the Sheriff would never let a Saudi sheikh establish the Ikhwan on his doorstep. It's not like it was in the old days when the tribes were separate; now the towns are all linked by commerce. You forget it's 1914.' Ferdhan's words reassured her, and Gymsha shut her ears to the noise outside because Ferdhan was always right.

Now he deposited two full money belts on the table and announced that for his next caravan the Sheikh of Bishah had agreed to provide guides. 'They will come tomorrow, *mahras* from the Shumran and the Beni Malik. I intend to go farther than I have ever been before, in fact to Abha itself.'

'What about the Qahtan?' enquired Gymsha, catching the new mood.

'The Qahtan are many sects. *Mahras* from each would cost a fortune and I shall have to manage without them. Get the girls ready for tomorrow.'

He smiled, oblivious to all else, for travel and its perils were the twin pillars of his happiness. Domestic comfort, and even sex, mattered little to him, except for the fornication of those upon whose concupiscence he could play the endless games of strategy that were his principal joy. He now demolished a plateful of ripe dates that Gymsha brought him.

*

The journey that lay ahead was a daunting one, for Abha was an enclave isolated from the rest of As'ir by mountains, and the Bedouin of the area lived mainly by robbing travellers. Therefore bodyguards were needed, and twelve *askaris* were recruited to assist the *mahras* sent by the Sheikh of Bishah. For the endeavour Ferdhan had bought new pack animals and five riding camels with a splendid *dhalal* for himself, as well as a camel in milk. Mabrak, who also acted as his storekeeper, had found provisions for the journey, flour for baking bread, strips of dried camel meat, dates, coffee and rice, and had made sure that all the goat and camel skins used for carrying water were well proofed against leakage. Finally, Ranya and Na'ema, for whom this elaborate caravan had been prepared, were given a final grooming by Etza to the accompaniment of a stream of advice from Gymsha on how to conduct themselves. Both had lost their voices when confronted by this abrupt return to reality.

During the first days of the journey they rode by easy stages, rising before dawn. It took two hours to load the camels, who protested continuously and many times managed to shift their burdens so that all had to be taken off and tied again. As they moved off, only the foreguard and the rearguard were mounted, and apart from Ferdhan and the virgins the rest went on foot, each man leading a camel. At noon they stopped for the midday prayer and then time was spent searching for enough *sidr* and juniper trees for the animals to be couched in shade. The meal was sparse, and coffee was brewed as the afternoon passed. After the *asar* prayer they resumed, and rode as far into the night as the fading light and the terrain allowed. By the time they halted the stars were up, and a tent was erected for Ranya and Na'ema, which Etza made comfortable with cushions and rugs. She cooked rice for them, although this often went uneaten.

In the Qahtan territory they were challenged often, and sometimes a volley of bullets was fired over their heads. When that happened Ferdhan and one of the *mahras* went forward together, and after an exchange of identity, and of course the news, they were able to resume their journey. They stayed for two days at the well with the name of Elbalus, and pitched tents in the valley, where the camels, in hobbles, were allowed to wander off to graze on the lush pasture. Ferdhan himself disappeared into the nearby town with some *askaris* and two baggage camels; there were many deals that came as a sideline to slave-trading, and since not all were within the letter of the law the loads with which they returned were suitably covered.

After Elbalus the country became more dangerous on account of roving Bedu robbers, consequently, the pace quickened and the journeys were harder and longer; no fires were lit by night and sentries were posted. Several times there were alarms and once it seemed that the camp was being encircled, but when daybreak came they found only the tracks of a hyena, and all were relieved that the camels had been couched tightly flank to flank.

Finally they reached the *dirah* of a tribe to which one of the *mahras* belonged, and they paused for several days at Khaiba oasis to rest the camels and allow the virgins to recover condition, whilst

Ferdhan, with a handful of men, set off for the purpose of selling the Africans that were being carried. It was a week before they returned, and then Ferdhan was scowling, for although he had sold the slaves one of the *askaris* had been shot dead when their camp was attacked by cattle raiders from the Dahm. This meant that Ferdhan would have to pay the man's family the compensation called the *'arf.* They buried the man in a shallow grave, using his *dishdasha* as a shroud, and left the bodies of four of the Dahm to the vultures.

All this time Ranya and Na'ema brooded despondently, but Etza encouraged them and brought them sweet melons and fresh spiced coffee. Although her own future was the least secure of the three, she alone remained cheerful, being hardened to discomfort and the shifting fortunes of being a slave. She had known strange places in her twenty-five years and worse masters than Ferdhan.

Time passed slowly, but the journey was nearly over, for five days after leaving Khaiba they ascended the great escarpment and entered the stone-built citadel of Khamis Mishait. It was the finest fortress that any of them had seen – until a day later, when they reached Abha and beheld the soaring Manadhir. They would have felt the same sense of awe that I myself vividly remembered. They passed, as I had done, through Abha's southern gate and entered the large caravanserai, which was bustling with activity. There, even before the *dhahurs* had begun unloading, Ranya, Na'ema and Etza were spirited away and stowed in lodgings which Ferdhan had somehow arranged in order that they should not be seen.

# Chapter 11

I TRIED TO imagine the picture that met Ferdhan's eyes as his caravan wound its way towards Abha, which must have been the first city he had ever seen that was entirely enfolded by mountains, unlike the cities of Nejd in their arid plains. The Bedu mountain folk must also have impressed him, for these are a wild and different breed altogether. At this time the city itself would have been quite different, for this was long before it had been affected by the banal influence of the modern world. It was also rich, more so than the cities through which he had passed, and this he would quickly have detected. His first sight of the Manadhir must have been overwhelming, and he would immediately have spotted that there was business to be done there.

When he had settled his caravan in the caravanserai, the priority after all arrivals, he would have set about making plans. As was usual his first act would have been to make discreet enquiries about the city's hierarchies, and the amir, who must certainly be his first target. He would have been struck by the openness of the people and the liberal way of life at Abha, shown by the fact that the womenfolk moved about freely and mostly went unveiled.

Talk of the amir would have been on everyone's lips, for at this time the star of Zeid bin Tahir was close to its zenith, and this for one excellent reason. He had just liberated Abha from the Turks. In his person, too, he would have been in his prime, a large man roughly made, famously quick-tempered, intolerant of authority in any form and given to outbursts of fury that made strong men quiver. By day he fought his battles and by night he would tell endless stories of a tribe famous for its sagas, and which loved its battles dearly. Such qualities would have endeared him to his people, although more would have been needed to dominate the Beni Mughe'id, especially the Ahl Yazid, the senior sheikhs with all their feuds. What enabled Zeid to do this, and to remain the undisputed master of his house, was the great milestone in Abha's history, the driving out of the Turks with their hated Mutaserrif, who took orders from the Grand Vizier and the Sublime Port in Constantinople. Zeid had achieved this with great cunning and little help from the Beni Mughe'id warriors, who were fearful of the terrible retribution of the Turks had they failed. In this he was supported by his sons and by Tabarhla in particular, who was the only one of them to survive the bloody encounter.

These details concerning the amir and the city's sheikhs quickly became known to Ferdhan, to whom it came as no surprise that such a man as the amir was on the look-out for new concubines; therefore he must certainly be Ferdhan's prime objective. He had examined the market place and had rented a stall from a spice dealer, where he could erect a platform for the display of his wares, which, as it happened, was carried on the backs of his baggage camels. This was now quickly unloaded and put together by slaves familiar with the routine from long practice. Ferdhan had long decided first to make a courtesy call at the Manadhir, which he did the following morning. What follows is of course the scene he had described to me on my visit to Khurma, when we first met. He was making his way there, accompanied by two camels each with a *dhalla* holding a maiden, when by chance he encountered Tabarhla, who motioned him to stop.

'I see that God has been bountiful to you, slave dealer, if one may judge by the splendour of your *dhallas*.'

'God's bounty is limitless to all,' replied Ferdhan evenly.

'Your litters seem to hide riches.'

'Riches worthy of a great amir.'

He drew back the camel's hair curtain with the point of his camel stick somewhat in the manner of a showman, and watched

Tabarhla's face as he looked at Na'ema and then at Ranya and then at Na'ema again. Such was the intensity of his gaze that Na'ema blushed and was grateful that she was wearing a *milfah* which covered the whole of her face.

He turned to Ferdhan. 'May I ask what you propose as their price?' His voice was casual but it failed to hide his eagerness.

'Six hundred riyals for each,' replied Ferdhan. 'This will be their starting price when they are shown in the market.'

'For the taller,' Tabarhla pointed to Na'ema, 'I will give you three hundred and fifty riyals.'

'Five hundred might attract my interest.'

'Then your interest attracts too great a price.' Inwardly Tabarhla despised slave dealers, but after a minute he added, 'It is possible, nevertheless, that a compromise might be reached.'

Ferdhan was savouring the conversation and would have liked to continue bargaining for longer, but the possibility of a quick sale tempted him as Tabarhla knew that it would. He closed the curtains of the litter and then hesitated, as though performing an elaborate calculation, but actually he was working out whether or not it might jeopardise the deal he hoped to make with Zeid. He decided to take the risk. 'If it would favour you for me to accept what you propose then it is your favour that I wish for. If I understand you to offer four hundred and fifty riyals, then let it be so.'

'Conditionally, upon one small matter touching the amir,' said Tabarhla.

'What is that?'

'Since you must show him both maidens you must contrive that his choice falls on the other.'

'How am I to do such a thing?'

'That is your own problem.'

'It is too great a problem.'

'I believe it could be overcome.' Tabarhla reached into the folds of his *abba*. 'Say for another fifty riyals.' He held out a bag of five hundred silver riyals.

'If God is willing then it shall be done,' said Ferdhan with a shrug.

'Let us pray also that He did not endow you with any lack of cunning.' Tabarhla counted out two hundred and fifty riyals and handed them to Ferdhan. 'The remainder when you have overcome your little difficulty.' He bowed formally, turned, and walked briskly on his way.

Ferdhan surveyed the silver coins for several minutes before placing them in his money belt. Certainly this was more than he had expected. He looked at the camels and the litters perched upon them, which were now tightly closed, wondering how he could fulfil the unusual part of the deal to his own advantage. After a while he continued on his way to the Manadhir, where he announced himself and waited in the antechamber, having ordered the camels with their *dhallas* to be rested in the nearby shade. One servant only accompanied him and this man carried three large boxes.

With the departure of the Turks from the As'ir, arms had become scarce, and the market had transferred itself to Mecca or Riyal, which had both been Turkish depots for supplies, and although it prospered there it did so to the great inconvenience of the mountain tribes. At Abha even the amir's personal bodyguards were affected, and whilst each man had his own rifle, bullets were strictly rationed. Suspecting this to be the case, Ferdhan had brought with him several thousand rounds suitable for their ancient Lebel rifles, and as soon as he had obtained an audience he presented these to Zeid with elaborate courtesy. It did a great deal to break the ice and it also heightened the curiosity of Zeid, who correctly assumed that Ferdhan must have a reason for offering such a gift.

'I trust that the fortunes of your trade have been favourable,' he said breezily, motioning Ferdhan to a seat opposite.

'By the grace of God I purchased two virgins.'

'And what is unusual in that?'

'They are white virgins.'

Zeid's expression changed and his eyes opened wider. 'You have them here at Manadhir?'

'For your inspection, before they are seen by any other. If I may venture to borrow the services of one of your servants they may be placed before your eyes.'

A guard was summoned and Ferdhan gave discreet instructions. The man left and presently reappeared, followed by Ferdhan's servant and behind him, heavily veiled, Ranya and Na'ema accompanied by Etza. The guard and Ferdhan's servant were dismissed and Etza was bidden to remove Ranya's *milfah*. This revealed her eyes, carefully touched with kohl, and her well-oiled plaits, which Etza now freed from the collar of her brightly coloured cloak. This allowed her figure to be easily appreciated.

Zeid stared at her and said not a word. Before he had fully taken in the spectacle a wave of Ferdhan's arm signalled Etza to replace Ranya's *milfah*, and Na'ema was brought forward in her place. As hers was removed in turn she quivered, not from fear but from fury at being shown in this fashion, and she glared at Zeid.

'You have indeed been fortunate in your purchases,' said Zeid, stroking his chin.

'Fortune bears its opportunity to others; I merely act as its agent.'

'Quite so. Pray tell me their price?'

'I fear they cost me dearly. The purchase was difficult, the journey long for first we had to ascend the great escarpment of ...'

'Quite so, but how much?'

'A thousand riyals,' said Ferdhan.

Zeid exploded, lust and anger fighting within him.

'A thousand riyals is the price of an army, not that of two virgins.'

'It is the price of one virgin. Each costs a thousand riyals.'

Zeid shook. He wanted to strike the man. 'You ridicule me,' he shouted. His eyes became bloodshot.

'I do you a favour by offering them to you before others have set eyes upon them,' replied Ferdhan coolly.

'Then ask a fair price or else take them away.'

'The point is, what is to be considered a fair price?' He began to taunt Zeid. 'A fair price for a negress such as you have in As'ir would be fifty riyals but I offer you something else, virgins such as the rich men of Jeddah own, white virgins whom you will never again have the chance to see, let alone to purchase.'

Zeid exploded. 'A fair price is what men are prepared to pay. You would see that if you auctioned them in the market.'

'If you would prefer that, then I shall do so, and we will find out their true value.'

Zeid stared at him. He had assumed that the figure Ferdhan had asked was no more than an opening gambit; it was inconceivable that the man was not even prepared to bargain with him. However, Ferdhan himself had become concerned at the promise he had already made and now realised the hidden risk: he had seen that Zeid had chosen Ranya, but he might be so consumed by greed and lust as to want both maidens, and then there would be trouble with Tabarhla. So he gathered his stock in trade and retired, unctuous in every step, enjoying the evidence of Zeid's frustration. The sight of the boxes of bullets only made this worse, for it meant that Zeid had a duty to give Ferdhan a gift in return. As this dawned upon Zeid it nearly caused him to have a fit.

*

After he had left, Ferdhan gave much thought to his moves the following day. He was sure that by then the news that he had two white virgins would have spread through Abha and it would be certain that the market would be filled with buyers and onlookers. In this he was not disappointed. The stall he had hired from the spice seller still carried a faint aroma and was in a corner of the market, visible from the Manadhir, at a suitable distance from the place where slaves were usually auctioned. Next morning he arrived early and couched the camels with their litters, with Etza standing beside in readiness.

A crowd gathered, but Ferdhan did not proceed until he was sure that enough sheikhs had arrived. He spotted Tabarhla on a horse at the back, and when Zeid appeared Ferdhan signalled to Etza to fetch Ranya on to the platform. She stood listlessly whilst the crowd stared at her but he still waited a minute before calling for bids, then set the starting price low enough to give himself time to see who was bidding. The pace quickened and Zeid bid eagerly, shouting an insult at Ferdhan each time. After a while this unsettled the sheikhs and one by one they fell silent, none daring to outbid Zeid in such a mood. The bidding stopped at a mere three hundred and fifty riyals, but Ferdhan had plenty of tricks to play in such a situation.

'The price is absurd for so fair a virgin,' he declared, stepping on to the platform himself. He flicked off both of Ranya's veils so that she was fully revealed, and poor Ranya covered her face with her hands. At this Zeid's fury knew no bounds and his voice roared above the cries of the crowd. 'Cover her this instant.'

Ferdhan quickly obeyed, but there was time enough for all to have seen how finely nature had made her and lust shone from the eyes of every man there. The bidding started again and now the Ahl Yazid sheikhs competed furiously until finally, at six hundred and ninety riyals, Ranya became the property of the amir, was paid for by his retainers and rapidly whisked away.

At the removal of Ranya's veil Na'ema had burst into sobs. It had added another dimension of terror to the situation in the crowded market. She put her hands beneath her *milfah*, felt for the thin veil underneath and somehow knotted it; she was seized with fierce indignation, and death would have been better than to allow herself to be displayed in this way.

At this point, Ferdhan revealed another of his wiles. He felt relief as he watched Zeid depart, for it spared him risk and still left the field open. He let his mind dwell on the possibilities: the price that Zeid had paid for Ranya, urged on by the sheikhs, was far higher than he expected, and he began to think that he had sold Na'ema too cheaply. After all, what he had received from Tabarhla was only part payment and the promise of more to come might not even be kept. The temptation to test the market finally got the better of him. He ordered her to be placed on the platform, and at this the crowd which had been restless, fell silent and stared at Na'ema.

'Unfortunately for all of you,' Ferdhan announced, 'an offer has already been made for this maiden which I am inclined to accept.'

A murmur of disappointment ran through the ranks of the sheikhs. Ferdhan made a casual gesture. 'Unless, that is, there is any here who would care to raise the offer to the same price as the last virgin.'

Here Ferdhan had overreached himself, for the next thing he knew was a dagger at his throat. Tabarhla stood behind him and hissed in his ear. 'Take her down this second or I will kill you!'

Ferdhan felt danger closing about him. 'Your bids will degrade you,' he declared. 'For this virgin no price is high enough.'

The sheikhs were sour-faced as he forced a laugh, and no one else shared the joke that he pretended. He felt a grip on his arm. 'I honour my debt,' Tabarhla hissed. He flung a bag of coins at Ferdhan, lifted Na'ema on to the croup of his horse and swept away. But Ferdhan could accept an insult when his money belts were full and he knew that Tabarhla's anger would pass, for no one wants to offend a slave dealer for long.

As they left, Na'ema burst into tears.

'My slave, Etza . . .' she sobbed.

'She will be sold in the town. She will be safe.'

The tears rolled down Na'ema's cheeks.

'Oh, very well, I will buy her for you tomorrow,' said Tabarhla, on impulse.

# Chapter 12

THE PURCHASE OF Na'ema had been the inspiration of Ayesha. For Tabarhla's wife, Ayesha, life had been hard. At the age of thirty she had borne eight children of whom only four had survived, three daughters and one son named Abdullah. Her spirit had survived the losses but she was tired, her body was aged before its time and her youngest child was six years old. She had not been pregnant now for three years, and so she had begun to doubt whether fate intended that she should provide Tabarhla with another son, let alone the many they had prayed for.

It had been a matter of much discussion between them, and Ayesha had pleaded with Tabarhla to take a second wife. But for all that he agreed with her, Tabarhla had found himself confronted by the problem of politics. The Ahl Yazid consisted of only three families, and for a sheikh of the bin Tahir it would have been possible to marry either into the ibn Aidh or the bin Mufarrih, for each had suitable brides. However, whichever family was not chosen would take offence. Ayesha had looked elsewhere and spoken to the wives of other sheikhs of the Beni Mughe'id, but always there were practical objections, or that at least was what Tabarhla claimed. In his heart he was divided about the whole idea of a second wife; he felt no need to have one for any reason other than obtaining a son, and besides, there would be much expense. To a man of greater domesticity such difficulties might have been overcome but in the case of Tabarhla all his energies were directed towards fighting, and towards the day he could rule Abha as he saw that it should be ruled; somehow this left little room for a small domestic matter such as this. Thus the disagreement between these two was the opposite from that which more usually affects married couples.

Consequently, it was Ayesha on her own who had decided that the solution was to find him a suitable concubine. There would be many advantages of such an arrangement, for Tabarhla, she felt, needed the novelty of a new partner, which might even cause him to spend more of his time at home at the Maqabil, and less at the Manadhir waiting upon his father. The concubine would bear him sons which would protect the lineage and make safe the position of the family. As for herself, Ayesha scarcely gave the matter any thought, for it was her nature only to consider her own needs after those of others.

When Ferdhan had brought Ranya and Na'ema to Abha she had learned of it within minutes, and had obtained an accurate picture of both from the family that provided their accommodation. She had even decided which of the two Tabarhla should purchase. He himself had demurred, as she had guessed he would, and so when it came to the point she had been extremely firm, more so, as it happened, than Tabarhla ever recalled her being, and thus the outcome was never in doubt.

Now, as Tabarhla lowered Na'ema from his horse and she was led through the courtyard of the Maqabil, Ayesha welcomed her like a daughter and took her at once to her own harem, where the womenfolk who had been attending her daughters fell upon her with an excess of attention. Almost before she knew what was happening her clothes were removed and she was being bathed, after which all manner of ointments and cosmetics were applied to different parts of her body, somewhat more intimately than she was used to. Finally she was dressed in new clothes, less gaudy and rather more comfortable than those she had stepped out of.

From these activities Tabarhla was of course excluded, nor was he allowed to see Na'ema that day or the next. At first she was speechless, but she adjusted to her situation by degrees and was relieved when two days later Etza reappeared. She had already changed ownership three times since arriving at Abha and had slipped unnoticed into the ranks of another household, where Tabarhla had difficulty in finding her. The reunion of Na'ema and Etza, when this came about, was a tearful affair for them both.

*

Following these events, Tabarhla considered it prudent to make an early call on his father, since he feared that his feelings might still be ruffled after the way he had been treated by Ferdhan.

'Ya *waludi*,' Zeid greeted him brightly. 'I see that you bought the other concubine.'

'I bought the other, Father, though you have only to command me and she is yours.'

'I don't see why you should want a concubine when I have just arranged a marriage for you. It will be to a daughter of the Idrisi, who at the joining of our families will become my ally against the tribes.'

Tabarhla was silent as he digested this extraordinary piece of information. Never before had Zeid taken an interest in his marital affairs, and that he should do so now seemed to him incredible, even presumptuous. Yet if this was his father's command he would have to obey it. As he considered the implications his anxiety increased; no one in the whole of As'ir had ever married an Idrisi and the thought that he should be the first made him reel. When he spoke he had difficulty in choosing words which did not betray his anger, for Zeid, he knew, would be watching his reactions closely and would seize on anything that he regarded as showing a lack of filial respect, and so he restrained himself.

'When have you planned the marriage, Father?'

'As soon as it can be arranged.'

'You have already chosen an Idrisi wife?'

'Very nearly so.' Zeid was lying and Tabarhla knew it.

'I will obey your decision in all things, Father.'

'Then enjoy your concubine in the short time available, for it would certainly be unfitting for her to be in your house when your bride arrives. Besides, you will have to sell her to pay the cost of your marriage: the Idrisi are hardly likely to part with one of their daughters cheaply.'

Tabarhla withdrew after kissing his father on the nose and then on either cheek, as was customary. He had never imagined that his father's jealousy of him could carry him to such an extreme course; it had been at the back of his mind that Zeid might be petulant, which was why he had visited him sooner rather than later, but he had been confident that if any wild ideas had entered his father's head he could dispel them and soothe his ruffled feelings. But now he was confronted by an accomplished fact, or one which soon would be accomplished, for he didn't doubt that Zeid would already have made an approach to the Idrisi, and once set on a course he knew that nothing would deflect him. He was appalled at his father's rashness and ineptitude: to order him to marry into a tribe who were amongst the most dangerous of Abha's enemies would be *aib*, or shameful, were it not so ridiculous. The advantage would lie entirely with the Idrisi, who would certainly seize upon it avidly. They would tie him into a marriage treaty that would force him to fight on their side and do so whenever they them-selves chose. Worse than that, they would plant one of their own at Abha, who would have access to its most private secrets.

He grew more and more angry, yet the worst thing he had not yet considered which was how he would break the news to Ayesha, for all her plans for the family would be ruined.

*

As it happened, he was able to avoid this, for when he returned to his house he found it caught up in festivities, and he soon put the future out of his mind.

It was all on account of Na'ema. In a short time her whole appearance had changed: she laughed, and light shone in her

119

eyes. As the desert grows green after rain he watched her youthful lustre return. One day, he thought, she would bear him sons, yet at present she seemed more like a daughter and his first duty would be to educate her, as his other daughters were educated, to write and read the Quran. Girls, he believed, should be properly taught so that upon marriage they were able to play a full part not only within the family but outside it. In this respect the customs of Abha were ahead of their time, for it was the practice for the sheikhas to attend his *majlis* at the Maqabil, and even on occasion that at the Manadhir. It was held that female intuition was an asset too valuable to be wasted and so their voices were heard. Reflecting this liberal attitude, the women of Abha went about wearing only a headscarf, and once married they were not confined to their own harems, as was customary, but suitably accompanied walked freely about the town.

Days and then weeks went by, during which nothing more was heard of the Idrisi matter, and Na'ema settled easily into the family and gradually became absorbed into it. She was a natural playmate for Ayesha's daughters, who regarded her at first as an object of curiosity but before long as an elder sister.

This happy state of affairs might have continued had it not been interrupted by Etza, who came one day to Ayesha, her mahogany face cast in gloom. She declared that the house was grievously threatened by some event that had to do with marriage and a ruler. The omens in the stars were very clear. 'It may apply to the Amir, for ruler and ruler of the house have the same sign, so it may be one or the other or both, but I know that there is great danger.'

The urgency in Etza's voice made Ayesha start. She was by now well aware that Etza could read the omens and that her prophecies had the habit of being right. She confronted Tabarhla with the information and learned what until then had been kept secret.

'Of course I am threatened,' said Tabarhla. 'We all are threatened, myself by an unwanted marriage and the whole of Abha by an absurd alliance. We should be fighting the Idrisi not marrying their daughters. For years they have had their eyes on Abha, wanting our stronghold for themselves, and it is perfectly plain that in the end war will come and we shall have to defend it.'

Then he wanted to know who it was that read the omens, and Ayesha told him, but what he had said only increased her anxiety. It was also quite clear that if anything was to be done it was she alone who would have to do it; but perhaps, on reflection, not quite alone.

After Tabarhla had left she sent for Etza, to tell her all that he had said. Ayesha had much confidence in Etza and although, as she reflected, it was an absurdity to confide in slaves, yet somehow Etza was different. She was clever, there was no doubt about that. She recalled how she had treated Abdullah, her son, when he was ill and how quickly he had recovered. There was something else that was unusual: she had noticed that whilst Etza's manners were perfectly correct she behaved as an equal and not as a slave, and the strange thing was that no one, least of all Ayesha, resented it.

Etza came at once and Ayesha gave her a full account just as she had received it from Tabarhla, seating her on a cushion beside her own. She knew instinctively that in Etza she had a resourceful ally, and as they talked she discovered how well Etza understood the workings of her family. As she finished, silence descended and Etza stared fixedly in front of her. Finally, she turned and faced Ayesha.

'*Ammati*, a way must be found to keep Na'ema in your house.'

'Of course a way must be found; my daughters are devoted to her and so am I.'

'That is not quite what I meant. A stranger is going to come into your house who may present a threat. Na'ema is a fighter and she will keep the family in balance if she is there.'

'What do you mean, she is a fighter?'

'At the moment Na'ema is young and may not seem to be so, but a fighter she is. Her star and the star of an ordinary warrior are very close.'

Stars once more, thought Ayesha, but she did not dare to say so. 'How shall I keep her in my house, then?'

'That is what we have to discover. There is always a way.'

So assured was Etza that this gave Ayesha heart, and from being distraught she actually smiled. The door was closed and curtains were drawn, and for two days the two of them remained in the harem alone. At the end of that time Etza discreetly left, and later Tabarhla took her place. He was morbid and introspective but fortunately in a mood to listen. She made him a proposal of a very unusual nature.

'If your father is ready to make a sacrifice of us all then I don't see why you should not resist him, filial duty or not.'

'What resistance can there be?' Tabarhla's voice was resigned.

'You will have to marry the Idrisi, that much is clear, but I don't see why you should have to get rid of Na'ema. She is part of our family.'

'I will have to. A new wife would not accept a concubine in her house. She would be outraged and her brothers would force the issue over it.'

'That is something we will come to later. Let us be practical. It took a long time to find Na'ema and I'm not going to give her up easily. Do you think it would be fair to impose an Idrisi wife on me if I have no support in my own house?'

'Support? I do not understand.'

'Na'ema is my support. At present she is like one of my daughters, but the time will come when she will bear you sons. Do you think I want only the sons of an Idrisi in my house? I may have to have them but I don't see why I should be quite outnumbered. Besides, if there is to be a war, whose side do you suppose your Idrisi wife will be on? And if she has sons, whose side will they be on?'

Tabarhla did not answer. He was not at all sure where the conversation was leading.

'A second loss, which is almost as bad, will be Etza, for Etza is devoted to Na'ema. If Na'ema goes, Etza will refuse to stay, which as a slave she is entitled to do. Then we shall lose a great asset.'

'Why is that?'

'Because she foretells the future.'

'What has she foretold?'

'Firstly that you are threatened by a marriage and secondly that there will be war. Ever since she has been here she has been foretelling correctly, even that Abdullah would catch measles. And when he did, she had a remedy for it. Etza's loss would be nothing less than a catastrophe.'

Tabarhla shook his head. He was confused, although he quite understood the importance of omens.

'Another thing,' Ayesha went on. 'How would we explain Na'ema's departure to our daughters, who love her? If she is thrown out they will never forgive you. They don't understand what a concubine is and they would probably start thinking that next you would get rid of them as well.'

Tabarhla looked at her despairingly. 'Then what in God's name are we to do?'

'I will tell you. You will marry Na'ema and then the Idrisi will have no cause to complain.'

Tabarhla turned to her in exasperation. 'Marry a concubine? Don't be absurd. How could I?'

'You could if her family were to insist and request a proper bride payment and the marriage was sworn before a *muta'awah*.'

'You are out of your mind. She has no family.'

'We know that, but who else does? No one. It can be given about the town that her brothers have come to Abha to demand either her return or else the *daf'a* for agreeing to her marriage. We shall have to invent their tribe.'

Tabarhla stared at her. 'Are the Ahl Yazid allowed to marry into this tribe?'

'Since there can have never been such a marriage there will be no rule. The *qadi* will talk about if for days but eventually they will decide that no objection is valid because there is no precedent.'

'Then how are we to find the non-existent brothers?'

'We will simply invent them. The rest of the Ahl Yazid are not going to be too much concerned with such details. If the *qadi* confirm that their honour has not been impugned they will lose interest in the marriage.'

'But the *muta'awah* will know the truth because he will see that she has no brothers.'

'The point is, will he see? You forget. There is a blind *muta'awah* who lives near Dhohyah, ibn Sawah.'

A smile appeared on Tabarhla's face. He threw back his head and his ivory teeth flashed against his black beard, then his whole body shook with laughter.

He got up and paced about the floor and then sat down again on the heap of cushions that served them for a sleeping place and for relaxing at other times, their geometrical patterns of red and yellow exaggerated in the filtered sunlight. Ayesha gazed at her husband and thought how much he reminded her of how he had looked when she had married him sixteen years before. With the mask of care removed his old nonchalance reasserted itself, and he tossed back his black hair, freed from its accustomed head cloth, and smiled at her, his eyes full of youthful cunning. She had little guessed at the time of her marriage that her husband would become not only the centre of her own world but that of everyone else in Abha. It had after all been conventional enough, marrying her *bint am*, her first cousin, who had the prior right to her hand. Yet from the moment she saw him he had seemed to her a perfect paragon, an event of nature, like a mountain, that had always been there. She had been in awe of him then and perhaps she still was, yet now she glowed in the knowledge that he needed her, for what she read in his gaze was gratitude.

'I think you have just saved our house.' He paused. 'Have you told Na'ema yet?'

'She will be told when we think it best.'

*

For a while, Na'ema was removed and placed in the care of Ayesha's aunt, to prepare her for the wedding ceremony and attend to details of dress and adornment. She did not return until the day of the wedding, and then, dressed as a bride, re-entered the Maqabil, where the ceremony took place. This was kept brief, as was conventional for a second wife. Ibn Sawah, the blind *muta'awah*, formally asked Tabarhla if he had chosen to marry Na'ema, and when he assented turned to where Na'ema's brothers were supposed to be standing and asked if the marriage had their permission. A deep voice answered, 'We offer no objection to the marriage.' Its owner was Etza, who managed to convey a coastal dialect in a masculine fashion. All this took place in Tabarhla's house and the only witnesses were the household servants, who displayed a genuine if uncomprehending happiness at the event. Afterwards there were no festivities for fear that others might wish to join in, nor was there any alteration to the domestic routine except that Na'ema became known as Sheikha and was given her own small harem.

Na'ema herself viewed the proceedings much like any other Muslim bride, enjoying the comfortable belief that it had always been thus intended. In her own family it had been the custom for girls not to be told when they were to be married and therefore the ceremony, although it was rather sudden, caused her no particular surprise. It all seemed to follow the natural course of events, although she was sorry that there was no feasting and dancing. However, Etza was quick to point out the many advantages in her change of station, for as wife she had a right to many things, including the ownership of all the jewellery she was wearing, a pair of gold bracelets, several necklaces of large amber beads, anklets of silver and an amulet to ward off the evil eye. With such a collection as these, Etza assured her, she could be accounted rich.

The only thing that Na'ema found strange was that the marriage caused no change in physical relations but this, Etza said, should be construed as a compliment to herself, and besides, the month of Ramadhan was approaching. Much more important was the fact that Na'ema was now a sheikha and would be allowed to pay calls on other sheikhas, starting with the wives of the Amir; it meant freedom and even the possibility that she might be allowed to see

Ranya. At this Na'ema's excitement was great and she at once set about preparing the two rooms of her harem so that they were fit for receiving guests, who would soon be paying return visits. She despatched Etza to the market with part of the small dowry she had received, and Etza duly returned with armfuls of fabrics to make carpets and cushions. She also purchased a *zarar*, a bronze medallion intended to be worn about the neck on a thin piece of leather, which Etza insisted she should present to her husband as a talisman to ward off evil. Tabarhla protested that it was unseemly for a man to wear such a trinket, but so abject a look came over Na'ema's face that he gave in to her wish and not only promised to wear it but actually did so.

When the news of the marriage was conveyed to Zeid, his response was just as Ayesha had predicted. He had forgotten all about Na'ema and he was unconcerned. The *qadis* were duly consulted and since they gave it as their opinion that the honour of the Ahl Yazid had not been compromised, Zeid thereafter forgot about it. He turned his thoughts to another direction, which was against which tribe he could most profitably go to war now that the fighting season was at hand.

He chose the Beni Bijad, who from time to time had stolen horses from the Beni Mughe'id, and as soon as the end of Ramadhan arrived, which Zeid had observed in a somewhat cursory manner, Tabarhla was ordered to make preparations. He organised a *gaum* of hundred and fifty men and horses which he led out of Abha with Zeid in the rear shouting orders. It looked like the rabble that it was for the horses were scraggy, still in summer condition, and the fighting tribesmen themselves had turned out with reluctance. They were clad in a motley of sand-coloured rags, with rifles slung over their shoulders, and the ends of their turbans loose in the wind. As in all As'ir, they rode on saddle cloths with a single rope to the headstall, and no stirrups, which were despised as an invention of the Turks. In this fashion they travelled along the line of the wadi where the Beni Bijad normally converged at the beginning of the season. However, before the *gaum* had made contact with the Beni Bijad it was set upon by robbers, who attacked out of the glare of the evening sun, and by the time they withdrew there were a number of casualties. At this, Tabarhla set off in pursuit, fought a running battle with the marauders, who turned out to be the Sa'er, commonly known as 'the wolves of the desert', and rounded up their riderless horses. Zeid meanwhile had returned to Abha.

After a celebration for which two baggage camels were slaughtered, the night was spent storytelling before a great fire of brushwood and *arfaj*. Next day the captured horses were paraded in the main square for all to see; they were examined in every particular, and the considered verdict was that the horses had been stolen from the Beni Bijad, who had stolen them from the Beni Mughe'id earlier.

Tabarhla, angered by the futility of the exercise, returned to the Maqabil, where he was greeted by Ayesha.

'You are not hurt?' she enquired anxiously.

'Not at all,' replied Tabarhla, 'though something nearly knocked me from my horse.'

He placed his forefinger on his chest and found that he was touching the bronze *zarar* that Na'ema had given him. It had a large dent where a bullet had struck and ricocheted. They both stared at it in silence. Tabarhla took the medallion from his neck and weighed it, first in one hand and then the other, and handed it to Ayesha, who examined it for a long time. The dent was left and from that day Tabarhla wore it always, underneath his *dishdasha*.

# Chapter 13

VISITS BETWEEN THE harems were governed by convention. Thus the first visit that Na'ema made was to Hazyah, the senior wife of Zeid; and after the lengthy formalities had been completed, and as this lady was of a tolerant nature, she was permitted to visit Ranya.

It took some time for her to be found as Zeid's palace, which occupied the whole of the western end of the Manadhir, had a number of harems with their attendant slaves. Na'ema found it somewhat overwhelming, and whilst she waited for Ranya to appear she began to reflect on the difference between Ranya's fortunes and her own. She felt that she must apologise for being so much the luckier and shuddered that it might have been herself that Zeid had chosen. To become an old man's concubine, a mere plaything – she thought that Ranya must certainly be very miserable.

But the reality was rather different from what she had expected, and from the moment that Ranya came tripping into the room it was clear that it was she who considered herself the privileged one. She was immaculately groomed and dressed and moved with the assurance of one who had found her place in the palace hierarchy. Her face lit up as she saw Na'ema, and she led her at once to her harem, seated Na'ema beside her and demanded to know all that had happened. It was some time before Na'ema could discover much about Ranya herself, for her curiosity was great, and when Ranya learned that Na'ema was now married she wanted to hear every detail of the ceremony and how it had come about, which, it must be admitted, Na'ema had some difficulty in explaining. As they talked she observed that a great change had come over Ranya: she was a girl no longer but a young woman of striking beauty, but beauty which was at the same time slightly unreal, so that it seemed that she might have been carved out of wax and then painted. Na'ema wanted to touch her face to be sure it was real, yet the thought of the other hands that must also touch her still appalled her.

Ranya seemed to read her mind and started to talk about Zeid as though to reassure her. 'He is wonderful. He tells such stories and he is so funny because he imitates all the others perfectly. Really, half the time I am laughing.' She lowered her voice and glanced at Na'ema. 'The rest of the time, well, you can't imagine. He is so strong and powerful as a man. Now I only think of how to please him. Do you know for the first week he hardly left my harem once!'

'Whatever did you do all that time?'

'What did we do? Shall I tell you what happened?' Ranya gave a nervous little laugh. 'The first night . . . you can't believe . . . it was like entering another world. It wasn't as I expected at all. First, I was bathed and toiletted for hours on end by three of Sheikha Hazyah's slave girls; I've never had such a grooming. One of them removed my hairs quite painlessly, then they dressed me in a white silk gown that was buttoned at the neck and down the front, and loosened my hair so that it fell over it. They put bracelets, lots of them, on my arms and ankles, and when everything was finished I was led to another harem, where Zeid was waiting. Of course I was very nervous and asked the slave girls what I should do but they said I needn't do anything. There was a scent of burning sandalwood and light came from a coloured lantern that hung in the centre of the room. It was very dim and it was a minute before my eyes were accustomed. Zeid was lying in a sheikhly way on a pile of cushions, dressed in crimson and gold, and he was quite the handsomest man I ever saw. I mean, he is handsome, isn't he?'

'Oh, yes,' said Na'ema, who had only seen Zeid once and not in quite the best circumstances. 'Yes, he certainly is very handsome.'

Ranya seemed to relive the scene, and her eyes shone. 'He drew me beside him and made many compliments to make me feel at ease, then he said, "Have you ever seen *salubas*?" Of course I had never heard of *salubas*, who are sort of gypsies, so I shook my head. He clapped his hands and after a few minutes some dancing girls came in, seven of them gorgeously dressed in billowing dresses of different colours. Then there were three more who carried drums and musical instruments and when they started to play you couldn't believe it. The music was so soft and dreamy to begin with, then it gradually grew louder and they all clapped to the beat. The girls who had been sitting got up, and danced two at a time, first as partners and then on their own with everyone else clapping their hands. You can't imagine how they danced. They had tiny silver pieces sewn on their costumes and as they moved their bodies quivered and the light glittered on them. They moved their bellies so their navels went in circles and backwards and forwards like this.' Ranya got up and gave a demonstration which was so expert that it made Na'ema stare. 'I am sure Zeid wouldn't like to see you do that,' she said.

'Oh, but you are wrong. I'll tell you, much more happened. One after the other the girls removed their silks until they were wearing less and less and finally just strings of coloured beads over their breasts and a fringe below. They danced closer and closer to Zeid until the beads actually touched him and he grew very excited, as I knew he must, and I did too.' She passed her hand through her hair, twisting her plaits and tossing them back. 'Finally Zeid had the curtains drawn around us, which made it like a tiny private room, but in a way not private because the curtains were so thin that we could still see the *saluba* girls dancing. It was all so unreal that I don't remember what happened exactly, but when he undressed me I know I blushed because his eyes were all over me. He whispered words in my ears and said he would make me just like an instrument, a special one for him alone, and with his hands he showed me what he meant. I don't know how long it was before he made love to me for I was really in a daze, but when it happened I was aching so much it was quite a relief, not a pain like I had expected at all. When it was over he said that if I really wanted to please him I should dance too, like the *saluba* girls, and next day he would have them teach me.'

'Whatever did you do?' whispered Na'ema, who could hardly believe what she was hearing. 'Surely that would be shameful.'

'At first I thought it would be shameful too, and I tried to say so, but Zeid said that it was not shameful but beautiful and seductive and would make him love me. When I looked at it his way I thought that he was right so I said I would.

'The next day the *salubas* were sent for again and they taught me the dancing steps until I ached all over, especially my back. But they seemed to know this would happen and made me lie on the floor and massaged my muscles so that when I danced again they didn't hurt at all. The whole day was either dancing or eating from trays of sweetmeats which the slaves brought, and Zeid didn't even stop to say his prayers. But I never expected what happened in the evening, for he made the *salubas* dress me in their beads and they really hardly covered me at all, especially when I danced. I think that he was trying to teach me, for he made me go on until I almost dropped, and then the *salubas* danced or played music while I lay on the cushions beside him. But I think I must be boring you to death? You suddenly look quite pale.'

'No, do go on,' said Na'ema. 'I want to hear.' It was all strangely disturbing yet she was too curious to allow Ranya to stop.

'Well, finally he sent the girls away, and that night he made love to me six or seven times; every time I tried to sleep he woke me up. The last time it went on for so long something happened to me that had never happened before, which I can't describe. It was like a sudden glow all over and I started shaking, which I couldn't stop, and that made him even more excited. Then something seemed to turn over inside me; it was a marvellous feeling. Did you ever have a feeling like that?'

'Well, I don't know. I don't think so, not quite like that,' Na'ema replied vacantly, her own fantasies working furiously.

'So, anyway, I'm not shy any more. I dance for him every night without anything on at all and he has promised me everything I want, so much you can't believe. Did you see my ring?' She pointed to a heavy gold nose ring that she wore in her right nostril. 'But really,' she continued without waiting for Na'ema to reply, 'I talk too much. Tell me what it was like with Sheikh Tabarhla. Was it wonderful?'

'Well, that was wonderful too but it was rather different. He is marvellous but . . . not quite in that way.'

'He will be, you see,' said Ranya encouragingly. 'You will give him sons.' She hesitated and blushed, then whispered, 'I think I shall soon give Zeid a son. I think it is already starting.'

'It can't be. Already?'

Ranya nodded. 'I think so. You will come and see me, won't you, because as soon as Zeid knows he will make me stay in my harem so that no harm can happen.'

'Yes', said Na'ema brightly. 'Yes, of course I will.'

*

She returned to the Maqabil lost in her thoughts. It was all so different from what she had expected. Ranya was different, the Manadhir was different. And Zeid . . . she tried to picture the scenes that Ranya had described. They were so different from anything she had experienced herself that she found them difficult to imagine and oddly disturbing. Yet Ranya had glided easily over her own relationship with Tabarhla and hardly noticed when she herself had said so little about it. Her brow puckered slightly. The fact was there was so little to say. She found herself blushing and suddenly realised that she did so because Ranya had made her feel self-conscious; then she knew that there was something badly missing. She started to touch her own body to explore all its parts, and after a while she made discoveries which enabled her to understand a little better what Ranya had meant. Yet this understanding only served to increase her curiosity, which in turn made her frustrated with her own situation.

She tried to talk to Etza but found she couldn't bring herself to explain the true source of her anxiety. Instead she turned to the subject of Ranya but then she found herself blushing, and did not tell Etza everything Ranya had said. She began to worry about Ranya being pregnant and clutched Etza's hand and asked, 'Will everything be all right?'

'God will protect her.'

'Will He, will He make her life happy?'

Etza paused and just perceptibly her expression changed. 'Her happiness is like everyone else's, it is not assured.' She would not be drawn further concerning Ranya, either then or later.

The next days were unhappy for Na'ema as she searched in her own mind for an explanation of Tabarhla's behaviour towards her, which was so different from Zeid's, and every night lay on her bed of *lahafs*, brooding about it. Finally she convinced herself that in some way she had disappointed him, and that he must now regret first having bought her and then having married her.

'But if he does not like me why did he go to the trouble of marrying me?' she asked herself. 'Why didn't he just ... throw me away?' At this she burst into tears and sobbed all night long, so that the next day her eyes were swollen and her face was still tear-stained when Tabarhla came upon her. Sensing that something was wrong, he drew her aside and asked if someone in his household had ill-treated her. Na'ema shook her head. At this he showed much concern, which surprised Na'ema, for by now she had concluded that she had ceased to be wanted, or indeed was of any importance at all.

'Whatever makes you so miserable?' he asked, taking her by the hand, and in spite of trying not to, Na'ema started to weep once more.

He led her into her harem and sat her down, drawing her beside him and signing to Etza to leave them. 'You must tell me what is wrong.'

'I don't . . . I don't know,' sobbed Na'ema. 'I feel so . . . so unwanted . . . so useless to anyone.'

'But you are not, you are precious. You are more beautiful than all my daughters.'

'But I am not . . . like . . . your daughters . . . I am your wife.'

He looked at the fragile trembling figure beside him and his brow furrowed slightly. 'Indeed you are, and you can have whatever you want.'

'But you are not . . . not . . . a real husband. I know it is because I do not please you. I know you do not want me because I am not beautiful like Ranya. I never was, and you took me in like a waif.' Her words came in a rush.

Tabarhla gazed at Na'ema, and after a moment a smile came over his face. 'How stupid of me to think of you as a child or a daughter,' he said quietly. He lifted her in his arms and carried her into the inner room. He laid her on the sleeping cushions and kissed her for the first time on her mouth, at first hesitantly, as if afraid it might frighten her, and then after a moment with passion, holding her tightly.

'I have waited so long for you to do that,' Na'ema murmured. 'I thought . . .' But no further words came forth.

*

As a result of this event, Tabarhla's attention became focused rather more on domestic matters than it had been before, and he forgot about the Idrisi affair, believing Zeid had done the same. So one day when he received a summons from his father, who announced that he had issued the *khutba*, at first he didn't know what he was talking about.

'What *khutba*, Father?' he said absently.

'The *khutba* payment for your Idrisi bride, of course,' said Zeid, beaming at him. 'The bride is chosen and the principal terms are all agreed.'

Tabarhla was horrified at this abrupt return to reality and it was a few moments before he could think of a reply. Finally he said,

'Father, if you insist that I marry the Idrisi I entreat you to let me handle the negotiations myself.'

Zeid waved his arms. 'Who else? I have made the *khutba*. Who but a bridegroom should bargain the *daf'a* and arrange the ceremonies.' He beamed again.

'Then have I your consent to conduct matters myself?'

'What is there to conduct beyond what I have said? Go forth and bring your bride into our house.'

'Father, I shall need money.'

'Indeed you will, and you should have thought of that before you bought the concubine.'

Tabarhla said nothing and left before his father started again upon the advantages to be gained from the Idrisi alliance. The prospect was nightmarish: it passed belief that Zeid should imagine that the Idrisi would ally themselves with him. They were not just a tribe like the Beni Mughe'id but virtually a state of their own, continually extending their territory and extracting taxes from the tribes they forced into submission. Besides, they were an alien people, not Sunnis like the rest of As'ir but Sufists who came from the Senussi mountains in northern Africa at the edge of the Muslim world. Their customs were notoriously barbarous: he recalled that their slaves were hamstrung to stop them escaping and they practised the circumcision of both sexes in an abominable manner forbidden by the Quran.

He returned to the Maqabil and talked to Ayesha, but all she would say was, 'You must obey your father, *insha'llah*, it is the will of God. I shall have a harem prepared for her.' These were to be her final words on the subject.

With Na'ema it was more difficult. He tried to explain to her that some marriages were not from love but made from duty or because of politics, but his words carried no conviction. 'They all make offspring just the same,' she said angrily. Tears ran down her face. 'Is she beautiful?'

'I have not seen her and I cannot say.'

'You are going to marry a girl you have never seen?'

'Sometimes it happens like that.'

'And you are content to marry someone you have never seen?'

'I cannot say that I am content but a son must do his father's bidding.'

'Then I hate it.'

There was nothing in the least submissive in her manner. Tabarhla looked at her and reflected that for one so young she was surprisingly forward. He left, and Na'ema sought out Ayesha, the awful prospect of another wife engulfing her mind. She stormed into Ayesha's harem heedless of manners and custom, and when she found Ayesha assailed her as though it had all been her fault.

'Why don't you stop him?' she cried. 'Stop him doing such a dreadful thing. You could if you wanted to, he always does what you tell him.'

'I cannot interfere,' said Ayesha gently. 'I know that you are hurt but you are young. There are rules which we have to learn to live by which as yet you do not understand.'

'Then I think the rules are absurd.'

'Nevertheless, you cannot change them. They have always been there and always will be and you will not know happiness until you have come to terms with them. Men control our lives absolutely, as it is written in the Quran that they are allowed to. For better or worse it is they who make every decision, and as women it is our lot to obey.'

'Then men own us both body and soul.'

'It is not as simple as that. It is a woman's best choice to obey, otherwise she has no protection in the world. To disobey your husband is to be divorced and sent back to your mother and father, which means that you are a failure, and as long as you live they will treat you accordingly. Sometimes it is hard to be obedient just as it is hard for men to obey their fathers or slaves their master, but that is God's will. Yet women are lucky because they have each other and there is much consolation in women's friendship. You must learn to find such consolation because it will save you much unhappiness and in the end it will give you the security which you will need, for you will meet plenty of enemies and your husband will often not be there. He may be involved in men's affairs or fighting or even begetting children by others, but to all this you must shut your mind for it shouldn't concern you in any way at all.'

With these plain words Ayesha attempted to console Na'ema, and whereas to a more mature person they would have seemed to state matters that were obvious, to someone as untamed as Na'ema they came as a terrible blow. She desperately needed Ayesha to defend her, yet Ayesha seemed to have no wish to resist or alter these customs, however much they might go against her. Too much had already gone wrong in Na'ema's own life to accept that everything was simply the will of God; surely it was her own right and every woman's to resist, and arm herself for the day she might fight these customs like any other evil.

But whatever God intended was in the future, and the awful event that presented itself was here and now and hideously threatening. She went to Ayesha and put her arms around her and wept, and as she wept she pushed her face deeper and deeper into the cleft of Ayesha's ample bosom so that Ayesha's black dress became wet with Na'ema's tears. She sobbed, and her fingers clutched Ayesha desperately like those of a drowning person.

For her part, Ayesha made no attempt to interrupt but settled comfortably amidst her cushions, allowing Na'ema to hide her face, and after a while, as the sobbing continued, she untied the plaits of Na'ema's hair, parted it carefully in three long bunches and tenderly plaited it again, taking a great length of time.

When the tears finally ceased, Na'ema started to put her agony into words and it was much worse than Ayesha had realised, for her words had a terrifying urgency: 'Once I had brothers and a father and mother, then suddenly I wake up to find that I am a slave. Here in your house I become like a daughter, then I am married but not properly a wife. For a few days I am a real wife and now I am cast off.' She began to weep again and through her tears cried, 'I don't know ... who I am. Please, please tell me what I am.'

Ayesha held her for a long time but in silence for she knew that was best. As the hours passed Na'ema became quiet again and curiously healed, as if in asking the questions she had found answers of her own.

From that time on, the friendship between Ayesha and Na'ema grew stronger, and each knew that as long as they lived it would be the same and would endure. In truth, Ayesha had a great capacity for taking the pain of others into herself.

# Chapter 14

So engrossed had I been in Etza's tale that the seasons went by unnoticed, apart, that is, from summer, for in Arabia there is no activity known to man that would make this pass unnoticed. At Ayinah, high in the mountains, there were always breezes to make it bearable, which of course is why the summer quarters of the Ahl Yazid had been made there. By contrast, in the great lowland expanse that is the centre of Arabia it is quite a different story, as in due course I was to discover for myself.

There the furnace heat of summer is so fierce that it will make grains of rice separate from each other and cook themselves. It is a threat to the existence of man and beast alike, and the first sighting of Suhail, the star that marks its end, has almost mystical significance, heralding the cooler days that come in late October. Then those that have survived pray in thankfulness and remind themselves that their annual deliverance comes from God alone. The new-found optimism affects not only man but all the creatures of the earth, from the camels to the insects, altering the manner of their movements, which in a single day become sharper and filled with a sense of purpose or a sense of hope. Handkerchief clouds appear with the promise that rain will fall once more on the thirsty earth. At such a time as this, Etza now explained, Tabarhla set forth for the Idrisi stronghold of Sabiya, a journey of a hundred miles that took three days. His retinue consisted of eight sheikhs of the Ahl Yazid mounted on horses, and behind them came baggage camels laden with gifts and supplies for the journey, guarded by a *fidawiyah* of twenty askaris. They passed through juniper scrub and then, as they reached the lower plateau of the escarpment where rain had fallen early, there were pine trees which filled the air with fragrance. They camped there and in the dark cicadas emerged from their burrows to set up their deafening chorus, until it seemed to Tabarhla that they were issuing a warning. He forced himself to relax, knowing that his nerves were over-stretched.

At the end of the second day they reached the Tihama plain, and at the town of Darb they were met by a party of the Beni Shi'bah tribe, who camped with them and then escorted them to Sabiya itself. It was not an impressive place. Its mud-brick houses, few of more than a single storey, were mean-looking, and the city walls were dilapidated, probably because the Idrisi thought they had no enemies strong enough to attack them. But if these gave an impression of poverty it was misleading for the Idrisi notables who rode about the streets were richly clothed and escorted by tall Sudanese bodyguards. Both masters and slaves wore carefully tied blue turbans, dyed from the indigo plant, which gave them a martial appearance.

The large house at the edge of the city which had been set aside for the visitors had a courtyard in which was a well with a good depth of water, and here the camels were unloaded and the askaris set up their tents. Nearby a field of fresh *hamdh* provided pasture. The upper storey of the house had been furnished for Tabarhla's use and from the open part he was able to survey the city and the sands of the Tihama beyond. There were crops of lucerne and *dhurra* husbanded by groups of black slaves with conical straw hats and a system of wells worked by blindfolded donkeys.

Their quarters were agreeable but this could not be said for the party of Idrisi that arrived to greet them. Their leader announced himself as Hassan ibn Ali, the bride's cousin, and after brief formalities he straight away started to discuss the *daf'a* payment expected from Tabarhla. The haggling took several hours, during which various facts emerged: the bride was a niece of the Idrisi ruler, the Seiyyid Mohammed ibn Ali. Her father had been forced against his wishes to provide one of his daughters and had chosen Nura, who was said to be sixteen years of age and hence old enough to take care of herself in so remote and primitive a place as Abha. The whole family shared his view that a sheikh of Abha was no fit husband for such a bride and this being the case the *daf'a* was set at two thousand riyals, and, Hassan added, he would if needed go himself to Abha to ensure to his satisfaction that Nura was given a harem suitable for an Idrisi princess. These terms, he declared, were a small price to pay for the great advantages of a marriage alliance with the Idrisi, as he was sure that Tabarhla would concede when the alternative was considered. At this Tabarhla responded that his idea of what Hassan ibn Ali referred to as the alternative was a declaration of war. 'That,' said Hassan acidly, 'was exactly what I also had in mind.'

The *daf'a* was finally settled at six hundred and twenty riyals and Hassan departed. The next day the *'aqd* was signed before an assembly of *qadi* and their scribes and then sent to the Seiyyid for his approval.

Mohammed ibn Ali was known also as Mohammed the Black; he had had a Sudanese mother who had been a slave. He had inherited power after his father had died, some said assassinated by his son, twenty years before, and was now in his middle years. His word was law throughout the tribes of the Tihama and his ruthlessness and extraordinary fighting record – he had never lost a battle – made him feared throughout the region and beyond. Many judged that he might one day succeed in making western Arabia his kingdom, and so great was the threat that he posed that there had been much talk amongst his three principal enemies, Hussein, Sheriff of Mecca, Abdulaziz ibn Saud and the Imam Yahya of Yemen. All these were agreed, in a unique display of unity, that the Seiyyid was much too powerful, although they could not agree what to do about it.

Mohammed the Black now entered the drama himself by holding a *majlis* for Tabarhla from which, against all convention, the sheikhs of the Ahl Yazid were excluded, and so returned to the guest house burning with anger at the insult. As Tabarhla waited in the antechamber sounds reached his ears of a man in a rage, and presently from the *majlis* scurried a group of cowed men, who hastily made their exit. The Seiyyid was still raging as Tabarhla entered, which made their customary embrace somewhat awkward.

'Emissaries of the Sheriff of Mecca,' he stormed. 'They come to seek my favours, forgetting that I whipped their sheriff like a cur when he dared to fight me.'

Tabarhla said nothing and was inclined to believe that the episode had been staged for his benefit. He looked around at the trappings of the *majlis*, which was adorned with painted columns between which hung rich carpets. The whole place proclaimed the wealth of the Seiyyid and was intimidating, as indeed it was designed to be.

'Is it not great and splendid, that which you behold?' demanded the Seiyyid, changing his tone. 'Our Senussi gold was surely bestowed upon us by God Himself.'

Tabarhla assented, although it seemed to him that God's munificence was more likely to have been in the number of local tribes who could be squeezed for taxes. They turned to the matter of the marriage. As a formality Tabarhla proposed that it would unite the Idrisi and the Beni Mughe'id in time of war, but to his surprise, instead of making a polite reply, the Seiyyid answered roughly: 'Naturally we will require you to fight with us in any war we decide to make.'

'I cannot answer for that,' said Tabarhla. 'That will be for my father to decide.'

'Apart from the *khutba* it is the one issue on which he has already agreed.' He watched Tabarhla closely as he spoke and Tabarhla realised that he was mocking him. It took him a moment to steady himself. 'The As'ir has long depended upon my father's good judgement.'

Mohammed flicked an eyebrow, then paused to enjoy his discomfiture. Tabarhla was furious at the disadvantage in which his father had placed him; he said no more, but rose, bowed formally and strode from the chamber, fearing that if he remained he would lose his temper. He returned to the guest house with a mounting sense of anger and frustration and was not even able to unburden himself to the Ahl Yazid, who, if they had known that he had been insulted, could not have been prevented from invading the palace and fighting a pitched battle. He shut himself in his room, and there, consumed by his anger, he cursed the marriage. He saw that the Beni Mughe'id and all the tribes that supported them would be drawn into the Seiyyid's grip, and he would grind them like harvest meal; it was extraordinary that his father should have so underestimated the Idrisi. The only consolation was that the Seiyyid Mohammed and Hassan ibn Ali plainly detested one another, and thus there was an outside chance that the Idrisi could end by destroying themselves, as had many another ruling family.

Next day he returned to Abha with anger still tearing at his heart. He swore that he would destroy the Idrisi and the threat they posed to Abha even if it took a lifetime to do so.

*

'Etza,' I said, 'I do not understand how you come to know all these things because you could not have been at Sabiya and seen what you have described.'

She stared at me for several seconds, her face blank with surprise. I shifted uneasily and was sorry I had mentioned the matter. When she spoke, her voice was sharp.

'The answer is quite simple. When Sheikh Tabarhla returned to the Maqabil he was in a rage for several days. He followed Sheikha Ayesha everywhere shouting, until the whole house knew about Mohammed the Black. In any case nothing happens in any household that is private. Everything that goes on is known to everyone.'

I had to swallow my pride and the fact is that I never dared to interrupt her again, however strange it was that she knew as much as she did.

*

A month passed, and Nura arrived at Abha accompanied by her three brothers and retinue of relatives, also a group of African slave girls who would prepare her for the marriage ceremony. In consequence the simple harem that had been provided by Ayesha had to be much extended.

The ceremonies that followed at the Maqabil continued for three days and after the formal preliminaries were over, to the surprise of all a lighter and more festive air came over the proceedings. As custom dictated, Nura was kept out of sight by her women relatives until the nuptials of the first night had taken place; however, the interest in her person was so great that the womenfolk of Abha strained to catch a glimpse of her, and although she was supposed to be hidden, reports of Nura soon spread.

Tabarhla himself was not allowed to see the person of his bride until the first night and even then, as was expected of her, she resisted unveiling for a long time. After that had been achieved there were so many of her women listening outside the bedchamber, and probably also covertly watching, that the preliminaries to their union were somewhat awkward. However, when the lamps had been extinguished Nura was so unexpectedly forward in their lovemaking that he soon found himself able to shut his ears to the sounds outside. Neither spoke a word and finally he had lain back and slept. When he awakened the lamps had been relit and he was surprised to find Nura fully dressed and whispering at the door to her relatives in a dialect that he could not understand.

He was not able properly to appreciate Nura's person until the second day, when convention allowed her to take part in the festivities, and she danced unveiled with the other womenfolk. He saw a girl of about eighteen, slim and dark-skinned yet not swarthy or negroid. There was a maturity about her which Tabarhla could not quite fathom. When he reflected on the night before he found himself wondering if she was truly a virgin, and had to drive from his mind the thought that the Idrisi could have cheated him.

On the final day of the marriage ceremonies it was usual for the bride to become the central figure and receive everyone's compliments. Nura handled this with easy assurance, yielding no hint that the marriage was a contrived affair, and in the dancing that ended the three days of festivities she took on a new vigour and with her dark-skinned retinue of slave girls quite dominated the scene. They danced and played music such as had never been heard in Abha before and its African rhythms had a strange effect, on Zeid in particular, who so far forgot himself that he stole one of the Idrisi slave girls and carried her off to his quarters without anyone noticing for quite a long time.

# Chapter 15

THAT YEAR SPRING came in early February and the wadis ran from the winter rains, making the surroundings of Abha green. It was a time for marriage celebrations, but now another event made Tabarhla's return happy for he found that Na'ema had become pregnant. His happiness was shared by Ayesha, who had prayed that this might come to pass; also by Etza, who assumed control and administered to Na'ema daily. As the pregnancy advanced potions were prepared and oil was liberally applied to keep the skin supple so that it would contract naturally after the birth. A little bleeding occurred but this, Etza assured her, was normal and she packed the birth passage with salt.

At times when there were no such complications Na'ema paid visits to Ranya, who had now been confined to her harem in the Manadhir for six months and bore the hectic flush of advancing pregnancy. Their chief conversation was on the subject of the names they would give their sons, for neither had any doubt that they would bear sons, although no confirmation of this could be obtained from Etza.

'But the stars, Etza, surely they will tell you,' Na'ema pleaded.

'No, *ammati*,' Etza had answered. 'Amongst the Galla we have a saying: that to seek the outcome of a birth from the stars is to court ill fortune. You must ask no more questions and if it is God's will He may give you a son.'

But Na'ema possessed a powerful insistence, and she sought out other fortune-tellers in the town, and when they told her opposite things she returned to berate Etza; but Etza would not be moved.

Besides, she had other things to do for there were many arrangements to be made, and an old part of the Maqabil that had not been used for years was turned into a new harem where there was ample room for the baby and the wet nurse.

In the midst of these preparations Ranya's labour began, and Na'ema persuaded Ayesha to call on Hazyah the wife of Zeid so that she could visit Ranya. At first the pains were weak and infrequent, as though nature had not quite made up its mind, and the midwives of Zeid's household were uncertain whether after all this might prove to be a false alarm. But when they tried to find out they found that the baby's head was firmly fixed in the birth position. Whilst awaiting the birth, the midwives set about their preparations and Ranya was put into a voluminous *thaub* of fine brown cotton, so coloured in order that bloodstains might not be seen. Na'ema was allowed to sit beside her to give her encouragement, whilst one of the midwives went away to fetch a dagger, which would be lain beside the newborn infant to ward off the evil eye.

When noon came Zeid appeared and ostentatiously knelt to say the *dhuhur* prayer in an outer room, and having done so, quickly departed. The pains now increased and during the afternoon came at intervals of a few minutes. Na'ema let Ranya clutch her hand and by the evening it bore deep marks from her fingernails, but as the waves of pain receded Ranya managed to force a smile and the midwives encouraged her, declaring that the labour would soon be over. As night fell there was no let-up in the contractions, which continued without result through the night, and at dawn Ranya began to show signs of exhaustion. During the morning a mare was brought into her room and barley was placed in Ranya's lap, a device that Bedu women used when childbirth was difficult, but the mare only sniffed at the barley and then backed away. The midwives cajoled the mare and after a few minutes led it to the barley again, but a sudden pain caused Ranya to let out a cry and at this the animal showed fear and backed away once more. The midwives looked at one another in dismay for this was not what was supposed to happen; for the mare to refuse to eat the barley was ominous, indeed, more so than anything else that had taken place since labour started. *Askaris* were summoned and they fired their rifles below Ranya's window, but even this had no effect.

Na'ema held Ranya in her arms, trying to comfort her, and demanded that Etza should be sent for as she would surely know what to do. The atmosphere in the room became stifling as well as tense since one after the other every woman in the Manadhir had come to Ranya's harem to offer advice and ply Ranya with questions, which she expended her strength trying to answer. When Etza came she placed her hand under the cotton *thaub* and examined the birth passage. Her fingers felt the womb and found its entrance, which was fully open although something seemed to be blocking it. She drew from her pocket a piece of ivory which was shaped like a curved hook, which in breach or other awkward deliveries was sometimes successful in pulling down an arm or a leg, but it did not seem to reach any part of the unborn child and only led to further bleeding.

The colour drained from Ranya's face until it looked like parchment. The pains were now so strong and continuous that perspiration collected in beads and trickled down her face though Ranya clenched her teeth and refused to cry. But by the middle of the day the pain became so intense that her courage gave out and she began to let forth screams so terrible that they could be heard in every corner of the Manadhir. Etza hastily produced some opium and placed a piece the size of a thumb-nail in Ranya's mouth, forcing her to chew it; quite quickly it relieved the pain and Ranya released her grip on Na'ema and briefly seemed to sleep.

The midwives became increasingly gloomy and in turn came and lifted her *thaub*, placing an ear on her belly; but what they were listening for they failed to hear, and one after another they stepped back and shook their heads. When all six had listened they withdrew and conferred in whispers in a corner, then sent to Zeid to tell him that the infant was no longer alive. They heard him pacing up and down in the outer room, muttering strangely.

Ranya began to scream again, screams so frightful that it was more than Na'ema could endure to hear as she held Ranya. She pleaded with Etza to give her more opium, but Ranya had difficulty in swallowing and Etza had to make it into a draught with camel's milk. Ranya grabbed the cup and emptied it in a gulp. She clutched Na'ema and Etza and tried to speak. Though her mouth moved there was no sound coming from it; they craned forwards, and Ranya whispered, 'Don't let me die,' then abruptly she sank back on the cushions.

All that night she remained conscious in spite of the draughts of opium and the pains continued to convulse her. Not a person in the Manadhir slept, neither man nor woman. When the third dawn broke Ranya's heartbeat was so rapid that its thumping shook her chest and could be heard in the room, but her face, which had been pallid, faded as though it were covered by a veil. Her screams grew fainter and she moaned continuously. Na'ema, who had held Ranya for two days and nights and was close to exhaustion herself, sat motionless and silent. She slept for a few minutes, involuntarily, and when she opened her eyes she saw that Ranya was unconscious. Her breathing became laboured and noisy and was the only sound to be heard. Na'ema cradled Ranya's head in her arms and gazed upon her face, which had once been so full of the promise of youth. She had loved her so much. Gradually a silence descended and before her eyes the colour of Ranya's face slowly changed until it was blue, and in that moment Na'ema perceived the spirit leaving the body.

In death the height of her beauty still lay upon Ranya and everyone who saw it gazed in amazement. Soon the womenfolk started their keening, and Etza led Na'ema away, for the harem had become an eerie place. Zeid was beside himself with grief and demanded of the midwives why they had failed to bring on the birth. At this, one of them examined Ranya; what she found was that the entrance of the womb was completely blocked by the afterbirth.

A great sadness fell as the news spread and it affected everybody in Abha. Grief took various forms and a mad man, a sort of palace fool, went about chanting obsequies of his own invention that somehow matched the general feeling. The whole palace went into mourning, but contrary to expectation Zeid hid his grief completely. When visitors came to commiserate he received them with equanimity: 'What God has given He has seen fit to take away. Praise be to God,' he would say, smiling. In fact he cared deeply, for Ranya, as all were agreed, had been the most perfect maiden Abha had beheld, and for Zeid it had been love.

*

In a short space of time the midwives had to turn their attention towards Na'ema. They said that her witnessing Ranya's death would have a disastrous effect and declared that when her time came fear could prevent her from giving birth. When Na'ema heard this she was angry. 'Old crows,' she cried. 'Scavengers of doom. I will confound them and their stupid prophecies.'

It was not long before she had the chance to do so. Her labour started and was quickly over; Etza delivered her single-handed, sewing up a tear with strands of her own hair. To everyone's delight she had given birth to a son, whom she named Zahl after her own father.

Three months later Nura surprised everybody. She had scarcely been seen since the death of Ranya and had secreted herself in her own harem. No one, not even Ayesha, had guessed that she was even pregnant, and now, with a minimum of fuss, she too gave birth to a son. Tabarhla, who now had three sons instead of only one, was overcome with joy and the Maqabil rang with happiness once more. Nura hid her emotions but inwardly she was proud, for in giving birth to a son she had made herself Na'ema's equal. She named him Bandar, and convinced herself that he would be the rival and enemy of Zahl. She, Nura, would provide the successor

– had not her father ordered her? And was not this the means by which such matters were decided among her tribe, brother against brother? But Nura kept these thoughts to herself, as was her nature.

*

*My Amir is a great lover. When I was shown off in the market I didn't mind at all. Though I hated my clothes I blushed when they saw me but then I knew that I would be bought by someone who was strong and powerful, and I could go on being myself, Ranya.*

*I love my body, my breasts, and where I am cleft to receive the seed. I did not think I wanted to become pregnant and was frightened, but when it happened I was happy and prayed that I should have a son. It will secure my place, for there are wives who are fat and bitter and do not like me. My friend is called Na'ema.*

*I was born near Tunis. It was on the Barbary coast, where there are pirates. They took me when I was fifteen and I remember the endless journeys in stinking boats. I love my mother and miss her still. Sometimes I think she is there. She would be proud if she knew that I am with child. I am happy and love looking towards the future. I love God, who will protect me and I will obey His bidding always. Whatever He chooses for me.*

# Chapter 16

A GREAT DISASTER now befell Abha, for it was struck by a plague the like of which had never been known, that carried off young and old in great numbers. This spread through all Arabia, as it had done through Egypt and the Levant and before that Europe, where it had received its name – the Influenza. For the Beni Mughe'id it was a great blow, for amongst its victims was Zeid. He died in a matter of hours, doubtless complaining about this obtuse stroke of fate, and with no family about him to whom to deliver a final speech.

For Tabarhla Zeid's death was a momentous event and he immediately realised that there was no time to lose. When it occurred he had been at some distance from the city, attending to quarrels amongst the tribes, and he had to return to Abha in haste. As he entered the city he was received with great acclaim and wherever he looked he saw on the faces of the townspeople the same emotion, relief at his return. It was a spontaneous and moving tribute which much affected him and he vowed that if it fell to him to become the new Amir the rod of rule should serve no other purpose than to preserve their happiness and freedom.

He had sent ahead of him word that a *majlis* would be held that same day, and as he rode now into the forecourt of the Manadhir, Zeid's *fidawis*, who now were his own, were waiting to escort him. Several sheikhs were there already and as the word spread others rode in from their outlying villages. Amongst the Ahl Yazid the bin Mufarrih arrived first, led by Ali, the oldest son of Mohammed bin Mufarrih, the most senior member of the family and now very old. The ibn Aidh came later and seated themselves well apart from the bin Mufarrih, their own leadership at the moment unsettled on account of Hassan ibn Aidh, who had laid a rival claim to Khalid as senior sheikh. Beside these two families, both with many members, the House of Tahir seemed perilously few in number, for besides Tabarhla there was Abdullah, his only son, grown to manhood, and eight other relatives of varying ages, but all for the purposes of fighting or leadership either too young or too old. Thus it was far from clear how the new balance of power would lie.

As soon as all were settled Tabarhla opened proceedings with the following words: 'It is plain that we are here to follow God's will, He who has taken Zeid from us but has spared so many amongst our greatest sheikhs. In thus caring for our city God has indeed been merciful towards us and we pray that He may guide us now in choosing a new amir.' There was a murmur of assent from the bin Mufarrih and the ibn Aidh, although Hassan, its second most senior sheikh, was notably silent.

'The fact of our general agreement,' Tabarhla continued, 'seems to show that God regards us as brothers of one family and would wish us to act, forgetting past wounds, and unite in common cause. If it were not so then why should so many of us be here as witnesses to this *majlis*? My brothers, it follows that if any hand is raised to divide us, it undoes the work of God and we shall justly demand that the hand be severed from our body. Now I ask you to heed this: although it was I who have summoned you I do not come among you as Asheukh nor do I set myself greater than any other. I have summoned this *majlis* for the purpose of deciding who amongst us we shall choose to be our Amir simply because I am the son of Zeid, but before any voices are raised I wish it to be known that although I have recently been much away from Abha, whilst Zeid lived I have been informed of all that has taken place here. Thus it has reached me who has died of pestilence, who at the hands of enemies and who as a result of feuds amongst yourselves.'

A stir ran through the assembled sheikhs, for there were some who had hoped that certain of their past misdeeds might have stayed hidden. That Tabarhla should so inconveniently be privy to these secrets caused a sudden concentration of minds, and those that had blood on their hands at once assumed that what Tabarhla had stated must be true, which of course it was not.

'But now let the past be laid to rest.' Tabarhla raised his arms so that his palms faced the audience in the traditional gesture of forgiveness. 'Our common aim now is to seek a leader who will make Abha prosperous and its defence strong so that no enemy shall ever enter its gates. And so let all who would be our liege lord and master speak now, and whoever gains the greater allegiance to him shall be the Amirate.'

No voice was heard, and an unease filled the *majlis*, for all feared to speak first lest he be accused by another who for other reasons sought revenge. The ibn Aidh looked at the bin Mufarrih, who stared back in silence, and the rest of the sheikhs looked in different directions or at the ground at their feet. A minute passed in silence as the atmosphere stiffened somewhat.

'In that case,' Tabarhla resumed, 'as the son of Zeid I offer myself as Amir and seek to know your will. Let the ibn Aidh say first.'

The oldest member of the Aidh clan took it on himself to be their spokesman and leaned forward. 'I think that we are of the view that as the son of Zeid it is your prior right to become Amir.' This drew a murmur of assent from the rest of the ibn Aidh, except for Hassan, who remained stonily silent.

'What does the bin Mufarrih say?' Tabarhla searched the inscrutable ranks of the bin Mufarrih, and Ali the son of Mohammed looked at him forthrightly and said, 'I believe that I speak not only for our family but for all the Beni Mughe'id. We have known you all our lives and to us you are a just and godly man who will be fair between ourselves. You possess the gift of good fortune and we desire no other to be our Amir. We pray that henceforth you may rule us and many generations of your house after. We will obey you in the good cause of the Ahl Yazid, all other sheikhs, tribesmen and citizens of Abha.'

Ali received an ovation for this fine speech, which plainly touched their hearts. The company rose to its feet and, with Mohammed bin Mufarrih leading, filed towards Tabarhla. Kneeling, they each in turn swore the oath of fealty in the time-honoured formula of question and answer.

It was a formality, but an important one, for at Abha it was the way that they liked things to be done. Thus was the place of Zeid filled.

*

*Here I lie by an abstruse stroke of fate, I, Zeid bin Tahir bin Zahkil bin Tahir, Amir of Abha, Asheuhk of the Beni Mughe'id and Sultan of all As'ir. Your camels will drop before they reach the limit of my kingdom.*

*I who drove the Turks from all Arabia struck down in my best years, no concubines nor even my wives at my deathbed, no son to receive my final order.*

*God is the only God. In His great wisdom and mercy He has cared for His faithful servant and guarded him in every danger. Many battles have I fought in His name. He has blessed them with victory, so why should He fail me now?*

*I do not understand. I must receive an explanation. A common pestilence.*

*

With the death of Zeid, a great change came over Tabarhla, which everyone noticed, indeed many were affected by it for there were practical consequences. Etza could see the change herself, for the ruler's stars grew brighter whilst those of the fallen Zeid faded so that they could barely be seen. It was as though Tabarhla's spirit was released from a lifetime of bondage and sword. Some perceived that even his person changed: he seemed taller and his manner bolder than ever. His manhood urges increased, which Etza could detect from the effect this had on Na'ema. It made her own womanhood blossom, and perhaps that of some of the other women too.

She became more rebellious, although she took pains to hide it. She welcomed the change in Tabarhla and seemed to try to match it with self-assertion of her own, which was expressed in her manner of speech, although this was never in the least disrespectful. For Ayesha the difference in Tabarhla was obvious too, not as regards herself, for she had withdrawn from such wifely duties, but in its effect on Na'ema. She questioned Etza as to whether she thought this was a good thing or whether it might lead to trouble between Tabarhla and Na'ema. Etza replied that it was a good thing for both of them even if, in the way of things, some eggs got broken in the course of the cooking. This drew from her a smile. Etza could not imagine Ayesha ever having been rebellious herself.

The consequences of these changes were partly practical. One of Tabarhla's first acts was to restore the family tradition of the yearly migration to the village of Nejidah, for with the onset of summer it had always been the custom that those that were able to do so left Abha for the cool of the mountains. There was a settlement called Ayinah, where the sheikhs of the Ahl Yazid and the more prosperous tradesmen had built summer villas, and higher still, by paths that rose twisting through the Jebel, here called Al Kaur, was the tiny upland village of Nejidah. This had once been an ancient stronghold retreat with its own water supply from cisterns cut in the rock, and now it was where the family of the bin Tahir had their villa, which was known locally as their palace.

Nejidah had been part of Tabarhla's existence since his mother, Zeid's favourite wife, had brought her three sons there when Tabarhla was six years old. They had quickly explored its secrets whilst the informal habits which the family adopted gave Tabarhla and his brothers the opportunity for adventure of every kind. Nejidah came to be a country of allies and enemies with fortresses and hiding places in which to fight their endless make-believe battles. Yet it was not all play, for Zeid had insisted that from their earliest years his sons should learn to shoot, throw spears and ride expertly both camels and horses, and in this way the rough and tumble of Nejidah was imprinted on their minds for ever.

When he was older Tabarhla had found himself brotherless, and instead sought out the company of the local *fellaheen*, watching their animal husbandry and learning from them to stalk and track. When bustards were seen he learned to hawk with a *shahin* falcon and *saluqis* and so became a useful provider for his father Zeid's feasts. This gained him his own position in the household and he was allowed to sit beside his father and the other sheikhs and listen to the stories that were nightly related. There were tales of battles, of honour and of love, the courage of youth, the wisdom of age and of the whole gallery of all of Abha's warriors that had ever lived, and above all these heroes the mighty Zeid towered, the single fixed point of Tabarhla's youth.

Zeid's villa, which was now Tabarhla's own, had not been used for some years. In the old days when it had been their summer retreat the annual migration of the Amir's court had been a ritual in which half the citizens of Abha seemed to take part. However, the custom had lapsed; Zeid was suspicious by nature and in recent times had chosen to remain in the Manadhir all year for fear that he might be deposed – on which account, considering Abha's past, history might decide that he may have been prudent. As a result the summer palace was abandoned and had fallen into ruin, but now the situation was changed; Tabarhla did not share Zeid's insecurity, for in the course of many battles he had forged bonds with the other sheikhs and he was confident that if troubles arose his enemies would be outnumbered and would not dare to challenge his authority.

The bin Tahir palace was an unpretentious building made of mud-brick, of one storey only, with a roof thatched with grass held in position by palm branches, like those of the peasants' *qasrs* below. By contrast its gardens were as opulent as the building was spare, fed by water which filtered through a series of stone troughs from the rock cisterns above. It was shaded by huge *sidr* trees, and beneath them a small tropical world existed where hoopoes, bee-eaters and humming birds darted and bulbuls and orioles sang from dawn to dusk. Hibiscus and oleander, bright with scarlet and magenta flowers, grew everywhere, and the blossom of sweet-scented lemon and orange trees filled the air. Here too insects of every sort abounded seeking nectar, hawk moths with their painted faces and butterflies in a confetti of colour. It demonstrated the ancient rite of nature: that in plenty all creatures should thrive and proliferate.

For Tabarhla, it was a pilgrimage renewed, for since Zeid had chosen to remain at Abha he had been forced to stay there too, and for years he had not visited Nejidah in spite of Ayesha's pleas. So the excitement upon arrival was great and can easily be imagined, and for Tabarhla's other wives it was nothing short of a miracle. A flurry of activity took place which rapidly transformed the ruin; the local peasants, delighted to find the new Amir's family in their midst, arrived bearing a whole bounty of materials with which to rebuild and decorate the place. In no time the roof was stripped and rethatched, the windows of fretted alabaster that screened the sunlight and let in the air were rescued and replaced, and a fresh coat of plaster made from mud and camel dung was put upon the walls. This was painted with ochre, ground from the rocks, and as it dried the slave girls covered them with all manner of designs until the harems were frescoed all over.

As soon as it was finished, camels were despatched to the Maqabil to be loaded with carpets and cushions, coffee-pots and cooking implements, together with a great quantity of belongings, as it was the tradition that when the household moved it took everything with it. When all was done, the younger members of the family were brought, and Bandar and Zahl quickly colonised the place after their own fashion.

*

Amirs, nevertheless, have their duties to perform at all times of the year, and especially the ritual of the daily *majlis* at the Manadhir. So at dawn each day Tabarhla rode to Abha, generally accompanied by his son Abdullah, and in the evening they returned to Nejidah.

The early morning ride to Abha was easy, for the animals were fresh and the way was mostly downhill. But on their return the sun was still high and by the time they reached halfway, at a well with the name of Zamzin, they were glad of the pause to water their mares and enjoy the *laun* dates that the peasants offered them.

It was at Zamzin one morning that they encountered a Bedu woman dressed in black, drawing water for her sheep; she seemed unaware of their presence. It was then, to their astonishment, that they realised that it was not a Bedu shepherdess at all but Na'ema dressed as one. When Na'ema saw Tabarhla's face she laughed and put the bucket of water in front of his mare. The mare drank it gratefully whilst Na'ema stood back and watched, her hands upon her hips exactly in the manner of a *fellaha*.

Tabarhla surveyed the scene and was temporarily lost for words.

'I heard that these were to be found here!' Na'ema took several cream-coloured truffles from the fold of her *thaub*. 'I thought you might enjoy them.'

'It is a long way to come even if you have found truffles,' muttered Tabarhla.

'It was easy, and I shall be back at Nejidah before you get there.' She gathered up the truffles and went skipping away so briskly that she was out of sight by the time the mares had finished drinking.

Tabarhla glanced at Abdullah, who was laughing. 'You can give her a lift on the back of your horse,' Abdullah suggested. He picked up the leather bucket, and they cantered until they caught up with Na'ema, who by now was out of breath.

'Jump up behind,' said Tabarhla. 'As you jump I will lift you.'

'Wait a second for me to recover.'

He drew up beside her and Na'ema looked up at him, her face catching the sunlight appealingly. 'Can I ride her alone for a little?'

'Heavens, no. You would fall off. At first it is very difficult to keep your balance.'

'Let me try just once. Please! Hold the truffles for me.' Her eyes were so eloquent that Tabarhla hesitated, dismounted and then took the truffles.

Abdullah was enjoying this. 'Let Sheikha Na'ema sit on my mare for a few minutes, Father. She is so docile that no one could fall off.'

He slipped from his horse and turned to Na'ema. 'Be careful. In those clothes you will have to sit sideways. I'll lift you up.' He made a stirrup of his hands and as Na'ema placed her foot in them he lifted her on to the mare's back. To his surprise she landed astride on the saddlecloth and then delicately drew up her skirts and adjusted them so that they covered her white *sirwals* beneath, which were tied at the ankles. Her sandaled feet hung down loosely either side.

'Please let me hold the halter rope so that I can balance better.' She took the rope from him and patted the mare's neck. 'Can I walk just a few steps?'

'Be careful, it's very easy to fall.'

Na'ema nodded. 'Yes, I know.' She walked the mare a few paces towards a clear patch of sand, then leaned forward and whispered into its ear.

The next moment, to Tabarhla's consternation, the mare broke into a trot and then into a canter and Na'ema disappeared over the top of the hill. 'Take my horse and go after her,' he shouted to Abdullah. 'She is sure to fall.'

Abdullah was grinning broadly. 'Father, can't you see? She knows how to ride.'

It was plain that Abdullah was correct. Tabarhla wiped his brow as Na'ema turned the mare and came cantering back, then reined to a halt and, gathering her skirts, vaulted lightly to the ground.

'That felt so good I can't believe it happened.' She smiled and handed him the rope of the *risan*.

'However did you learn to ride a horse?'

'Where we lived we used to race them on the sands. I learned when I was seven or eight years old.'

'You never fell off?'

'Of course I did, we all fell off. That's what taught us to stay on.' The absurdity of the question escaped Tabarhla. He mounted the mare and bent over to lift Na'ema up, but Na'ema scarcely needed any lifting, and a second later she was sitting behind him on the mare's crupper, from which position she kept up a lively conversation all the way to Nejidah. There, having retrieved her truffles from the saddlebag, she slipped away almost unnoticed in the bustle of servants that came out to greet them.

*

Some hours later, in Ayesha's harem, Tabarhla related the incident. It had not occurred to him that a woman could ride a horse and, he added, it did not seem entirely proper. Ayesha stopped what she was doing and asked him to repeat the story in every detail. It made him realise that this was not a trivial matter after all, and he exclaimed, 'Why does she always have to do what everyone least expects?'

'Perhaps,' Ayesha answered, 'because that is her nature. It's not that she's disobedient, she's just high-spirited, so it's best not to make an issue of it.' Then she added, 'It is quite interesting that where she came from they taught the girls to ride horses as well as the boys.'

But this was not how she answered when Na'ema in turn raised the matter, fearing that she might have incurred Ayesha's displeasure and behaved in a way above her station. 'No,' said Ayesha. 'I don't think that you did, but it would have been another matter if you'd been pregnant and as a result had a miscarriage. Then you would certainly have been both foolish and sinful in your husband's eyes.'

Na'ema nodded thoughtfully and had to admit that what Ayesha said was true. She turned it over carefully in her mind and then waited until it was her turn to receive Tabarhla, who followed the custom of visiting his wives in their harems in strict rotation. In Na'ema's there were three rooms, for herself, Etza and two serving women, one of whom attended to the cooking while the other looked after the youthful Zahl, who was always carefully prepared for these occasions. On these nights Na'ema would spend a long time with Etza, who dressed her hair and helped her decide what to wear.

It was Tabarhla's habit to come to the harem in time for the sunset prayer and to eat a meal. Much care was put into its preparation, and on this occasion Etza had obtained the head of a spring lamb from the market nearby. This was cooked whole and served on a bed of scented rice with the eyes, which were the choicest delicacy, each encased in a truffle. After the servants had brought the bowl for washing the hands, and the linen towels, the lamb's head was carried in on a huge brass tray and set before Tabarhla, who sat cross-legged on a rug which only he was allowed to use. Na'ema knelt behind him, in the formal manner, but whilst the meal always began with this ritual it was Tabarhla's habit to draw his wife down to eat beside him as soon as he had taken the first mouthful.

Na'ema obeyed his gesture and sat down, but did not eat; instead, she made little balls of rice and meat which she rolled between her palms and placed in Tabarhla's mouth, as fast as he could eat them and sometimes a little faster. This made it impossible to speak, but on this occasion he did not protest because he happened to be very hungry. After a period of silence whilst he ate, Na'ema remarked that she hoped this was not the wrong moment to raise such a subject, but there was something important she wanted to ask him.

'Go ahead and tell me what it is,' said Tabarhla, between mouthfuls.

'I have been wondering,' Na'ema hesitated. 'I mean, just thinking, whether you might allow me to have my own horse.'

Tabarhla wiped his hands on the linen towel. 'I think that there would be a lot of difficulties. Perhaps I could arrange for the *fellaheen* in the valley to graze their horses nearer Nejidah so that you would be able to look at them.'

'I did not mean having a horse to watch it eat lucerne, I meant, to ride it.'

'But wherever could you ride?'

'Around Nejidah, perhaps as far as the well.' She hastily rolled another ball of lamb and rice and placrd it in Tabarhla's mouth.

When he was able to speak again he tried to grope for an answer. 'I hardly think ...' he hastily swallowed the rest of the lamb '... that it would be seemly for a wife to ride in public. It might not be shameful but I think it would be unseemly and in any case if you had an accident Ayesha would blame me.'

'Oh, there would be no question of her doing so or of my having an accident. I learned not to when I was young.'

Tabarhla thrust his chin forward although the gesture was not as assured as he meant it to be. 'I really don't know, but let us leave the matter for the moment.'

Na'ema made no answer and resumed the wifely task of making further morsels and pushing them into his mouth. She still ate nothing herself, for she was much too preoccupied with her own thoughts.

The evening passed and they lay together for some hours. It was an evening when she found him hungry for her, and she satisfied his appetite so thoroughly that he soon fell asleep. She waited patiently for several hours until he awoke, then she whispered, 'You did promise me, didn't you?'

'What did I promise you?' Tabarhla tried to escape the two brown eyes that drilled into his.

'That you would think about it.'

'Think about what?'

'My horse.'

He scratched his head, forced himself awake, and then sat up on the cushions that formed the top of their bed. Na'ema lay looking up at him, her eyes unusually wide.

'I don't see how you could have a horse,' said Tabarhla.

Tears filled Na'ema's eyes. 'Never?' she faltered, trying to choke back sobs. She put her arms around his neck. 'Not ever? Ever?'

It was a fact that ever since childhood, when his sisters were always crying, Tabarhla simply hated the sight of a woman in tears. He looked away from Na'ema, first at the floor and then distractedly at the candle that still burned. The tears were now flowing noisily.

'Oh, do stop crying!' he said in exasperation. 'If it makes you cry so much then if God wills it you'd better have your horse.'

Na'ema stopped crying and her face glistened. She raised herself until she touched him, then put her arms about his neck.

'When?' she whispered, releasing him a little.

'I don't know. Whenever it is possible.'

'Tomorrow?'

He could see the tears might start again at any moment. 'Oh, tomorrow then. Abdullah will bring you one from the *rabat*.' Having made this pronouncement, he fell asleep once again. Na'ema herself was still awake long after the candle had flickered and gone out.

*

Tabarhla's *rabat*, or stable of breeding mares, was a jealously guarded possession inherited from his father and his father's father and it continued to produce, as it had done for many equine generations, a steady supply of fine mares. Those with the greatest promise received a thorough training, although the true quality of a mare was not known until it was tested in battle.

The *rabat* was kept at a village close to Abha, but for the summer a number of mares had been brought to Nejidah and it was from these that Abdullah chose one that he thought would be suitable for Na'ema. He had been enjoying the situation hugely from the moment his father had asked him to fetch a mare. He did not dare to ask how Na'ema had won such a favour, but it was a great joke which he longed to share with his friends at Abha. A woman who could ride a horse, what would they say to that? He was so enthusiastic in carrying out his task that he brought not only one mare but a selection of three, so that Na'ema could make her own choice.

Na'ema accordingly did so, and it did not go at all as Abdullah had expected. She began by carefully inspecting each mare, and the way she went about this surprised even so experienced a horseman as Abdullah. She examined their teeth first to assess their ages and got these correct without being told or for that matter asking, then she examined the various points of their conformation. It would have been hard to find much fault with these for the *rabat* was bred to a high standard; nevertheless, Na'ema found some things more to her liking than others and pointed them out. The eyes of one mare were judged too close together, another's chest was a shade too narrow for staying power. Then she produced a pair of canes with which she measured each mare, drawing imaginary pyramids with one line from the point of the shoulder through the withers and the second upwards from the rear hock past the rim of the thigh bone. All the pyramids were judged to be low enough and secured approval, somewhat to Abdullah's relief. But it was when she came to the markings that she really impressed him. She gave a running commentary: 'This has a *saur* line on its neck, that is good; it has three white fetlocks, which is also good, but then let us make sure she has no *sa'ad* on her forehead, which would cancel the advantage. Bays like these are always calm and sensible so long as they were born by day and not by night. Were they?'

Abdullah had to admit that he did not know, since it was not recorded in the *rabat*. Na'ema showed irritation at this important oversight and at length placed the mares in order of *hajil* or merit. The inspection had lasted for most of an hour and now Na'ema asked for a saddlecloth. The act of jumping astride a horse's back whilst wearing a long black *thaub* was not easy, but Na'ema accomplished it so adroitly that Abdullah couldn't see how she managed it; when she looked down at him, her dress seemed to fall equally on either side without any visible division. He was too polite to comment but it seemed to him to defy logic, and when she moved off everything remained exactly in place.

There was a sandy path that led towards Zamzin and there she chose a place to put the mare to trial. She walked, trotted, cantered and then galloped, controlling all the motions by means of the *risan* alone. Then she brought the mare back and dismounted in front of him, and still he could not see how she kept her *thaub* in place. He watched more closely when she mounted the second horse and then realised how it was done – the garment was cunningly divided so that what looked like an ordinary *thaub* divided like a pair of outsize *sirwals*, yet when she walked it hung just like any other dress. She saw him watching her and laughed. 'You never saw a riding *thaub* before?' Abdullah shook his head.

She was off, putting the next mare through its paces. It was late before she had finished and Abdullah had the impression that it was only because she had to be in her harem for the sunset prayer that she stopped when she did. Her final choice was the mare she had placed first for its points. It performed exactly as she had predicted; its stride was the longest and it had a perfect action at canter and gallop. He took the animal back to the stable and ordered a new *risan* and a light saddlecloth to be made for her.

The opportunity to report this to his father came when they rode to Abha the following day, and then Abdullah could hardly contain himself. 'Father, she is amazing, Sheikha Na'ema.'

'Why, what has she done now?' Tabarhla was slightly edgy.

'It's not that, it is just that nothing, absolutely nothing escapes her. She has the eye of an expert.'

'Oh, about the horse, you mean? You found one for her?'

'She did the choosing. She told me lots that I didn't know myself.' He related what had taken place. 'Especially the markings, she knows exactly what is lucky and what is not.'

'That is what a *rabat* is all about, I admit. First speed, then endurance, and most important of all, luck. Who would want to be thrown from a horse in the middle of a charge?'

Four days later, when they watered at Zamzin, they found Na'ema there once more and this time Tabarhla did not hide his anger. 'Go home immediately,' he said curtly. 'I forbade you to ride beyond Nejidah.'

Na'ema looked crestfallen. 'But the mare is so frisky I couldn't hold her.'

'Then find one that you can. Think what people will say if they see a sheikha riding around the countryside.'

'Of course you are right, it would be shameful.' Na'ema was the picture of meekness.

Tabarhla made no reply, relieved that the issue had been disposed of, and in order to be sure that Na'ema had a proper sense of her unseemliness he made her walk her horse behind them as they rode, excluding her from the conversation. On reaching Nejidah he retired to Ayesha's harem, but on this occasion made no reference to having found Na'ema at Zamzin.

Domestic routine was resumed and for some time the harems were taken up with painting and adorning their rooms ahead of receiving visitors. On the night when it was Na'ema's turn for Tabarhla's visit, he found her subdued, suitably, so he thought, and plainly eager to lavish her attention upon him. He concluded that she had learned her lesson and that in future she would keep her riding within suitable bounds. In that case, he decided, it had been a good thing to let her have a horse for her amusement, especially since she knew so much about horses.

However, it was not long before he realised that this judgment might have been premature; indeed, it began to look as if it might be totally wrong. Once again it was the well at Zamzin that sparked off the new incident. One morning they came upon a youth riding a fine mare which, even in the distance, seemed familiar, and when they got closer it was obvious to them both that it was the one that had been given to Na'ema. When they got closer still, to Tabarhla's intense irritation, it was apparent that the youth was not a youth but Na'ema dressed as one.

He did not know what to say. To make matters worse Abdullah began to laugh. The delay in speaking, as Tabarhla should have realised, proved fatal. The initiative passed to Na'ema, who looked at Abdullah and promptly challenged him to race her to the top of the hill. There was a flurry of hooves and Tabarhla was left to contemplate this new turn of events on his own.

Even when they returned, with the mares breathing heavily, he could not think of the right way to reassert his authority and the moment for decisive action passed again. Na'ema, once she got back her breath, took the initiative. She pleaded to be allowed to ride with them to Abha. 'Like this, I'll just look like any other of your servants, won't I?'

'No,' Tabarhla cried in desperation. 'Heaven forbid such a thing.' If this was what doing the unexpected meant, there and then he decided that he had had enough of it. 'Do it once more and I'll take your horse away,' he shouted, losing his temper.

Having reached this impasse, Na'ema decided to beat a retreat. 'Of course, if you say not ...' She hung her head and murmured an apology, at which Abdullah began to laugh again, although he did so behind his hand, turning to one side. There the matter rested and a week went by in which nothing happened to disturb the daily routine. Several times Tabarhla wondered whether he should ask Ayesha to say something suitably stern to Na'ema, but did not do so for fear that somehow Ayesha might take Na'ema's part. He dismissed it from his thoughts in favour of more important matters.

He did not refer to the incident again with Na'ema, either. However, she did. She started what he saw could be a carefully calculated new offensive, although she began with deceptive simplicity: 'Do let me ride with you to Abha,' she pleaded. Tabarhla promptly refused but it didn't stop there.

'Surely,' she said, 'it is an established custom that the sheikhas of the Ahl Yazid can take part in the *majlis*.'

He admitted that this was so but added, 'It rarely happens. As I recall it, in my father's *majlis* few sheikhas ever attended and they were very senior ones.'

'Perhaps that was because the others didn't have anything to say at the time.'

'Probably.' It was essential to remain calm. He could not resist adding, firmly, 'Even if a younger sheikha had spoken she would certainly not have come to the *majlis* dressed as a youth!'

'No, I quite see what you are saying. That would indeed be shameful.' She lowered her head submissively. 'Sheikhas should be dressed like sheikhas if they are not to bring disgrace upon their husbands.'

'Precisely.' Tabarhla saw to his relief that he had headed Na'ema off and that there would not have to be an argument after all. Na'ema stayed silent, fingering the plaits of her hair, and he took advantage of the pause to change the subject and enquired about Zahl.

Three mornings later, Na'ema was waiting for him when he came out of Ayesha's harem after the dawn prayer. She was dressed in a conservative black *thaub*, and, unusual for her, she was wearing a veil. Or that is how it seemed, for it was not possible to be sure since she was perched high above his head in a curtained camel litter about which two camel men hovered with their *dhalals*.

Tabarhla raised an arm and placed it across his face. 'By the grace of God, my eyes deceive me.'

'Please don't be angry with me,' said Na'ema, looking down and doing her best to convey humility. 'It is most important that I should attend the *majlis* because I have something urgent to say.'

'What?' said Tabarhla tartly.

'That the wells of Abha will run dry before the winter rains.'

'How do you know that?'

'Because that's what the omens say and Etza knows. Besides, the wells here and at Zamzin are falling steadily. It is the first time all summer that they have done that, just in the past week.'

'Very well, I will tell the *majlis* myself.'

'They won't believe you because they know that you don't read the omens.'

'Then they certainly wouldn't believe you either.'

'Not this time, but after the wells have run dry and they haven't drawn any water for a week they will remember and next time they will believe me, you see.'

He did not like the way she said it and found himself looking away from her.

'Of course, if I thought you wouldn't believe me, or rather Etza, I wouldn't ask you to let me tell the *majlis*.'

Tabarhla did not reply. Instead he turned and hurriedly went back to Ayesha's harem and searched for her. He found her kneeling at her prayers, which he interrupted with a flow of rather incoherent words. Ayesha got up from kneeling, stretched herself painfully, and then sat down cross-legged on a mat. Very carefully she thought it over, after acquainting herself with all the facts (with the exception of Na'ema riding her horse at Zamzin which Tabarhla didn't dare to admit that he had forgotten to tell her).

Finally, she said: 'I think that you had better allow her to have her way, for this reason. If the wells of Abha do run dry the Beni Mughe'id may learn that it has been foretold. They may also learn that an attempt was made to warn them, and then they will certainly blame you if they discover that you have concealed it.'

'I could perfectly well tell them myself.'

'You could, but then they would never act upon the warning because they know you do not read the omens, whereas half of Abha knows that Etza does and therefore her Sheikha, but no one else. It comes down to this: the people are your responsibility. If the city goes thirsty infants will die when their mothers' milk dries up. Besides, Etza is always right.'

Tabarhla walked up and down the harem several times, then, without a word, bent down and kissed Ayesha's forehead. After that he went outside.

'Get down from that contraption,' he snapped.

Na'ema looked at him in some alarm.

'Don't dally. Fetch your horse.'

# Chapter 17

THE LOCAL POPULATION of Nejidah, who, if truth be told, would not have questioned it if an elephant had emerged from the bin Tahir gardens and proceeded to eat their crops, took little notice of the black figure of a woman on horseback. Equally, the elders of Abha, or such as were there, did not object to her presence at the *majlis* and they listened to what she had to say as they would have done to anyone else. The only dissenting voice came from Nejidah itself and that was Nura's. When an opportunity came her way she challenged Tabarhla: 'How is it that this woman, a mere slave,' which was her usual way of referring to Na'ema, 'is allowed to ride about Nejidah or wherever else she chooses?'

Uncertain what to say but hoping for the best, Tabarhla replied that he had asked Na'ema to check the level of the wells, and for this purpose it was easier for her to have a horse.

Nura was vexed. She complained that she had not been consulted and if anyone knew about wells she did, since she had grown up in a place where wells ran dry as a matter of course. Tabarhla listened without comment, humoured her as best he could and inwardly congratulated himself for not falling into the trap of playing off one wife against another, as a less prudent husband might.

One result of this incident was that the long-standing competition between Nura and Na'ema for Tabarhla's favour intensified, but since it was covert it did not spoil the atmosphere at Nejidah. The stakes were subtly raised as the two harems vied with each other, and for Tabarhla it was an opportunity to enjoy it. The dishes placed in front of him by Na'ema were ever more delectable, but it was what Nura provided that was the wonder of all, for although the harems were supposed to be private, in practice the servants and slaves who came and went between them shared their secrets and thus everyone knew what was going on.

What caused the gossip was Nura's slaves, who provided nights of entertainment such as had never been seen at Nejidah. Tabarhla had watched the slave girls on an earlier occasion when there was dancing at the celebrations when Nura arrived, but this was something altogether more spectacular. In the first place, the slaves themselves were different; they were younger, not above fourteen or fifteen years old, chosen for their personal beauty, which was of a kind that arises when the African and Oriental meet. Their style of dancing was also novel, not at all like that of the *salubas*, and the music, played on strange instruments, had stronger rhythms. It was one with the dancing, which was polished and provocative and bore the mark of careful training; it was evident that Nura was unusually experienced in such matters. Exactly how she had acquired her troupe was something of a mystery, but it was generally agreed that from the varied delights they provided the battle of the harems was won by Nura.

As Tabarhla watched he recalled Nura dancing on the day after their wedding night, but now, he noticed, she remained a spectator, directing the girls as she lay on a heap of cushions, leaning against his shoulder. He thought as he watched the scene about him that Nura must have considerable resources which he did not know about, for the slaves wore a profusion of necklaces and bracelets of gold and silver encrusted with coral, amber and turquoise, and the instruments were elaborate and lavish in number. It was quite unlike anything that had ever happened at Nejidah before.

As the evening went by the music grew louder, its beat became insistent, and in the half-darkness the four dancers seemed to be wearing less and less. At intervals bowls of nuts and sweet-meats were placed in front of Tabarhla and each time he looked up from eating something else seemed to have been shed. By degrees glistening bodies were revealed until at length all four were bare-breasted and almost naked; not quite naked, for like a uniform each slave wore a string of beads which fastened at the waist and passed between the legs. Now that they could be fully appreciated it could be seen that their movements were choreographed, not in the least abandoned like those of *salubas*, and as the dancing continued those beads or whatever they were became quite unbearably provocative.

'Are they professional entertainers?' Tabarhla asked absently, turning away for a moment since his head seemed to be overheating with strange sensations.

Nura was horrified. '*Fainnat*,' she exclaimed. 'Is it possible that I should offer you *fainnat*? Really, you underestimate me. They arc the finest dancing girls that money can buy, chosen out of hundreds, and all my training . . .' Her voice softened and became filled with pride. 'Tell me which one pleases you most.'

Then, without waiting for an answer, she gestured to one of the slaves, who stopped dancing and came and stood beside her.

'This is Zala,' said Nura. 'She's Ethiopian. Don't you think she's very beautiful? Look at her skin. It's not quite black, it has a blue sheen.'

She made Zala sit beside her and placed a hand on her leg, at which Zala rested her head against Nura's shoulder. The action struck Tabarhla as oddly mechanical, and when he looked at her blue-black face amidst its jewellery and decoration it was quite expressionless.

After a moment, Nura rose, catching the light of the reed lamp that hung above, and led him to the principal couch, where she stood beside him, helping him to remove his *dishdasha*. Then, with an expressive tap on the shoulder, she beckoned Zala, who unfastened her string of beads and stood before him quite naked, as though awaiting approval. By now Tabarhla was so aflame that he scarcely took in all that was happening. He floated in a mist of lust, and all the time Zala stood there with those huge expressionless eyes; finally, he motioned her beside him and swiftly released the mounting tumult that surged inside him.

For a moment, pleasure overwhelmed him, but the next minute Nura was there. She took off her robe and lay down beside him, and Zala rose from the couch and, delicate in all her movements, slipped away. The next thing he knew was that Nura had insinuated herself where Zala had been and was grappling with him. That was the only word he could think of, for she was not just ardent but voracious, as though he was to be the pleasure object and she the succuba, dragging out his virility and consuming it until she had drained him.

Next morning, when Tabarhla finally left the harem, the hour was late and Abdullah had already set of for Abha. However, Na'ema was waiting for him. She sat there silently on her mare, who restlessly threw up her head and pawed the ground. He looked at her but said nothing, feeling in no mood for another argument, and so it happened thereafter that the riding party was increased by one. He adjusted to the new arrangement, and later added a couple of *askaris* with spare horses in case they ran into trouble, although it was a remarkable fact that on the road to Abha not a rifle had been fired all summer except at game for the pot; for once, As'ir was peaceful, and for those at Nejidah there was nothing to disturb their serenity.

\*

It was a summer that would linger for long in the memory of all who had been part of it, whatever the times that lay ahead might bring for them. This was how it had been each summer before Zeid's time and it would, they were sure, be like that in those ahead; but now a new season was about to begin. It was marked by the moment of the first sighting of *suhail*, which signalled the end of summer's heat and a joyous celebration of the blessed rain that would follow.

On hearing Etza recount this beautiful story I found it impossible not to find myself sharing in the general happiness of the time. I rode to Nejida to talk with this local Bedu in their humble *qasrs* and found that they recalled every detail, almost as well as Etza herself. I was saddened to find that the palace itself had become once more a ruin. That was all that remained as a reminder to any who might one day come back of that precious gilded summer, just one season which was not destined to be repeated. Crows had replaced the bulbils and bee-eaters.

*Mohamed my uncle is a lecher. So is my father; but he is clever and I didn't mind when he apportioned me off when I was fourteen. He married me to a sheikh, but I did not please him and after a year he sent me home to my father. I had to leave my baby. Then my father arranged another marriage for me, although this one was far away at a place called Abha.*

*My husband is kind but I am not drawn to him for he is of a tribe which was always our enemy. I have a son who is four years old whose name is Bandar and he is the joy of my life. I have a large harem and plenty of slaves whom I have chosen myself, still children really, barely in bud but beautiful and very attentive.*

*I enjoy grooming my slaves and dressing them so that I can offer them to my husband when he visits my harem. They divert his attention because for myself this is not always welcome. As I have said, I have given him a son. My girls are as soft as sugar. I play with them and have trained them well. I cannot tell more because this is my little secret.*

*My heart is still in Sabiya, not Abha. One day Abha will fall and my father and brothers will ride through the Bab el Shastri. I send my father reports on everything that happens here so as to hasten this, and in turn he is generous to me, which is as well since my slaves cost me much.*

# Chapter 18

THE HIGH SPIRITS engendered by the months spent at Nejidah did not long survive the return to Abha since the new season brought new problems. It was usual for the wells to be depleted by the time autumn arrived but then soon replenished by the rainstorms that came regularly with October. Now, even in December, not a cloud appeared in the sky. It was all too clear that the predictions of the omens were correct.

The water levels in the wells were so far down that it took much labour to draw up the water, which was no longer clear but cloudy, and soon the tribesmen had to work all day fetching water in skins that leaked from villages ten miles away or more. This was a recipe for trouble at the wells and disputes arose concerning which tribe had the right to water their animals. Soon patience began to give way and each side hurled insults at the other; it was the same with the grazing, where only scant salt bushes remained. The Wada'a were especially arrogant, arguing about the boundary of their *dirah*, and it was only a short time before bullets flew. Tabarhla had to set encampments of Beni Mughe'id to guard each well, even the tiny one at Zamzin.

At Abha citizens began to pray in the streets with arms held aloft, beseeching God to intercede, whilst others of a more practical mind talked of migrating like nomads to search for rainfall. A fever known as *hasbah* broke out and a great number of infants, especially those that suckled, were snuffed out like candles. Soothsayers in the marketplace averred that God was angry and was punishing Abha for its sins. They persuaded simple folk that animal sacrifices should be made, following the ancient practices, and when at last rain did fall they claimed that it was the result of these sacrifices, and went about noisily congratulating themselves on their achievement. But by then seventy or eighty were dead, many at the start of life, and a number of Beni Mughe'id had been killed at the wells.

Grief filled the people's hearts and many wept at their impotence in the face of disaster; nevertheless, they noticed that had it not been for the warning from the omens many more would have perished. Thus when Na'ema attended the *majlis* she found that the sheikhs' manner towards her had subtly changed, and she was welcomed. She remained in the shadows, listening and learning much about the character of the sheikhs and the conduct of Abha's affairs, often being amazed at the lack of logic in the arguments and the unpredictable impulses of the sheikhs when the wildest schemes were proposed with the utmost gravity.

All this was duly reported to Ayesha, but to Na'ema's surprise that lady perceived matters differently; she explained that such debates were fruitful since after the safeguarding of the *haj* the first duty of an amir was to engage the energies of the Beni Mughe'id. This was not difficult, provided that something was found for them to do, since they lived for excitement, especially retrieving animals that had been stolen and traced by the trackers, or better still, making raids in order to steal horses and camels from others.

*

The delay in the rainfall certainly had a disturbing effect on the citizens of Abha, as it was the act of God, as they perceived it, that they most feared. However, as natural survivors they had acquired resilience and soon their mood changed again. This was prompted by an event which, according to Etza, was the most extraordinary that had ever befallen Abha. A mysterious Bedu appeared and the manner of his appearance was stranger still, for he simply came walking down the mountain; indeed, some said he came from higher still. With his shaggy beard he looked like a Bedu wanderer but as he grew closer a cry arose, for somehow the figure was familiar, and before long they realised that it was none other than the *nasara* they remembered of old, whose name was Ullobi. Needless to say, I had already guessed this and my heart leaped for it was a perfect picture of my father, and certainly it was time for him to enter the story. It was exactly how he might have chosen to make his entry.

Evidently, Etza was not familiar with the passage of history that had gone before and was unaware that Ullobi had been a prisoner of the Turks. I was able to tell her the story of how he had been released from a dungeon in the Manadhir when the Turks were driven from Abha, and how Tabarhla had sawn off his chains and himself carried my father to the Maquabil, where he was restored to health. The two warriors had become as brothers, and in gratitude for his release Ullobi had sworn that he would one day return to place himself at the service of Abha. Tabarhla had never forgotten Ullobi's stories of the desert war in the Hejaz, the explosives he had used and the guns with barrels as thick as a man's arm.

For Etza, it explained much that she hadn't understood and the reason for such a celebration at Ullobi's return; but now she was able to give a good account of what followed. These years were famous and much recounted in the sagas, for the combined power of Tabarhla and Ullobi carried all before it. Abha came once more to dominate the mountains of As'ir whilst Ullobi himself was established in a house of his own and given all the appurtenances of comfort that Abha could provide. After all their battles, the defeated sheikhs were made to swear oaths of allegiance to Abha's Amir and since the penalty for breaking the oath was death, as they well knew, by and large the oaths were kept and the province became peaceful.

In the course of these years of dominance it would have been surprising if Tabarhla, at least in his imagination, had not at times returned to the idea of striking at the Idrisi, but he knew that the siege of a stronghold like Sabiya was beyond the resources of the

Beni Mughe'id and no alternative had presented itself. And so for a time it had rested, and at Sabiya itself there was no sign of fratricide or any other sort of coup; Mohammed the Black evidently had no brothers, or at least no brothers left.

Yet the melting-pot which was As'iri politics continued to simmer, and it was now the turn of Ullobi to occupy himself with the problem. He reasoned that if Sabiya itself was impregnable, on which both were agreed, an alternative target must be found. Sabiya and the surrounding Tihama were largely barren, and so most of the staples of the Idrisi, their grain and rice and in particular their Sudanese slaves, had to be brought from Africa. These were landed at the port of Jaizan, where a local tribe, long since subjugated, was given the task of transporting the Idrisi supplies to Sabiya, a journey of some twenty miles. Ullobi had concluded that altogether Jaizan was a tempting prospect.

He proposed in the *majlis* at the Manadhir that he should attempt a reconnaissance, for if the harbour, constructed by the Turks for their invasion of Yemen, could be destroyed, much of the Idrisi threat would vanish. It was a matter for much debate and the sheikhs of the Ahl Yazid all had different ideas on whether and how it should be done, but in the end it was Ullobi who carried the day and he was offered a *ghazzu* of a hundred warriors to try his luck. For the *ghazzu*, competition was keen. He declared that he would make his base at Jeddah, where he could rely on the military stores remaining at the old British arsenal, although this was a long way from Jaizan and how he might reach it was far from clear. For Tabarhla and the sheikhs it seemed that this would require the hand of God; however, Ullobi had his own ideas on the matter. He was adamant that his departure must be delayed until the next pilgrim season, which puzzled the sheikhs. It became a running joke at Abha that Ullobi must have become a true believer and was planning to make the pilgrimage himself. At this point, everything had to wait until the end of winter, which was the timing of the *haj* for that year, and when it arrived Ullobi and his *ghazzu* set forth. To me it was obvious where the story was leading, for this must be the episode that Vartak had described during our voyage, and I would now be able to discover the outcome which Vartak had been unable to tell me.

*

The *haj* itself now occupied everyone's attention, and they quickly forgot about the *ghazzu*, the *haj* being an altogether more urgent matter. It occupied their minds to the full because upon it the entire city depended, both the prosperity of the merchants and the livelihood of the ordinary citizens. It was a joyous annual event, for no city in southern Arabia was so blessed by its geography as Abha, lying as it did on the main southern road from Mecca, and at this season its caravanserai filled with camel trains. There were other pilgrim routes such as the shorter one which followed the coast of the Tihama, but there the pilgrims had to contend with bandits and fevers and most chose the safer one which followed the mountain spine, and this was the route that passed through Abha.

The city lay at the junction of the road to Mukalla, the port for Africa, and the road that led westward to the Hadramaut and the other ports of the southern coasts of Arabia, through which passed the pilgrims from Java and India. Some of these now travelled by more modern means, such as ocean liners plying directly to Jeddah, but there were still plenty of caravans to provide the annual bonanza at Abha. Some of the tribe acted as *mahras* to protect the caravans as they passed through the long *dirah* of the Beni Mughe'id, whilst others, the merchants, provided supplies for the pilgrims, hoarded throughout the year to await their arrival. At such a time of excitement, whatever might happen at Jaizan was furthest from all their thoughts.

As it happened, the *ghazzu* itself, or at least part of it, also managed to enjoy the *haj* in the traditional way: those who were given the task of collecting the camels that had been left behind at Jeddah seized their chance to act as *mahras* for the returning caravans, and in the end accompanied them from close to Mecca all the way to Abha. Being well armed with rifles and bandoliers seized at Jaizan, they fought off the rightful *mahras* of the other tribes through whose *dirahs* they passed, and by the time they reached that of the Beni Mughe'id they had received record payments. These were shared in due course with the less fortunate section led by Ullobi, with the field gun from Jaizan, which returned home several days later.

By this time, Abha had found out everything it wished to know about the raid. At Jeddah a steamboat that sailed the Red Sea coast was in port; it belonged to a friend of Ullobi and the captain had agreed to take them to Jaizan. Before they sailed, a field gun that Ullobi had found in an old British arsenal was put on board. There had been some difficulty in fixing it to the aft deck so that it would fire properly, but after extra welding this was overcome and the gun was tested. It made a thunderous noise and the shells landed at a great distance; their effect on Jaizan was not hard to guess. The camels were left in safe keeping at Jeddah, and the *Alhambra*, which was the name of the boat, set off. It sailed down the coast and after three days reached Jaizan, where they anchored offshore within range of the mud-brick citadel which defended the port. The *Alhambra* was well known there and no suspicion was aroused until they began the bombardment. By the end of the day all that was left was a ruin. White flags were run up by the garrison and everyone on board became excited at the prospect of storming the citadel.

Apparently, this was not what Ullobi had planned; what he was after was the port itself, which had stone quays for moorings and four ancient cranes for unloading the boats, all built by the Turks before they departed. The *Alhambra* went close enough to make sure the remainder of the garrison had fled, then anchored with its gun still pointing at the citadel whilst Ullobi and the *ghazzu* went ashore. Explosives attached to long fuses were placed all over the port, and when all was finished and Ullobi had checked everything they lit the fuses and the *Alhambra* sailed away. Before they had gone far, a series of mighty explosions rocked the boat, and as they watched, the cranes and large parts of the stone moorings fell into the sea. The *ghazzu* later dwelt on this drama in loving detail, and the assembled citizens of Abha strained to hear, making them retell the story several times over.

After this, some of them returned to Jeddah for the camels and the others took the gun apart, put it back in the chests and loaded them on to mules which they found at Jaizan for the journey home. Sometime later, back in Abha, after the tale of these adventures had been told, Ullobi emerged from his quarters. The gun was reassembled and drawn by the *ghazzu* through the streets of Abha amidst cheering crowds, who touched it and examined it in loving detail. After that, it was placed on the Bab el Shastri, the gate which faced towards Sabiya, and then to the delight of the citizens shells were fired in that direction. It was intended to serve warning to Mohammed the Black, who would soon hear about the gun from his spies at Abha, although such was the excitement that Ullobi did not dare to reveal that these were the last shells in his ammunition boxes.

The celebrations lasted for days and the considered verdict of the citizens was that God had blessed Abha and had created the guns Himself so that Ullobi should bear them to their city to protect it in His name.

# Chapter 19

THE FIRST INTIMATION that trouble lay ahead came from what Etza was reading in the night sky. At first she hid her concern, but as the signs grew ominous she confronted Na'ema, her mahogany face doubtless cast in gloom.

'There is much trouble, *ammati*, for I see an army on the move. Two rulers confront each other. Their stars nearly touch, they move together and then they move apart, but night after night they are there and much turbulence is there too, *ammati*. I know there is trouble in the eastern mountains.'

All this was repeated by Na'ema to Ayesha, who went to Tabarhla and told him of Etza's reading of the omens, but his reply surprised her.

'I heard the same from my spies in Khamis Mishait,' he said. 'The Wahhabis are on the move and are encamped at the oasis at Khurma. What this means is that the Saudi Asheukh intends to make war on the Hashemites and will lay siege to Mecca for the control of the pilgrimage. He will probably occupy Taif first and use it as a base from which to fight Hussein. If he wins the battle he will enter Mecca, no doubt dressed as a pilgrim for good effect, and then he will attempt to take Jeddah, but even if he conquers the whole Hejaz we have little to fear because it will keep him occupied for a long time and he will have no interest in As'ir. One day we may have to have dealings with him, but meanwhile you may tell the harems that there is no cause for alarm.' But in spite of this reassurance Ayesha would not be comforted.

However, the signs from the omens made Tabarhla pause, and he resolved to send the Beni Mughe'id trackers, whose knowledge of the camels of Arabia was prodigious, to find out which tribes made up the Wahhabi force. On their return they reported that the camels belonged to the Mutair and Ateiba, and that mares were attached to their tails. They bore the green flags of the Wahhabi and were moving up the Wadi Bishah and were close to the city itself. Bishah was not on the road to Taif or to Mecca, and the camels were those of the Ikhwan. The fighting mares tied behind told their own story.

To Tabarhla it seemed that after all the Asheukh was not intent upon the Hejaz but Yemen, which he would approach through Bishah. He summoned the Ahl Yazid and Ullobi. In the *majlis* the clamour was great and all the sheikhs tried to speak at once, but eventually the general opinion seemed to be that the Wahhabi would not dare to attack fearsome Yemen without conquering As'ir first, and thus there was no time to lose. Once the Wahhabi reached Khamis Mishait their objective would be clear: if they took the road to San'a it would mean an attack on Yemen, but if that to Abha then As'ir was the target and ambushes must be set up without delay. However, as Tabarhla pointed out, ambushes had never been successful on the road from Khamis Mishait to Abha since there was nowhere for the Beni Mughe'id to conceal themselves. It would be better to fortify the Bab el Hara, Abha's eastern gate, and attack the Wahhabi as they tried to enter the city. Ullobi was called upon, but his verdict was different again: a Wahhabi force of such a size could not be resisted by the Beni Mughe'id, who would be outnumbered by ten to one. There was no alternative but to negotiate. However, if the final decision was to fight the Wahhabi he would be at their side. At this proposal, which amounted to surrender, there was much protest, but opposing arguments came from every quarter and as a result the *majlis* ended without any decision having been reached. In the end it fell to Tabarhla and Ullobi to decide the matter for themselves.

It was the hour of the '*asar* prayer and shrill calls came from Abha's mosque, which seemed like the city's cry of pain. Tabarhla swore that he could never bring himself to bear the shame of surrendering Abha; he would rather die than do so. He was deaf to all logic; the chance of a reprieve to fight another day meant little to him and nothing Ullobi could say persuaded him otherwise. However, Ullobi himself was just as intransigent as Tabarhla. He could not alter his view that for the Beni Mughe'id to try to resist an army of ten thousand Wahhabis was futile and would lead to the pillage of Abha, whose citizens could expect no mercy from the Ikhwan. They would all be put to the sword.

The stalemate remained. Events thereafter had to take their course and as it happened Abha did not have long to wait to find out what this might be. The road the Wahhabi took from Khamis Mishait was theirs.

The Wahhabi force that arrived at Abha was much smaller than they had expected and it set up camp just out of rifle range from the walls. Then, amidst rising tension, the two sides confronted each other for a day and a half. No war cries were heard, and finally three horsemen left the Wahhabi camp and rode towards the Bab el Hara with the city's eyes upon them. None carried weapons, and from the casual pace at which the horsemen rode it was clear that they were peace envoys.

The Wahhabi terms were offered by Faisal, the second son of Abdulaziz ibn Saud, and were better than expected. Oaths of fealty to the Saud must be sworn, and thereafter Tabarhla and his sheikhs could continue to rule at Abha. An 'ushr tax would be levied and a governor with a garrison of Saudi would remain at Abha for the purpose of protecting it as a fief of the Saudi kingdom.

This was good news for Abha, but it was soon clear that acceptance of the reprieve was not going to be as straightforward as it should have been. Another *majlis* was held and interminable arguments were heard as the sheikhs vied with one another to demonstrate their bravery and daring. From Tabarhla, there was disdain for compromise. At this point, the voice of Ullobi was heard once more. He pointed out that the terms were those of a political settlement, not a defeat. Plainly the Wahhabi did not intend to interfere with the customs and daily life of Abha nor the leadership of the Ahl Yazid. The price they would pay would be the presence of a Saudi governor in their midst, but this would be mainly symbolic and the Amirate would remain intact. The gain would be the added protection they would undoubtedly receive against attack by other enemies: the Idrisi, when they had recovered, or the warlike tribes in the southern mountains. They should swallow their pride and accept terms.

This argument may have persuaded some of the sheikhs, but for Tabarhla the shame remained hard to bear, although even he had in the end to agree that there was no alternative to negotiation. It was put to the vote and by a fine margin it was decided to accept terms, although the ibn Aidh excluded themselves from this decision and Hassan ibn Aidh lost his temper and stormed out of the *majlis* chamber. Further uncertainties followed, but finally an *askari* was despatched to convey the keys of Abha to Faisal ibn Saud.

There was no immediate response. The Wahhabi commander was a hardened campaigner named ibn Mussaud and he was in no hurry to claim the fruits of victory, so he waited. He was a cautious man with plenty of experience of ruses and he knew that surrender was not the same as victory. Thus it was not until the following day that he despatched a *gaum* of a few hundred Saudi as a foreguard to confirm that the surrender was genuine and make preparations for the large retinue that would accompany Faisal to receive the oaths of fealty. Having done so, he ordered the tents to be struck and the camels loaded whilst he awaited the report of the *gaum*.

\*

In the day that had elapsed since the offer of surrender the citizens of Abha, believing that they were now safe, had crowded the walls to await the arrival of the great army of the Wahhabi. It caused disbelief and no little wonder when what they beheld was a small *gaum* of Saudi horsemen and not the army of thousands they had been led to expect. They were tempted to conclude that the threat to their city had been greatly exaggerated. One who was watching events from the Bab el Hara was Hassan ibn Aidh, and for him initial disbelief turned to wild excitement, and extravagant bellicose notions began to form in his mind. He had at his command several hundred Beni Mughe'id horsemen, and from such a position of advantage he believed that he himself could defeat these Saudi and remove the threat to Abha once and for all. In any case, had not God promised that He would protect Abha and why should not he, Hassan ibn Aidh, be his servant? A great victory was his for the taking.

And so when the portcullis of the Bab el Hara was raised to admit the Saudi *gaum*, Hassan and his Beni Mughe'id horsemen charged forth firing wildly, their horses gathering speed as they galloped down the slopes. To their surprise, the Saudis did not react as expected, but with perfect precision the *gaum* divided and allowed the Beni Mughe'id to ride through them without resistance. After that the charge continued, passing through the Wahhabi *gaum*'s encampment, where they scattered the camels and their loaders.

It was all just as ibn Mussaud had predicted: the offer of surrender was only a ruse. He also knew what would happen next, for a Bedouin charge once released has no way of stopping, since the horses, ridden with only a halter rope, take control. Consequently, the Beni Mughe'id horsemen charged onwards until finally they came to the main force of the Wahhabi, who were hidden from view. What followed was a brief encounter, and nothing could save the Beni Mughe'id from annihilation. Their horses were gratefully retrieved by the Wahhabi and very few Beni Mughe'id returned to Abha to tell the tale. By an irony of fate, Hassan ibn Aidh was amongst them and managed to escape despite his wounds.

The effect of this intemperate action was predictable and calamitous. Although the Ikhwan tribes were restrained from sacking Abha, which would have been the likely outcome, the punishment was no less severe: the freedom of the Amir and the sheikhs of the Ahl Yazid would be forfeit and they would accompany the Wahhabis as hostages to Riyadh. Ullobi, although not of course a sheikh, was judged to be one and went too, although little did the Wahhabi realise they had taken prisoner a *nasara* and an Englishman at that.

It was the end of a chapter. On this day in the year 1921 the might and pride of the Beni Mughe'id and the freedom and independence of Abha passed into history for ever.

# Chapter 20

THE ROOM WHERE we had been sitting each day for so many months, during the telling of Etza's saga, was small but in an isolated part of the house, which we had entirely to ourselves; I had become attached to it. It was now approaching dusk, a time when the summits of Al Kaur were silhouetted against the fading sky, and I realised with regret that my days of watching this familiar and reassuring sight were nearly over. I could tell from the tone of Etza's voice that her own record had to end here with the passing of the old Abha.

It was a sad moment for everyone who cherished this mountain citadel with its idiosyncratic ways and especially so for Etza, who had shown me what a proud and careful custodian she was of the story of its final years. Yet so far as Abha itself was concerned, could it really be the end of the story? Somehow I rather doubted it, for Arabian history had never been quite as neat as that. Certainly it must signal the beginning of the end of tribal Arabia; it also led us into a period which was well recorded in history. As I had learned from Professor Monaghan, this year 1921 was of crucial importance in the rise of the House of Saud, but would that really prove to be quite as straightforward as it seemed? I was determined to find out.

My first piece of good fortune was to discover that whilst Etza's story was finished it had in effect a coda. Somehow she had found out later a lot of what happened when the sheikhs of the Ahl Yazid were taken from Abha as hostages, and I can now set this down.

Their journey to Riyadh was long and dispiriting, although relieved to some degree by the courtesy and respect all were accorded by the victors. At nightfall when the sheikhs ate together the hostages were treated as guests rather than captives, and after the meal was finished an exchange of stories took place in the way as it always had done. Every night this began with Faisal's tale of the storming of Riyadh twenty years before by Abdulaziz, of which mighty deed no one, Saudi or Beni Mughe'id, ever tired of hearing.

Riyadh had been seized by the Rashid, the hereditary enemy of the Saudi tribe, and for ten years the ruling family of the Saudi had been in exile and given shelter by the Sheikh of Kuwait. Their prospects were poor, and the family had to wait until a new generation had grown of age and were ready to challenge the might of the Rashid. Finally it found its leader in the person of Abdulaziz ibn Saud, twenty years of age, who in the year 1901, entirely dependent on the favour of fortune and with forty warriors, assaulted Riyadh by stealth. The full story of this mighty deed must be reserved for another place but against such overwhelming odds the storming of the city and the killing of the Rashid governor followed. After this Abdulaziz became the Asheukh of the Saudi and had governed in Riyadh thereafter.

The tale of this heroic endeavour was barely matched by the sagas of the Beni Mughe'id, which were related in turn by the sheikhs of the Ahl Yazid, but these were set in the mountain fastness of the As'ir, which until now was unknown to the Saudis, and hence these tales proved just as popular. As a result bonds of comradeship soon began to form between the two sides and once they reached Riyadh the sheikhs of Abha were given their liberty and villas were provided for them with slaves in attendance. No doubt they were covertly watched but in any case escape from so remote and inhospitable a place as the Nejd was impossible. In quite a short time they melded into the scene and were seen about Riyadh, becoming part of its everyday life and indistinguishable from the rest of its citizens.

For Tabarhla and Ullobi, who shared the same villa, boredom was their chief concern; however, they had found friends amongst the Saudi sheikhs with whom they had travelled, and at times were visited by Faisal ibn Saud. A bond of comradeship formed between the three men and after a while Faisal even came to believe that in Tabarhla and Ullobi he might have found useful allies, or even warriors, in the larger endeavours of the House of Saud. However, there soon arose an unexpected difficulty.

During the journey from Abha Ullobi had been inconspicuous at the times of prayer, which were rigorously observed by the Wahhabi, and had tried to disguise the fact that he did not take part. In this he believed that he had been successful, but now it seemed that his absence had been observed by Faisal. It was a delicate matter, and Ullobi had long decided that if challenged he would have to confess that he was not a Muslim, that he had been born a Christian and brought up as one and would always remain so. To Faisal he admitted that he was also an Englishman.

An uncomfortable silence followed as Faisal tried to come to terms with this novel admission; finally he said, 'I praise your frankness but for us this raises a profound problem.'

Tabarhla interrupted him. 'We must accept that the wisdom of God is revealed to men in different ways.'

'The problem,' continued Faisal, 'is not the different ways in which God's wisdom is revealed. What concerns me is the fact that Ullobi is an Englishman. My father will be mortified. If it became known, or was even rumoured, that there was a British prisoner in Riyadh it could jeopardise the agreement he is trying to reach on our frontier with Kuwait. At the moment my father is negotiating with the British Resident in Basra, Sir Cox, or he may be called Sir Percy. If he found out about this the talks would be ended and the British could even despatch a gunboat. I must send at once to my father to find out what action he wishes me to take.'

An unexpected diplomatic crisis loomed with Ullobi at the centre of it. When the messenger returned, the response from Abdulaziz ibn Saud was brief and to the point: 'Send him back at once to wherever he came from. Give him some *askaris* to make sure that he gets there. Let it be known at Riyadh that he is a sheikh of a distant tribe whom we do not wish to offend.'

It was a reprieve for Ullobi, but for Tabarhla the loss of his comrade in arms was a great blow; his present misfortune was now doubled and he could not prevent himself from brooding over the times they had shared at Abha. Suddenly, it seemed that his best years were passing. He became depressed, for what was the past anyway but an illusion without substance of its own? It was some consolation that Ullobi's freedom would be in the best interests of Abha; nevertheless, it was a long time before he became reconciled to the loss of a comrade who was the closest he had ever had, a brother in all but name.

As Ullobi was leaving Tabarhla took from his neck the bronze *zarar* which hung there. 'Take it,' said Tabarhla. 'You may need it more than I do, and may it protect you as it has protected me.' With this the two men parted, and both felt that there lay upon them the heavy hand of fate.

*

'You may wonder how I know these things that happened after the fall of Abha,' said Etza. 'I will tell you. Close to the house of the ibn Aidh where you stay lives a man called Nasrulah. He is the servant of Sheikh Mohammed bin Mufarrih, the head of the family who is very old, and you may wish to talk to him yourself. When the sheikhs were taken to Riyadh Sheikh Mohammed was amongst them and Nasrulah refused to leave him and went to Riyadh with him. He had been sworn as a *fidawi* and a *fidawi* never deserts his master. Because of this Nasrulah was in a position to tell me what followed the fall of Abha, the journey of the sheikhs to Riyadh where Sheikh Tabarhla and Ullobi lodged together and their friendship with Faisal ibn Saud. When on the order of Abdulaziz Ullobi was sent home he asked that Sheikh Mohammed should be released at the same time in view of his great age, which was agreed. When the party reached Khamis

Mishait Sheikh Mohammed and Nasrulah returned separately to Ayinah because it was considered a safer place than Abha.

'This was as well, for soon we all had to flee from Abha. As I told you it was the time of the great troubles and everyone feared for their lives. It would be difficult for you to find out what happened next but I expect that somehow you will succeed and when you do so you can explain everything to me. They were times of great confusion, and I cannot imagine that anyone at Abha will know the whole story, for much of it happened elsewhere.

'Now there is something else I want to mention. There is in my possession a curious object which I have long since promised myself that I must show you and I have brought it here for you to see.'

It proved to be a simple wooden box, unadorned, practical and capacious.

'When Sheikha Ayesha died, which was the same year as Sheikh Tabarhla, I was given everything that was precious to her, because she loved me. Amongst it all was this box, but I have no idea what it is or why it was so important to her; it only contains packets of papers. I often looked at them and wondered what they were and why they had been sent to her. They came separately every month or so, one after the other, and this is where she put them.'

She opened the box, took out a packet and gave it to me. I sensed immediately that this might be something of importance, but I was quite unprepared for what followed. I stared in amazement, for written on the first package in a careful Arabic hand were the words, 'To be sent to my brother Tabarhla at Riyadh.'

I fell on my knees, seized the package, kissed it and tore it open. Inside was a very long letter, my father's words written by his own hand. I picked up the box and emptied it on the floor and package after package fell out, all addressed in the same way as the first.

I could not understand why they had not been sent to Tabarhla, as Father intended. It was a treasure trove, like someone finding Troy in the sand. I turned to Etza, whose expression and manner had changed. She looked abashed, even guilty. I became angry.

'Whatever are these doing here and why were they not sent to Tabarhla in Riyadh as instructed? Did neither Ayesha nor yourself realise how important they were? Can't you read?'

Etza stared vacantly at the packages and then at me, and a tear began to run down her cheek. I was mortified. Etza weeping; I could not have imagined such a thing. I could think of nothing to say.

'I haven't told you . . . you see, I cannot . . . I cannot read what it says . . . I cannot understand Arabic letters. Sheikha Ayesha could not read them either. We did not know what to do with them so we put them in this box as they arrived.'

'But, Etza, you could have asked anyone and they would have told you. It is so simple, send to Sheikh Tabarhla in Riyadh.'

Etza's head moved slowly from side to side and she continued to weep. 'No one in the harems can read; no one ever could.'

I could have hugged her. 'Etza, when I have studied the letters I shall find out everything and then I shall be able to tell you, because they will be a diary of events. Father was writing to Tabarhla so that he would know what had happened when he returned.' I began to laugh at the absurdity of the situation. 'The complete story of Abha exactly where you left off. I will tell it and you will listen. This is the most marvellous moment in my whole life; it is my father's voice, which I never dreamed to hear.'

At once, I began to sort out the packages and assemble them in a proper order. His touching relationship with Tabarhla was evident at every turn in this series of epistles.

# Chapter 21

FATHER WAS CLEARLY unhappy at leaving Tabarhla behind and says so. He writes as follows.

*

My reprieve has left me with much confusion of mind. To have been singled out in this fashion makes me feel guilty, and the sense that I am deserting you strikes like a dagger in my heart. I know that you live for the companionship of others of like mind and this was ever so. It has made me resolve that, whatever else, I will make a record of what happens at Abha in your absence so that you are well prepared when you return. I shall send the letters to the Maqabil; the Saudi governors can forward them to Ryiadh for so long as you remain there.

At my departure, the Saudi were as good as their word and assigned me twelve good *askaris*, together with camels of the blood stock that could gallop all day. I took with me old Mohammed bin Mufarrih, who rode like a man half his age, so eager was he to return home. We soon reached As'ir and stopped at Bishah, where the new Wahhabi governor provided fresh mountain camels. He also gave me disquieting news: As'ir was full of unrest, which had followed soon after the Wahhabi army left Abha. He could not account for this, although rumour had it that there was fighting in the mountains.

It was spring and flowers lined the wadis, but when we reached the mountains the nights were bitter, and we lit fires with thorn branches which we kept alight through the night. In four days we reached Khamis Mishait, where I planned to lodge the *askaris* and get local news from Suleiman bin Kabit, the Sheikh. At this point, Sheikh bin Mufarrih wanted to proceed to Ayineh, so I lent him two *askaris* for the journey.

The sun was well up as we reached the gates of Khamis Mishait, which to my surprise were still closed. I thought that the people must have become so zealous that they shut the gates at prayer times in the manner of the Wahhabi, yet no sound came from the city's mosque. I announced myself, and we were admitted by a stony-faced guard. I took the Saudis to their lodging, and went to the Sheikh's palace at Dhahban, where I waited alone in the receiving room. It was unlit, and as I sat there I felt ill at ease and sensed that I was being watched from the shadows.

I had not seen Suleiman bin Kabit since before the Wahhabi came, and when admitted to the *majlis* I was struck by the change in the man; he was no longer the proud sheikh that we remember but spoke in a whisper and kept glancing nervously about the hall. I hid my concern as we embraced, and the conversation was as follows.

'I had not expected you to be alive,' said Suleiman. 'It is a miracle.'

'In Riyadh it was prudent to be patient.'

'You were lucky to be at Riyadh. If you had been at Abha they would have killed you. Perhaps you do not know that the Riyal el Ma captured the city. Another of the tribes, the Sa'er, a band of brigands known throughout the As'ir as the "wolves of the desert", then besieged the Manadhir. They have threatened to attack Khamis Mishait if I do not pay them taxes, which I have naturally refused. Therefore I guard my walls and have placed outposts on the road to Abha. Their spies are everywhere.'

I was aghast. 'How could the Saudi governor have allowed such a thing to happen?'

'He was murdered together with most of his garrison by Hassan ibn Aidh after he had recovered from his wounds,' Suleiman said.

'How could the Riyal el Ma have known this?'

'They arrived within days of the murder. They must have had their own spies at Abha and reckoned that when the Saudis returned they would first settle accounts with the ibn Aidh. By that time the Riyal el Ma would have stripped Abha bare.'

'I shall at once go to Abha. Until I see it with my own eyes I cannot make a plan.'

'They will recognise you and kill you.'

'I shall go in disguise. I shall go dressed as a Bedu woman and say I am of the um Bina.'

'Better to wait here and gather a force from the outlying tribes. I will lend you my Shahran warriors and horses.'

'I am afraid it wouldn't help. If the Manadhir is defended by the Sa'er it is impregnable. There is no other course for me to take. I will buy women's clothes in the market.'

'Better let me send a servant to buy them. As I told you, there are spies.'

With some difficulty they bought for me a black *thaub* of double length. I applied henna to my hands and feet and I rubbed my eyes until they were rheumy and watered like those of an old woman. Then I shaved off my beard and drew markings of the um Bina on my nose and cheeks. Next day, I lodged the Saudi *askaris* at Khamis and set off alone the ten miles to the western gate of Abha. As I arrived, storm clouds were gathering over the city.

I was barefoot, leaning heavily on a stick to disguise my height, and hid my face beneath the head shawl. At a distance someone shouted at me, but I ignored him and went on until I reached the gate. The guard studied me and shouted to know my business. The accent was unmistakably that of one of the Riyal el Ma tribes, probably the Beni Zeidin.

'I am a daughter of the um Bina,' I replied. 'I come to seek food and shelter, for my son has been killed by the Sharan and the goats that I pastured were all stolen.' My expression was the picture of despondency. The guard had a belt stuffed with cartridges and a rifle slung over his shoulder. He unbolted the small inset gate and I stepped carefully through, gathering up my *thaub* whilst trying to conceal the size of my feet. To my relief, he let me proceed without more questioning and I shuffled on my way.

The town seemed strangely quiet and the streets, normally filled with a chaos of citizens and animals, were now almost empty. On the city walls groups of wild tribesmen were ostentatiously holding their rifles, and although few were to be seen in the city itself their presence pervaded the place. I began to wonder what had happened to cow the Beni Mughe'id, whose black forms slid into alleyways at my approach. I reached a well where normally there were scores of women drawing water and found it deserted, its leather buckets hanging buckled on the ropes; evidently it had been rendered unusable. I walked towards the poor quarter and met only a single unattended camel that plodded by. I doubled back several times in case I was being followed and finally came to the house of a baker I knew called ibn Musa and knocked at the door.

A woman appeared at an opening in the upper storey and shouted to know my business.

'A poor widow as God wills it,' I called back without raising my head. 'Thieves have stolen my goats and I need bread or I shall die.'

The baker himself came to the window, stared at me and threw down a crust of bread, which I grabbed.

'May you be praised, but as God is bountiful I need water for I thirst.' I looked upwards, holding out my hands to form a bowl in a gesture of supplication.

The baker disappeared and his footsteps could be heard on the wooden stair; the door was unbolted and he beckoned me to enter. I took a few steps, then sat down cross-legged on the floor with my back against the wall and lowered my gaze. After a few minutes the baker's wife came and handed me an earthenware mug which she filled from a water jar. I was thirsty and drained it at one gulp, then I held it out to be refilled, knowing that as a beggar she would not refuse me. I drank the next jar more slowly, then bent forward, touching the ground with my forehead, and called a blessing upon the baker and his house.

'Go now in God's peace,' rasped ibn Musa uneasily.

Relieved that my disguise had deceived him I drew the folds of my *thaub* around me. 'Something tells me that there has been a pestilence here.'

'A pestilence there has been indeed, not once but twice.' Ibn Musa looked at me, his once jovial face creased with grief and fear. 'The Ahl Yazid fell to murdering each other and Hassan ibn Aidh killed ibn Mussaud, the Saudi governor. The bin Tahir would have stopped it but the Amir was taken away to Riyadh by the Wahhabi.'

'Who then rules Abha?'

'The Beni Zeidin. They seized the city and all the Beni Mughe'id that remain live in fear of them. When the Sa'er came and captured the Manadhir many more were killed that had been spared before.'

I was beginning to understand. After the Beni Zeidin and the Sa'er had finished with Abha I had little doubt that other tribes were waiting their turn. I was about to reveal my identity to ibn Musa when there was the sound of footsteps outside, followed by banging on the door. The baker's face went pale.

'Open,' said a rough voice.

'Trouble,' hissed ibn Musa, glaring at me, 'and it is you who have brought it on us.' He went to the door and unbolted it and several tribesmen wearing blue turbans entered.

'Where is the Bedu woman of um Bina?' one demanded.

'She is here,' I replied before the baker could speak. My heart beat fast, but I had to retain my composure. 'What do you want of a poor woman that you should address her in such a godless manner?'

The man made no answer but moved threateningly forward. Before he reached me I rose slowly to my feet with the help of my stick and thanked the baker with carefully chosen formality. Ibn Musa was trembling.

I stumbled into the street and the turbaned tribesmen closed about me. They took me through the alleyways, and I wondered if I should make a dash for it but no opportunity presented itself. Finally, we reached a guardhouse and I was pushed inside. The place was dark and filthy, but although I had no inclination to do so, I sat down on the floor as a peasant woman would. After half an hour two men entered, one of whom I recognised as the guard at the city gate who had admitted me. He pointed to me, then moved away.

'You are the um Bina woman?' demanded the other.

'I am of the um Bina, yes.'

'You entered by the Bab el Harra this morning?'

'I did so.'

'Get up.'

I rose slowly, brushing the dust from my *thaub*. The man spoke in the coarse dialect of the Beni Zeidin and was brutish like others of that tribe, although even the Beni Zeidin must have had difficulty in finding a man of such villainous appearance. One of his eyes was blind, white and staring, while the other squinted, giving him an air of such craftiness and evil that it made me shudder.

'You were pasturing goats, I believe. Where was this?'

'On the high ridges above Abu Ranzah.'

'And you met the Sharan there?'

'The Sharan killed my son and stole my goats. As God is just let him be avenged.'

'Would you be willing to return there with another flock of goats?'

'Why should I? The Sharan may come back.'

'Precisely. I wish you to spy on the Sharan and report their movements.'

I pretended to consider the matter. 'What will you pay?'

'Two piastres a day.'

'I cannot live on less than four.'

'Very well, woman, four. But first a simple precaution – I must be able to recognise your face.' He reached forward and pulled the shawl from my head, a sinister grin spreading across his face. There was an outburst of laughter. It was obvious the whole thing was a charade and they had simply been playing with me. They must have been warned of my coming by spies in Khamis Mishait and probably hadn't taken their eyes off me since I arrived.

'I see that you are dressed for the part,' the man rasped as the laughter continued. '*Ya*, Ullobi, we hoped you might return and save us the trouble of seeking you out like a rat in the corn.'

I thought they would kill me then, but instead the Beni Zeidin turned his back and barked an order to the guards. 'Take him to the Manadhir and put him in the Turkish dungeon.'

The storm clouds that had hung overhead now released a monsoon. Normally such providence would have been a cause for joy, but now it was of no consequence except that it soaked me to the skin. They took me to the Manadhir and forced me down a long stone stairway. At the bottom was a door which was open and all that I could see was a black hole. They bound me with cords, trussing me like an animal for slaughter, then pushed me through it.

# Chapter 22

WHEN I BECAME conscious I was aware only of pain in my head. I tried to touch the place where the pain was but found that my hands were tied behind me. The discovery brought me back to reality: my whole body was trussed. To be left to die in such a place, ignominiously; how much better would have been a quick thrust of the sword. I saw now that I should have forced them to kill me, I should have attacked them with my bare hands and taken one of them at least with me, perhaps more. For the first time in my life I felt without hope, my mind empty of all but despair, and for a while I lay motionless like a spent animal that had been hunted down. You will not be surprised when I tell you I uttered a prayer for God's forgiveness and resigned myself to death.

The place was dark and the only feature I could distinguish was the stench. When I tried to look up I could just make out an outline of light around a door, about twice a man's height above where I lay. It was evidently from there that I had been thrown.

I examined myself, moving each limb in turn as best I could, and discovered that one of the cords that trussed my legs had snapped with the force of the fall. After a while I managed to loosen the others and wriggled free, although my wrists were still tied behind me. I stood up and tested myself. I couldn't straighten one knee but the bones seemed to be unbroken and I took some steps to see if I could walk. I was overcome with dizziness and fell backwards on to a mass of soft debris that had reduced the impact of my fall when they pushed me through the doorway. I lay down and wrestled again with the cords that bound my wrists. A gurgling sound of something being emptied came from above, and a moment later there was a splash nearby: it was all too plainly a long drop into a sewage pit. I moved away from the rising stench until my foot struck a wall, then turned and leaned my back against it, touching the stones with my fingers in the hope of finding something sharp. I kicked against something hard in the debris and knelt to feel for it with my hands, but couldn't because of the cords binding my wrists. I sat down to search for it with my bare feet and found an object the shape of a melon; my toes found a hole, and then a second one and it dawned on me that it was a man's skull. I broke it with a blow from my heel and then searched with my fingers until I found a sharp piece that could be used for cutting. I twisted it so that it just reached the cords and sawed at them, but my fingers quickly tired. Once again I heard water splash into the dungeon, which made me pause and consider the implications. It must be falling into some sort of cistern and was evidently something more than a simple long drop for excrement; it must receive storm-water from the roof, for otherwise it would have dried and there would be no sound of splashing. I recalled the monsoon that had struck earlier.

I wrestled once more with the bonds but still there was no give in them; it occurred to me that there must be other bones, and, searching, I found a thigh bone which I placed against the wall and stamped on until it broke. I knelt and held the splintered end of the bone between my heels and forced it into the binding cords of my wrists. I sawed until my fingers were numb, but eventually I could feel one of the strands giving and after a while the whole binding suddenly parted. Suddenly I was overcome with weariness and pain.

I lay down on the debris, and the dungeon and its ghosts closed about me as I slept. I seemed to be in a coffin with hammers driving nails above my head. I awoke when the door above opened and the light flooded into the dungeon, which seemed as bright as sunlight although it came only from an oil lamp. A man was silhouetted, holding a bucket, which he emptied, and its contents fell with a slopping sound close by. Then the light narrowed to a chink and the door was shut. I felt among the slops and with disgust realised that these were animal entrails. I decided to search the dungeon, starting at the sewage pit which was opposite the door, examining the walls stone by stone. It curved slightly towards me; after three or four paces I found there was water trickling down the stones; it tasted brackish but at least it was rainwater. I found one of the broken bones and used it to hollow out a trough where two stones met. I was so thirsty that whilst waiting for it to fill I sucked water from the stones themselves, and so came across another excavation hollowed out by some earlier prisoner. This was full and I drank it gratefully.

I continued my search and made a survey of the whole dungeon, feeling my way along the walls. It appeared to be circular, for whichever way I moved I came back to the sewage cistern without encountering any corners, which made me realise that I must be at the bottom of one of the three towers.

I concentrated on the cistern, which was topped with a row of steyning which projected from the face of the cistern; it was logical that storm-water would fall inside the building because of its outward slope. Since it was built upon solid rock the only direction the sewage and storm-water could seep away was through the wall itself, which would have softened the mud in which the stones were laid.

I felt around the stones below the water level, and found that this was so. I wondered if I could use a sharp piece of bone to scrape with, and gradually tunnel my way through the wall, stone by stone. However, I would need to lower the water level in the cistern, for only the mortar below this would be softened enough for the stones to be movable. I fetched a bone and levered a block of the cistern's steyning free, and found I could remove the whole course.

I went and drank again at the water holes. By now I could find my way about the dungeon as a blind man does, by learning the shapes of the stones in the walls, helped by the minute amount of light filtering through the cracks around the door, to which my eyes had become accommodated. I searched for the bones again and distinguished two complete skeletons long since desiccated and put the long bones in a pile. The ribs splintered easily and I shaped one into a pick for removing the mortar and broke a long bone to make a lever. At this point I grew exhausted, and it seemed to be night again.

I was still sleeping when the door above opened and another bucket was emptied into the dungeon. I examined it and amongst the offal found a kidney, which I forced myself to eat, then returned to the cistern and found that the water level had dropped by a foot or more. Now, unless the monsoon intervened, I could lower the water level by removing all the steyning and then perhaps start to tunnel through the main wall. I began to scrape away the mortar from the nearest stone where the water had receded. After much work I managed to get the bone far enough into the wall to free the first stone, and began to work at the next one. By what seemed to be the end of the day I had removed the whole of the stone face and then found that in the deeper part of the wall the mortar was saturated and quite soft.

I slept again until awakened by the offal man and decided that I must reckon the hours more carefully and be awake at the time the door opened so that I could make use of the temporary light. I returned to the excavation and found that the water level had dropped, and I could now prise out the stones of the course below. The infill was made of smaller stones thrown in during the construction of the Manadhir with bucketfuls of mud, and by the end of the day I was far into the wall with a mounting pile of waste which lay against the side of the dungeon.

I stopped and studied each aspect of my situation. First, it was imperative that no clues were left to betray my activities to the guards; secondly, the spoil from the excavation must be put out of sight of the door. I laboriously shifted it, using my discarded *thaub*. Somehow I had to maintain my strength and therefore must force myself to eat something each day; I went to the water holes and licked the stones around them, searching for salt that had been drawn out of the mortar by the damp.

So long as the water did not dry up and the offal man came I could survive. The guard invariably shouted at me, evidently to see if I was still alive and I realised that it would be better to shout back to ensure the next bucket. I began to have a vision of what I would see when the tunnel was complete. There would be trees below, where I could hide when I slid down the rocks that must lie below the dungeon wall. The air would be fresh and there would be water everywhere from the monsoon.

On the fourth day I came to a large stone that blocked the way ahead and had to extend the tunnel sideways to avoid it, but this only uncovered another large stone. Then it dawned on me that these must be the blocks of the outer face. I carefully picked away the mud around one of the stones and all at once, miraculously, daylight came through a tiny hole, and it seemed as if it would blind me.

I was still in a state of elation when I heard the offal man unbolt the door. Hastily, I covered the point of daylight and concealed myself, but when the guard shouted at me, for the first time I could not reply. It seemed an age before the door was closed again and I was worried by the thought of what the guard might have observed, so I closed the light hole with mud and climbed out of the wall, almost falling into the sewage. I found my *thaub* and the original trussing and had just hunched myself in position below the door when it opened again and this time the guard held a lighted torch into the dungeon. He looked down and threw a bucket of slops over me and I vented my feelings with a curse. I recalled the evil reputation of the Sa'er and realised that the guards were relishing my plight and the slow death which they had prepared for me. One day I would kill them all.

I got up, found the offal and ate some of it, hoping that it might be for the last time, then climbed into the tunnel and scraped away the mortar around the first of the six stones that formed the end of the tunnel. I went back to the pile of bones and chose two of the largest ribs with hook-shaped ends, and when the stone was loosened I hooked it towards me and freed it altogether. It caused a devastating burst of light.

I freed another stone and managed to get my head through the hole. The evening air was fresh and carried the perfume of the mountains and the spicy smell of the town, which was so intoxicating that it was several moments before I could take in the view below. When I did so I was appalled: there was a drop of some fifty feet, sloping downwards to the rock on which the castle was built. I withdrew my head and replaced the stones and filled up the light cracks, then climbed back into the dungeon.

It had never occurred to me that once I had reached the outer face I would have a problem descending the wall. The dungeon should have been at the lowest point of the castle with the bedrock directly below it, but the masons had evidently taken advantage of the rock bluff and had clad it with their masonry when they built the Manadhir. With awful clarity I now surveyed the prospect of climbing down the immense stone face.

I found my *thaub* and measured it; it would yield twelve strips of cloth of a hand's width about ten feet long. The material was coarsely woven but in order to take my weight it would have to be plaited. I climbed into the tunnel again, unblocked the hole and examined the face of the wall below. There was a green mould from the sewage that had seeped downward where the mortar between the stones would be softened; it would be possible to hammer pegs into the cracks if enough could be made from the bones. I returned and examined them by the light that came into the dungeon. There were two more thigh bones besides those which I had used to lever out the last stones, which, suitably broken, would provide eight pegs. The shin bones would make eight more and the arm bones would be usable although the pegs would be short; the smaller bones of the forearms likewise if they were paired together, and this would add up to sixteen pegs from each skeleton.

I fetched one of the steyning stones and carefully broke several of the bones, then drove the sharp ends into the wall and tested their strength by swinging on them. The larger pegs held well, although some of the smaller ones would have to be reserved for places where the joints between the stones would grip them tightly.

Instead of a single rope, which would not be long enough on its own, I decided to make two, each tied in a loop to form a sling which could be anchored a short distance apart, sideways and vertically, so that I could cross from one to the other to hammer lines of pegs down the face. I picked up my *thaub* again and used one of the splinters to cut the hem and tore it into strips. Then I plaited these, knotting them at intervals with the truss that had bound my wrists. Finally I had two loops of about five feet each and I tested them by swinging on them so that the plaiting tightened and lengthened.

I returned to the wall and removed all six stones at the outer end. The completed tunnel was a massive twelve feet from end to end, which meant that it must be part of a corner turret and therefore would be out of view of the guards who patrolled the walls between the turrets. I remained in the tunnel until it grew dark, and made the sleeves of the torn-up *thaub* into pockets to hold the pegs and the flat stones to hammer them with. When all was completed I went to the water holes and drank them dry, then waited until the stars showed at the end of the tunnel. I counted the number of days I had been in the dungeon, which seemed to be either seven or eight, by which reckoning the moon would be past the full and rising at about midnight. I gathered all the gear into the tunnel and set to work to rebuild the wall behind me, using the blocks from the outer face and making new mud mortar. It gave me a novel sense of security, for when complete there was no longer the fear that if a guard were to open the door he would be greeted by a shaft of light. I had built a barrier between the gaolers and myself.

I crawled to the outer end of the tunnel and drove two pegs into crevices on either side of the opening, and hung first one sling then the other, using a double hitch, and cautiously tested their strength. Then I looked down the wall to accustom myself to the height and to plan where to set the two lines of pegs. I would place them at intervals of about three feet, staggered so that one sling would hang lower than the other, and I could cross between them, descending to drive in pegs, then climbing to unhitch the sling above. In this way I could work my way down the wall, always keeping one hand on a peg in case either a sling or the fixing broke.

It was a long time before the moon showed and had risen high enough in the sky to cast light on the wall, for it was more days on the wane than I had expected, but as soon as the light struck the opening I heaved myself into one of the slings and swung over the void. For a moment time seemed to stop, but the peg held as the rope tautened and I was seized with new confidence.

I reached across to the other sling and tested it with my full weight, and then transferred myself with the help of a foothold in the wall. I looked upwards and was relieved there was no point from which I could be observed from the parapets, which meant I could afford to move slowly. The only risk of being seen would be from persons approaching the city by the southern gate, but they would hardly expect to see a man clinging to the face of the Manadhir and I would be taken for discarded rags.

I drove in another peg as far down as I could reach, attached the second sling, then climbed upwards again to unhitch the first. I had to heave myself up, gripping the knots with both hands, and was surprised at how much effort it took to raise myself. I went on hitching and unhitching the slings, standing in one to remove the other and then sitting in it to hammer another peg lower down. As I became more practised I lengthened the vertical distance between the pegs as much as I dared; eventually I had to use the smaller arm bones driven in pairs deeply into the wall. When tested they held, but when I had used all of them there was still a drop of nearly twenty feet and the rocks beneath looked uninviting although the slope was in my favour. It had to be the moment of truth. I flicked off the top sling, somehow untied the knot and made it into a rope of about ten feet. I anchored it with a hitch to a strong peg I had kept for this purpose and lowered myself, holding the rope with both hands and feeling for crevices with my feet. I reached the last knot, said a prayer and launched myself into space.

Time seemed to stand still. I bounced off the wall time after time where it sloped away at the foot and finally landed on a pile of rubbish that took the worst of the impact. I was dazed from the shock but found that no bones were broken and I was able to clamber painfully down the rocks below. I reached some sand and lay there, spent in body and mind. Then dawn broke and as the sun rose it warmed me and slowly brought me back to life.

The three round towers caught the first rays of the sun, which made them glow like yellow amber. I gazed at the Manadhir in wonder, as if seeing it for the first time. The great castle defending its city, half as old as time, as the poet described Petra; it was certainly that, but also much more, more than I had ever comprehended and for a moment I forgot all about my escape. It was mine, the Manadhir, in spite of all the hardship it had brought me; Abha was my own city, my last attachment and nowhere else was my home. Somehow, some day, I swore I would retrieve it. With such wild thoughts racing through my mind, I found cover and lay down and slept.

After an hour I awoke, and for an instant the light confused me and I thought I was in the dungeon and the offal man was coming. I jerked myself back to reality and found a rock pool. The water was cool and delicious, and having drunk I splashed it over my face and hands and washed my feet, which were covered in blood. I retied the cord of my *sirwals* and put on my shirt again, both now so tattered that they barely held together. It mattered not that I was cold and hungry and that all my bones ached; for the second time I experienced the astonishment at being free.

I felt my strength returning and with it the will to leave whilst my luck held, for the guards of the dungeon must now believe I was dead. I smiled at the thought of the tattered rope left hanging on the wall which they would take for rubbish thrown from the parapet, yet which in reality had held my life in its tiny threads.

# Chapter 23

I WAS NOW wearing only a *dishdasha* and *sirwals*, with my shawl in place of my *thaub*. I walked painfully towards Khamis Mishait, not daring to use the road, picking a way over the loose rocks for the rest of the day and into the encroaching dusk. Owls hooted eerily on either side, but apart from these the *jebel* belonged to me alone. Hunger began to gnaw afresh.

I heard a dog barking in the distance and made a detour in its direction until I could make out some black tents. I walked towards them, but at a distance a shot rang out and a bullet spattered the sand; I shouted a greeting and went on walking towards the tents. The only response was a second bullet, which made me jump aside in case others followed. It was most unusual for Bedu to behave in such a fashion, for they must have seen I was alone and unarmed, and by custom I should have been welcomed and fed in exchange for news. It must mean that they were frightened.

I rested until dawn and could see Khamis Mishait in the distance. Footsore and consumed by hunger and fatigue I reached it an hour later, but was surprised to find the western gate was still closed, and at the sight of me one of the guards waved his rifle and swore.

Even to a beggar this was insulting. I waved my stick at the man and went towards the postern cut in one of the gates. 'Unbar it and let me enter, miserable wretch, and know that I carry news for your Sheikh.'

'Filthy beggars do not carry news.'

I was incensed. 'Send to your Sheikh forthwith and say that the woman from um Bina wishes to speak with him.'

'You are no um Bina woman.'

'Tell him what I have said or before this sunset he will have your head.'

There must have been such menace in my voice that the guard did not argue and moments later unbolted the postern. Two men signalled me inside and bolted the door, then led me through back streets to Dhahban. The smell of freshly baked bread coming from one of the *qasrs* almost made me faint. At length, leaning heavily on my stick, I was led into the *majlis*. At the sight of me Suleiman bin Kabit leaped to his feet, but I placed a forefinger on my lips. 'I am still the woman of um Bina,' I whispered. 'Give me food and water and let us speak where no one can hear.' We went into an inner room where bread and a bowl of camel milk were brought by a slave, who withdrew silently, closing the door behind him. I seized the bread, crammed it into my mouth and drained the bowl, then went to the door to check that no one was listening.

Suleiman was staring at me.

'Your disguise would certainly have deceived me. At least let me send for a cloak.'

'It is better that I remain as I am for I will have been taken for a beggar with news. Every movement that we make is watched.'

'There may be spies in the town but not here in Dhahban.'

'In the town, in your house, everywhere. You will soon understand why I say so.' I related the story of my encounter with the Sa'er, speaking in a low voice not far from his ear. Suleiman listened in silence and when I had finished drew his breath and swore.

'By God, I will rid this town of spies and kill all of them.'

'First we have to uncover them, which may not be easy. Tell me where I can find my Saudis.'

'Wherever you left them when you went to Abha.'

I left Suleiman, borrowed an *abba* and head covering and went by a roundabout route in case I was followed to the two houses where the Saudis were lodged. I knocked upon the door and began droning out a long plea of misfortune like a beggar, with suitable invocation to the mercy of the Almighty. It certainly deceived the Saudis, for when the door was opened I was bidden to go away. At this I uncovered my face so that it caught the light.

'By the mighty power of God …' exclaimed Mubarrak, the leader of the Saudis. I quickly stepped inside and they gathered about me excitedly. 'We had given you up for dead and were about to return to Riyadh.'

'I had to find out what was happening at Abha. As it turned out, it took longer than I expected.'

'Tell us,' they chorused, crowding around me.

'*Bishara*, doesn't matter. It is quite a long story. First tell me what has happened here.'

'The town is quiet and we have been well provided for by the Sheikh. Also we have found a new recruit, another Saudi.'

'Indeed. Tell me about your recruit.'

'Bin Shah. He is from the north. He came with the Wahhabi but caught a fever and was left behind when they left. He came here to seek work at Dhahban and Suleiman sent him to us.'

'You know his tribe?'

'None of us has heard of it but it must be one of the Wahhabi tribes from the north because he fought with them at Abha.'

'Bring him to me.'

'Let us feast you first.'

'Bring him now.' My tone was sharp and made Mubarrak start. He left to fetch bin Shah.

Meanwhile, I was occupied by another matter. For the first time in many days I washed, trimmed my beard and put on fresh clothes, a *kefiyah* and head ropes. I did so at leisure, enjoying the sensation, and when I descended the stone stairway I must have looked more like the man they remembered. I accepted a cardamom then scrutinised the young tribesman brought before me, taking in every detail. The man wore a brown *thaub* and sandals such as were worn in Riyadh and thus far resembled a typical Wahhabi from one of the outlying tribes. He was no more than sixteen years old and his face, scarcely bearded, was honest, yet there was something in his manner that seemed out of place. I looked at him intently for a full minute: the man reminded me of a Bedu of the Beni Shi'bah, one of the As'ir tribes.

I took a string of beads from my pocket and casually flicked them so that they parted evenly in two rows. 'Tell me, bin Shah, which is your tribe?'

'We are nomads. We herd sheep to sell in Riyadh.' His accent was unmistakably that of As'ir and it was obvious that bin Shah did not come from Riyadh.

'How is it that you are in Khamis Mishait?'

'I was with the Wahhabi at Abha. I caught a fever and had not the strength to return so I came here to look for work.'

'Which flag did you fight under at Abha?'

'The flag of my sheikh, naturally. Now I hope it will be yours.'

'I am asking the colour of the flag.'

'It was the colour of the flag of the sheikh. Each sheikh had his own colour.'

'A yellow flag for example?'

'Certainly, red, yellow, many colours.'

'So the Wahhabi fought under many colours?'

'I don't know what you mean.' Bin Shah began to shift his feet and small beads of perspiration began to appear on his forehead.

'You don't know what I mean because you have never fought with the Wahhabi or you would know that their flags are green. You have never seen a Wahhabi. You are a spy sent here by the Riyal el Ma.'

Bin Shah threw himself at my feet. I gave an order, 'Take him to an upper room and guard him.'

Mubarrak looked downcast but my reproof was gentle. 'It is enough that you have discovered that we are surrounded by spies who watch our every movement. Now, if your recruit will sing for his supper, we may start to catch them.'

'How will we do that?' Mubarrak managed to find his voice.

'That we will discuss after I have slept,' I said.

*

Late in the afternoon, the call to the *asr* prayer came from the mosque. I awoke and ate a meal of freshly baked bread and a bowl of rice broth, then summoned Mubarrak to bring bin Shah.

'Release the prisoner and bring him to me. With his help we shall catch every spy in Khamis Mishait.'

Bin Shah came stumbling in and stared at the ring of hostile faces. He assumed he was about to be executed and prostrated himself once more. 'Get up, bin Shah, you shall keep your life if you do as I say. You are not, I think, the only spy in Khamis Mishait. The Riyal el Ma sent others whom you must know. How many others?'

'Many, a dozen or more.'

'Of which tribe are they?'

'Beni Shi'bah and Beni Zeidin.'

'Then you can identify at least the Beni Shi'bah? And with the help of the others you can identify the Beni Zeidin?'

'Yes.'

'Bin Shah, I will spare your life if you will reveal them. I mean all of them. You will lead me to where they live, one by one call them by name, and when they come down we will take them. It is a fair price for your life, is it not?'

'Afterwards you will kill me.' Bin Shah looked up and his face was that of a callow youth.

'I will set you free, the others likewise.'

He led us to an alley where a man was beating copper and above the din called to the upper storey window, 'Sharif!' Sharif appeared at the window. 'I have brought some friends who carry news.'

Sharif came down to the street and was promptly seized by Mubarrak and pushed into a side alley. I was beside him with my dagger at the man's throat. 'We know that you are a spy. Make no sound or you will die.' Sharif blinked in disbelief and did not try to escape. 'You will die, Sharif, unless you agree, as bin Shah has, to lead me to another spy. When every spy has been found you will be freed to return to Abha as I have promised bin Shah.'

Sherif hesitated, looked at bin Shah's face and made a swift calculation of the odds. I turned to Mubarrak. 'Take him back to our quarters and let bin Shah lead you to the others. Offer each his life on the same terms but if any resist kill them. By nightfall we shall have a full house.'

They went through the market and in the houses of the merchants uncovered spies of both the Beni Shi'bah and Beni Zeidin. Some emerged unsuspectingly as they were called by name, others sensed trouble and tried to escape. Either way they were seized, for the *fidawi* had grown adept, and each in turn was offered the same terms. In this fashion they collected eight Beni Shi'bah and eight Beni Zeidin; only one spy made a dash for it but for him this proved to be his last mistake. At the lodging I interrogated them with Mubarrak and under threat they provided a list of the rest. Some were already prisoners but four remained unaccounted for and it did not take long to establish that all of these were at Dhahban itself.

Sheikh Suleiman was evidently a trustful man and refused at first to believe that there were spies in his own household. However, when offered the evidence he ordered the doors of Dhahban to be locked whilst the whole of his retinue was identified one by one. By this means the missing four spies were quickly found, but Suleiman was too angry to let them go on such easy terms; he declared that amongst the four must be the spy that betrayed me to the Sa'er and swore to have him executed in front of me. It took much persuasion on my part to prevent this, and I had to draw Suleiman apart and explain that it was vital that they all returned to Abha since I wished them to convey a message to the Riyal el Ma.

For the captives an uncomfortable night followed, twenty-three men under guard in a single room, but on the following morning they were escorted to the western gate that led to Abha and released. No doubt their deliverance must have seemed miraculous; however, before they were freed they were given a message for the Riyal el Ma. The Wahhabi would shortly return to Abha and would take no prisoners. This news, together with the extraordinary fact that the um Bina woman was free once more, reached the Riyal el Ma at Abha that same day. Their response was to withdraw from the villages surrounding Abha and place most of their warriors on the road between Khamis Mishait and Abha to await the Wahhabi army which would shortly pass that way, after which they set themselves to fortify the city walls in readiness for a siege. In this fashion the Riyal el Ma, quite against their nature, became defensive.

One of the spies did not go back. This was bin Shah, who pleaded that his tribesmen would certainly kill him for giving them away. Indeed, this was likely, and it also occurred to me that he might prove useful, and so, having sworn an oath, bin Shah was allowed to join the *fidawiyah*. It might have been expected that the Saudis would have been hostile to this decision but in fact they were much relieved, for bin Shah, who was a baker by trade, had become extremely popular as by general consent he was the best cook the *fidawiyah* had ever had. Nor was it long before I too became aware of bin Shah's value, for he provided excellent intelligence of what was happening at Abha. It seemed that when the city fell the Sa'er, a warlike tribe of outcasts, greatly feared, had fought the Riyal el Ma for the possession of the Manadhir with its armoury and stores of supplies.

*

That the Riyal el Ma should choose to remain at Abha rather than return to their own city and their families was unexpected and presented me with a great opportunity: the battle that the Riyal el Ma would assume they had to fight at Abha could be fought somewhere else, at a place of my own choosing. In that case the element of surprise could outweigh any disadvantage I might have in numbers, since it was unlikely that I would muster more than a few hundred warriors. So first I must return at once to Riyadh to persuade Abdulaziz ibn Saud to let me have as many as possible, which he could hardly refuse if the object was to retrieve Abha for the Saudi.

A plan was beginning to form in my mind: the battle would be in the mountains at a place well known to us all and perfectly suited for this purpose. We had never, as you know, had much contact with the Riyal el Ma since the only pass, the Sha'ar, a mile long and in places narrow, is a hazard that both tribes have preferred to avoid for fear of ambush. However, if the returning Riyal el Ma could somehow be lured into it, the resulting Battle of Sha'ar Pass would go down in history and outshine all others in the sagas of the Beni Mughe'id.

This intoxicating prospect I shall discuss with you when we meet on my return to Riyadh, where I shall seek the support of Abdulaziz.

# Chapter 24

I HAVE ALWAYS believed that the city of Riyadh owes its existence to its oasis, although on my return there were so few palm trees to be seen that this might not have been obvious. Since you were not to be found as I arrived we proceeded to the palace fortress of the ibn Saud, a mud-brick structure with square towers at the corners, not at all impressive like the Manadhir. The *fidawis* were known there and I was allowed to make my way to the quarter where ibn Saud's secretary, Youssuf Jassim, sat surrounded by a large number of boxes in which he was frantically searching; evidently these held the documents of state, as it happened in their entirety, which I discovered later. He knew all about me and showed concern that I had returned to Riyadh, but when he learned that the Saudi garrison and the governor of Abha had been killed, he went at once to report this to his master. And so it came about that later in the day I was ushered into the presence of Abdulaziz ibn Saud.

Like others before me, I felt a sense of awe. The great warrior prince, immaculate in spotless white *abba*, head robes and *kefiyah*, radiated an aura of tranquillity and charm; I am tall myself but ibn Saud towered above me. He listened in silence to what I had to say with no change in his expression. It had seemed to me that the news I carried would be a severe blow and a serious setback for the Wahhabi cause, but if this was the case Abdulaziz gave no sign of it and finally appeared to dismiss the whole episode with a shrug of the shoulders. Perhaps, I concluded, it was not the first time that a Saudi governor had lost a city and his head. Nothing more was said about the matter.

After a moment's pause ibn Saud rose to his feet and beckoned me to follow him. We entered another room, empty except for a large wooden box standing on the floor, which he pointed to with pride.

'Before we consider the problem of Abha perhaps you would care to see a gift I have just received. It is from your countryman, the British Resident at Basra.' He knelt to open the box and took out a machine, and began to tinker with it, much like a child with a new toy. It had three black knobs, each with a pointer that moved on a white disc with letters and numerals; below these were an assortment of knobs, switches and red glass bulbs that lit up at his touch.

'When Youssuf has learned to use this machine you can scarcely imagine what it can do. It can make noises that can be heard as far away as Jeddah, and another machine in Jeddah can make noises that can be heard by this one.' He pointed to another box, still unopened. 'That one is called the receiver and this the sender, and although the noises that come from the sender are tiny they can be made into words by the receiver.' At this he pressed one of the buttons and the machine emitted a sharp note like that of a bird. I recognised a wireless telegraph.

'In a short while when these machines are made ready they will carry in a minute what takes a messenger two weeks, and so the wireless telegraph will be the master of the kingdom. Some say that it must be the work of the devil but I tell them it is a gift from God. I asked the *ulema*s to pronounce on the matter. Since the machine can be made to utter the words of the Prophet they agree that however strange it may seem it must indeed be the gift of God. What you have seen will one day make Arabia a state that can be ruled from Riyadh, even in its remote parts. Now I will tell you something else. A prospector from America who seeks my permission to search for oil has promised me that he can drill wells so deep that water can be found anywhere in Arabia, even in the Rub el Khali. This means that the tribesmen will be able to grow their own food, nomads can settle and all will stop killing each other. Now let us turn to the matter of why you have come to Riyadh.'

'In the first place to ask for the release of Tabarhla, our Amir. In the second to seek your help in providing warriors and the means to pay them so that we may recapture Abha for the Wahhabi.'

'I am sorry to say that both these are impossible. Tabarhla is not in Riyadh and in any case he cannot be released. He has chosen to help us fight the Rashid at Hail and is one of my most valued commanders. As for the warriors, mine are all engaged in the war. There is also the small matter of your *askaris*, whom I shall need.'

'My own *fidawiyah*!'

'Your *fidawiyah* indeed, sworn to fight for you until death. That is a fine compliment to you and if you have earned such respect perhaps I will let you keep them. They can help you to recapture Abha as I once recaptured Riyadh with but forty men. As for money I have none, or so little that my whole treasury is carried in the saddlebags of one camel.' He was smiling. 'I myself always managed to find the means, as you will have to now. However, I promise that tonight I shall make sure that you and your *fidawis* are properly fed.'

He turned to leave, then a thought struck him. 'I meant to say that I heard about your escape from the Manadhir. It is the least I would have expected from an Englishman. Should you be successful in recapturing Abha I will give you one of my daughters in marriage.'

'That is indeed an honour,' I replied, 'but the fact is that I have a wife already.' Abdulaziz paused to consider this novel complication and then proceeded on his way; evidently it was not a predicament that he had ever encountered.

*

I found Mubarrak, who was loading supplies on to the camels. He read my expression. 'What did he offer you?'

'Nothing except a free meal.'

Mubarrak shook his head. 'He'll still come up with something, you'll see.'

'He hasn't got it to give, that's plain. There isn't any money and no warriors either. They're at war with the Rashid so we might as well go back to Khamis Mishait.' In spite of my gloom I noticed that in my absence Mubarrak had been active, for a number of new *askaris* had mysteriously appeared and all the *fidawis* now wore belts with rifle bullets draped about their shoulders.

Sometime after sunset slaves arrived bearing trays of rice and mutton and camel meat, food enough to feed twice our number. Fires were lit and the meal was eaten as the *fidawis* exchanged their news. Later, for the benefit of the newcomers, the story of my escape from the Manadhir was told by Mubarrak once more. Next day I left Riyadh with the *askaris*, much saddened that once more you were not amongst us.

We rode across the emptiness of sands which belonged to the Shahran tribes in the direction of the southern mountains. The general mood was bleak. I had given up all hope of receiving help from ibn Saud and had put him out of my mind whilst busily trying to think of a way to capture Abha with twenty men. Then, one morning, we were awakened by the sound of horses' hooves, which brought me hastily out of my tent. Coming towards us were a group of wild-looking men on horseback whom I took to be bandits, but some distance away they stopped and a single horseman broke from the others and rode towards me.

He reined to a standstill. 'Abu Hamesh. Us Naha,' he announced. 'Look for Saudi come from Riyadh with *nasara*. Must be you, saw the sandmarks They said *nasara* had fight to be done. That right?' His speech was a sort of pidgin Arabic I'd not heard before, so of course it was barely intelligible.

'We're on our way to Abha, where I come from, to sort out some trouble with a tribe that's taken it,' I said.

At this moment another horseman wheeled beside Abu Hamesh. 'What's he want?' The Arabic was even more atrocious.

'Tribe took man's place when he not looking. Must get it back by fight. Wants us do fight. S'all it is. Get Nahas. Hear what man say.' There was something infinitely disparaging in the tone in which he spoke, even allowing for the strange language.

Abu Hamesh got off his horse and handed the head-rope to the nearest Saudi. 'Don't mind him speak rude. Can't help it.' He gestured towards the other Naha with sublime disregard for his own 'speak'. 'This your place for talk?' He pointed to my tent, which we used as a *majlis* and was open on all sides except for the screens at the back, where I slept. Abu Hamesh leaned against the tent pole. 'Say you not got man for it that right?'

'Quite right. How many are you?'

'Ninety left our sands, all never came don't suppose.'

At this point more cries were heard and the rest of the Nahas arrived. They came at full gallop, stopping at the last minute in a flurry of sand a foot from where we stood. They were all exactly alike, short and scruffy, with small wiry beards that jutted forward, and ragged hair. Like Abu Hamesh they were dressed in rags and had no head-cloths, yet there was certain discipline about them.

'Make things clear from start,' said Abu Hamesh. 'Naha don't want food, Naha find food themselves, nor we ask money but we look that you find us good chances, proper ones right for Naha, not dirty Mecca caravans. Them we leave for common thieves.' His sharp eyes were everywhere and he studied me as though estimating what I might be good for.

'As it happens I have a good opportunity in mind,' I said, turning to address the Nahas as a whole. 'It is the largest market for rifles in the As'ir and at present is not properly guarded.'

'Khamis Mishait,' the Nahas shouted in chorus.

'Not Khamis Mishait. The place is Riyal.'

'If you think Riyal not guarded, then you never fought Riyal el Ma,' said Abu Hamesh.

'Perhaps not, but there is good reason to believe that the Riyal el Ma are busy elsewhere. They happen to be at Abha, which is my place.'

A sinister grin spread across Abu Hamesh's face, revealing an assortment of broken teeth. 'Comes to this, if you know where there's quality stuff to be had Naha do fight for you. If you lead right we follow, if not we go back to sands we come from.'

'I ask for nothing better,' I replied. I rose and walked with Abu Hamesh to where his horse stood. Abu Hamesh vaulted on to its back and reached for the halter rope. 'When we leave?'

'As soon as we can break camp.'

As the Nahas moved away Mubarrak and the *fidawis*, who had been watching from a distance, came into the tent, clamouring to know what had been said. I explained and then took Mubarrak to one side.

Mubarrak shook his head. 'In the name of God, who are these Nahas?'

'Who knows? Men say they were part of the Shahran though to me they look like villains, but maybe that's just what we need.'

It was quite true that the Nahas had once been part of the Shahran, although it was a long time ago. Now they had ties with no one and were nomads, or if they had villages no one knew where they were; indeed, for all that the rest of Arabia knew about them they might have come from another planet. How exactly ibn Saud had summoned them was something that I never discovered; indeed, it was possible that they just arrived without being summoned at all.

\*

As we reached the mountains the going southward was arduous since we were riding along the mountain spine. We climbed through juniper forests, camping at small pastures where the horses thrived on the fresh *nassi* and *hamdh* grasses, and met only shepherds whose villages, which we avoided, could be seen in the valleys below. The route provided perfect security, which is what had attracted me in the first place, and we were soon lost to the world. Gazelles, hares and bustards abounded, and each evening lavish feasts were held when we all ate together. At length we found a *hajnah*, the flat top of an extinct volcano, and a small spring which ran to waste in the sands below the eastern escarpment. Here we set up camp and stayed for several days to rest the horses.

However, the Nahas soon became restive. One dawn we were awakened by the sound of their war cries and I seized my rifle and rushed from my tent. A strange sight met my eyes, for the Nahas were wheeling their horses to either side of the *hajnah* and brandishing spears.

'What on earth . . .?' Mubarrak came to join me.

'God knows but it looks as if they mean to settle some quarrel, or else they are planning to kill us. But wait, what is that in the middle of the *hajnah*?'

It was a bundle of dead thorn bushes tied about a sapling. The Nahas were now drawn up facing each other, and as we watched, a single horseman from either side separated and galloped towards the other, shrieking their war cries. At the last minute they diverged and each threw a spear at the bush pile; after that others followed in pairs until the target was a mass of spears and resembled a giant porcupine. When all had thrown the spears were retrieved and the game started anew.

I fetched my horse, rode to one of the groups of Nahas drawn up in readiness for the next round and borrowed a spear. My mare was prancing and tossing her head with excitement so I steadied her, but she wanted to gallop so I stuck the spear in the ground, released the head rope, and let her take me where she wished. We galloped twice round the *hajnah*, after which I retrieved the spear and rode towards the target; I threw but missed, having underestimated the horse's momentum. I turned and leaned to retrieve the spear whilst all around the Nahas yelled excitedly. On impulse I rode towards Abu Hamesh, dropped the head rope, stuck the spear into the ground and raised my arms into the air in mock despair at which there was general laughter. I retrieved the spear and galloped at the target again, throwing earlier, and this time the spear embedded itself in the brushwood. A roar went up from the Nahas and in a moment they were all galloping towards it to set their points next to mine.

*

It became clear that the ways of the Nahas were entirely their own. If like the *salubas* they came from another country no one knew or cared, least of all the Nahas themselves, but clearly they had preserved their own traditions and had not married into other tribes; perhaps it was this that accounted for their strange appearance and extraordinary similarity. As I contemplated them it seemed to me no surprise that the Shahran, with their conservative Bedu traditions, had driven the Nahas out, since their wild behaviour and savage appearance would have seemed undignified. Nevertheless there was a curious consistency about the Nahas, for they always seemed to know exactly what they were going to do and without any direction from Abu Hamesh proceeded to do it. It was little wonder that confronted by these wild men many took fright, just as for a moment I had myself, for if their manner was alarming so were their weapons, and I could see that both would cause confusion and uncertainty to any enemy. I realised that if I could control the Nahas and discipline their fearsome ways they would be a formidable foe for anyone, even if they were in a minority.

It was something which caused me much thought. However, as it happened Abu Hamesh was having ideas of his own, and had evidently decided he had not quite finished with his fellow leader – for that is how he viewed me. Some days after the spear throwing he had the opportunity he was looking for. We were riding through rocky defiles when suddenly one of the Nahas sighted a mountain leopard crouching upon the rock above our heads, and, raising his rifle, shot it just as it sprang. The bullet struck behind one ear and the huge creature came crashing down in front of us, which caused pandemonium amongst the horses. The Naha who had fired the shot stood triumphantly astride the dead leopard, whose huge claws, as long as a man's finger, were still outstretched in readiness. At once Abu Hamesh drew his dagger and started furiously to rip open the carcass, cutting out the heart, which he held up for all to see. The next moment he tore into it with his teeth and drank the still warm blood, which, as he believed, bestowed on him the life force of the beast. No one else took part; it was the leader's right but the strength he so gained, according to their primitive belief, was everyone's gain as well.

Another ritual followed: Abu Hamesh put his finger in the blood and drew lines across my forehead and down my cheeks. 'Let be witness,' he cried. 'Swear this moment *nasara* my blood brother.' At this there was great acclamation from the Nahas and also the Saudis.

For me it was not so much a matter of brotherhood as the recognition of one outcast by another.

# Chapter 25

THE SHA'AR PASS was in the heights of the Jebel al Durbah as it rose south-west of Abha. It was not part of the natural caravan route to the south, for this was through Khamis Mishait and lay further east, crossing the line of the wadis that flowed from the mountain spine towards the central sands. It connected Abha with a cluster of villages about the small town of Riyal, which lay some miles to the south of the pass on the western slopes of the Jebel al Durbah. The pass was mainly used by local shepherds who herded large flocks of sheep and goats to the summer pastures in the mountains and returned with them to Riyal in the autumn.

There had never been contact between Abha and Riyal either in trade or concerning the boundaries of their respective *dirahs*, which were decided by the mountains. By the standards of the Beni Mughe'id the Riyal el Ma were an impoverished tribe, but recently they had found an unexpected source of prosperity: the Turks had made a base there and when they left had no time to retrieve their ordnance. This was seized by the grateful Riyal el Ma, and in consequence Riyal had become the arms market of the southern As'ir and Tihama. Nevertheless, the Beni Mughe'id and the Riyal el Ma still kept their distance, each respectful of the Sha'ar Pass and its perils.

However, the scene was now greatly changed, for with the murder of the Saudi governor, the Ahl Yazid absent in Riyadh and the Beni Mughe'id leaderless, no tribe that valued its reputation could properly have been expected not to fill the vacuum thus created. Certainly the Riyal el Ma, with no citadel of its own, would hardly have forgone the chance to get its hands on Abha, even if it was a case of a minnow swallowing a swordfish.

The pass was serpentine, about a mile from end to end, and lay between the twin peaks of Damir and Tuwayra where the devil was said to roam. The track had been cleared of fallen rocks and these now littered the margins, providing a measure of cover for anyone brave enough to take up position in the pass itself. Smaller rocks scattered on the mountainsides would also have helped, but there was little vegetation and for this reason no one had ever tried to use this natural site for an ambush. At the northern end where it debouched towards Abha the pass was wider, and here the slopes were shallow and rideable by horse or camel; by contrast the southern end was narrow, its walls sheer, and its entrance guarded by two enormous rocks known as *nuhaidain* for their imaginary resemblance to a virgin's breasts.

As soon as we reached the Sha'ar I rode the pass from end to end with the Saudis, and by the time the reconnaissance had finished it was late afternoon and the late October sun was directly in the face of anyone approaching from Abha. Above us on the western side we found a plateau which could not be seen from the pass itself and here the Nahas made camp and concealed the horses. It was called *um laj*, which means the mother of *laj*, in other words a well, for although the plateau itself was waterless there was a wadi that flowed westward in season and was sufficient to nourish it. Here there was water throughout the year, although it could only be carried to the plateau above with much labour since the dried-out bed of the wadi could not be ridden. The problem for us was that the pass was inconveniently wide, for although the shallow slopes would allow room for cavalry to manoeuvre they could also be used as a means for escape, and so it might be difficult to contain the battle within the pass itself.

At the northern end of the pass, where it led to Abha, an unusual feature caught my attention, for on one side a whole section of the mountain had fallen, or been cut away, the sheer walls showing the strata of the rock. I had passed it many times without realising its significance, for it must have been the quarry where stone was cut to build Abha and the Manadhir, and indeed it still showed the marks of the masons' axes. The base of the quarry had been flattened by use and was now partially grassed over. Evidently it was being used by shepherds for corralling their sheep, but it was obvious that it would also make an excellent place to conceal horsemen who could attack an enemy's rear once it had entered the pass. The southern end at the *nuhaidain* would be easy to defend even against a large force and the way to Riyal would then be blocked.

I would discuss it with Abu Hamesh the next day and decide our tactics, especially the need to conceal the Naha spearmen who would play a crucial part in the ambush. Even now they were to be seen foraging for saplings, which they were splitting and shaping into spear shafts with their daggers. The spearmen would have to be positioned throughout the whole length of the pass to check the Riyal el Ma, whilst the horsemen in reserve at the quarry could charge their rear as the ambush was made. Much would depend upon timing and upon whether the Nahas would follow a proper battle plan, which must be put to Abu Hamesh with much firmness and tact. I set the Saudis to find poles with which to move rocks to provide more cover close to the *nuhaidain*.

The other matter was the need to devise a ruse by which the Riyal el Ma could be lured into the Sha'ar Pass. This depended on how many of their warriors remained at Abha and how many had been left to defend Riyal, and so the first step must be to send a *gaum* to find this out. I would have preferred to lead it myself, but Abu Hamesh had insisted it should be left to him and as a result had gone to Riyal, accompanied, it seemed, by all the Nahas. If they found, as I hoped, that most of the tribesmen were at Abha, a diversion could be made by setting fire to some *qasrs*, which would cause messengers to be sent hurriedly to Abha to alert the Riyal el Ma. They would then rush to defend their city and would be trapped in the Sha'ar. Much care would be needed to prevent them from escaping up the shallow slopes before the Saudi horsemen charged from the quarry whilst Abu Hamesh sealed off the *nuhaidain* and the Nahas held the slopes. Everything would depend on the discipline of the Nahas, who, if defeat loomed, were likely to leave us to our own devices; success, on the other hand, would allow us to go straight away to Abha and the Nahas could be left to enjoy the fruits of victory at Riyal.

*

It had grown dark by the time Abu Hamesh returned. We could hear the Nahas talking excitedly in the distance, but when they rode into the camp at *um laj* Abu Hamesh offered no more than a brief greeting and it was not until they had eaten that he said anything about his mission; even then I sensed that there was much that he withheld. However, the general picture was clear: there were few tribesmen left in Riyal itself and most of those that remained were not of fighting age. The women and children had left the city and gone to the villages when their menfolk went to Abha. The *qasrs* were built of stone and could not be set alight but there were large storage barns on the outskirts with roofs made from branches. When these were fired – Abu Hamesh's eyes gleamed – the Nahas would gallop through the town and make such chaos that anyone that remained would flee to the mountains.

'Where did you find their store of arms?' I was all too aware that our own ammunition was limited.

Abu Hamesh's expression was enigmatic. 'Didn't 'ave time to look, just lifted some corn sacks and mares.'

I turned to the matter of tactics. 'Can we discuss how many Nahas should be put in the pass to make the ambush?'

'You'll be plenty,' said Abu Hamesh staring in front of him. 'You watch pass and we'll do fightin' after we leave Riyal.'

'But most of us must be at the ambush if we are to hold the Riyal el Ma in the pass.'

'You do that with your Saudi.' Abu Hamesh was picking his teeth.

I was horrified. 'But we agreed that firing Riyal would be just the start and after that we would all be at the Sha'ar.'

'Oh, Nahas be back in time for ambush, you not worry.'

'But what about the spears stacked on either side of the pass? They will be wasted.'

'Wasted? You good thrower yourself.'

'None of the Saudi have ever fought with spears.'

'Can learn. We've left plenty practise with.'

'You cannot mean you're taking all the Nahas to Riyal.'

'Not fair take some leave some. They'd fight each other.' Abu Hamesh continued to pick his teeth.

'It sounds like you will ransack Riyal whilst I am left to fight the Riyal el Ma single-handed.'

'No,' said Abu Hamesh. 'We come in good time to kill Riyal el Ma and capture Abha for you.'

On receiving this insult, I seethed. I paced up and down, fighting to stop myself from making a reply which would destroy the harmony we had been at pains to create. Finally I sat down without saying a word and Abu Hamesh added, 'You watch for messengers with news to Abha that Riyal's on fire, then when they leave the pass you cork it up and leave the rest to us. It'll be late and they'll have sun in their eyes.'

Plainly, it was useless to argue. I realised that I would now have to hold the *nuhaidain* myself as best I could and hope that a few of the Saudis could make the ambush so that Mubarrak and some horsemen at the quarry could charge from the rear. Whether the Nahas would arrive in time or would stay in Riyal helping themselves to loot was a chance that had to be taken, although I judged that when it came to it they would not want to miss the battle. I resolved to strengthen the defences at the *nuhaidain* next day and conceal the quarry entrance where Mubarrak would be waiting with his horses. The spears which the Nahas had spent hours fashioning and were piled on the slopes below *um laj* would now be wasted; it made me wonder what had made Abu Hamesh change his mind. With these thoughts I retired to my tent.

*

The instincts of the Nahas were similar to those of a swarm of bees in that they seemed to act in unison without any signal from a leader. On this occasion they were also noiseless, for at dawn next day we awoke to find that the Nahas' camp at *um laj* was empty, with nothing except a litter of bones to show that they had passed that way.

I now had to plan afresh, and with Mubarrak rode the pass once more from end to end, finding it empty except for a pair of vultures which circled above, drawn perhaps by some instinct to be the first for the pickings of war. Looking at them I found that my vague optimism of the night before had evaporated and the birds seemed like an omen. Mubarrak voiced all our thoughts when he said, 'They don't look as if they greatly care which side they make their meal out of.'

We reached the *nuhaidain* and levered some more rocks to provide extra cover. Since the battle would be won or lost at this narrow end of the pass I decided to defend it myself and took two of the Saudi to help me, choosing Fuad and Daud, who had shown themselves the bravest. The passage was wide enough for just five or six horses abreast and here at all costs the Riyal el Ma must be contained until the Nahas arrived. Our only advantage would be that in the latter part of the day the sun would blind the Riyal el Ma horsemen. I rode to the top of the pass where it led to Abha, finding positions where the cover was best for the few Saudis that could be spared to make the ambush. Finally I reached the quarry where I planned to conceal Mubarrak's horsemen and there I found a new disaster: it no longer belonged to us. It was occupied by several hundred sheep, and shepherd boys were still herding more from the mountain pastures above, whilst those they had corralled in the quarry were contented eating the grass.

The whole plan had now to be changed once more, for there was nowhere else that the horses could be hidden, and now there could be no charge at the rear of the Riyal el Ma when they had entered the pass. It meant that the horses could no longer be used at all and would have to be left, their only purpose being for escape if the worst befell; but at least it allowed for more Saudis to make the ambush. We placed them where they could move from rock to rock, to give an illusion of numbers amongst the piles of spear shafts left by the Nahas, which littered the pass from end to end. No tribe in As'ir had encountered such weapons and they would not know how to respond. As I rode back to *um laj* with Mubarrak I was bitter at the chance that we had lost; it was a parody of what had been agreed with Abu Hamesh. We reached the plateau, tied the horses to the posts left by the Nahas and began our wait. All day long the pass remained empty, silent but for the calls of those heralds of impending battle, the vultures.

At evening a pall of smoke could be seen over Riyal and presently there was the sound of horses' hooves. Three horsemen came into view and galloped into the pass, old men plainly not used to such a strenuous mission, for they constantly looked over their shoulders in anxiety. 'Have all the more effect when they get to Abha,' said Mubarrak, surveying them.

We waited until the horsemen had ridden the pass, then Mubarrak and the snipers moved to take up position. I went to the *nuhaidain* with my two Saudis, then levered more rocks to narrow the entrance now that the messengers had passed. I placed Fuad and Daud on ledges of rock overlooking the narrow entrance and close enough to fire effectively, then concealed myself and checked my rifle again, ejecting and reinserting cartridges. It was a fine .275 Rigby, no doubt looted from the British, for it had once been the property of a Turkish officer whose name in unfamiliar letters was carved on the rosewood butt. It was reliable and could fire clips of either five or six rounds in succession. I settled down to wait with what patience I could muster for the length of time it took for the messengers to reach Abha and for the Riyal el Ma to react.

It did nothing for the nerves, and after a while I fetched a horse and rode through the pass, speaking to each of the Saudis and joking to relieve the tension, then returned to Fuad and Daud, who were visibly taut with their burden of responsibility. I laid a hand on Fuad's shoulder.

'Is this your first battle?'

Fuad nodded.

'The worst is the waiting; after it starts it gets better. Don't shoot until you are sure of hitting and when you knock a man off his horse you'll take heart and feel brave.'

It was evening, as Abu Hamesh had predicted, before there was evidence of a reaction by the Riyal el Ma, when faint sounds reached us from the direction of Abha. These grew louder, and soon we could hear the battle cries of the Riyal el Ma echoing from the mountainsides. Before long they would reach the pass, and I moved forward to the edge of the shadows cast by the *nuhaidain* and strained to listen. I tried to imagine the scene in the pass and waited tensely for the sound of the snipers as they opened fire, signalling the start of the ambush.

I stayed there for several minutes but no shots were heard and instead the battle cries grew fainter and seemed to be strangely muffled. I rode away from the *nuhaidain* to find out what was happening, and had not gone far before I discovered the reason: the pass was full of sheep. A thousand or more were being driven towards Riyal by shepherd boys, and they had brought the Riyal el Ma to a halt as they vainly tried to drive through them.

A great opportunity presented itself, for effectively the Riyal el Ma were in a trap. I was tempted to stay and direct the ambush myself. I rode towards Mubarrak but before I could reach him a splatter of rifle fire was heard and I knew the trap had already been sprung. As I got nearer I could see that the Saudi had taken control of both sides of the pass; half of them were firing at the leading horsemen and the rest were hurling the spears, with no great accuracy, it must be said, but sufficient to terrify the Riyal el Ma. Like the sheep the tribesmen were leaderless, and, confronted by the spears, they stopped trying to drive a way through the obstructing sheep and turned back.

I decided to leave Mubarrak to hold the pass for as long as possible and returned to the *nuhaidain*. It could only be a matter of time before the Riyal el Ma, in such numbers, would succeed in forcing their way through, and once they had regained momentum the main battle would still take place at the *nuhaidain*.

I rode back there, and as I had guessed they would, a hundred or more Riyal el Ma extricated themselves and came galloping towards us. They must have thought they were through the pass, but as they reached the *nuhaidain* they were met by bullets and found themselves in a new ambush. They became desperate and charged regardless of danger but were hampered by the narrowness of the pass and its vertical walls, and this caused the horsemen to obstruct each other. In the chaos that followed Fuad and Daud fired at them at a range of only a few yards and before long the exit was blocked by fallen men and horses. This checked the Riyal el Ma, who in desperation turned back into the pass and attempted to climb the sides where they could, with the intention of avoiding the *nuhaidain*.

In the end this tactic proved successful and I found myself under attack from the rear. The battle hung in the balance, for three men could not hold out for long against so many desperate Riyal el Ma, and the defence of the *nuhaidain* began to give way. Finally, our ammunition gave out and I drew my sword and dashed into the pass, shouting to Fuad and Daud to roll down the rocks which we had kept in reserve as a last resort. However, at this moment a new barrage of thunder came from behind us.

It was of course the Nahas. From their appearance they might have been taking part in a carnival rather than a battle, for each wore five or six cartridge belts and was festooned with sheaths of daggers sticking out at crazy angles. They scattered the horsemen who were upon me, cleared the *nuhaidain* and drove them back into the pass itself.

Here once more the Riyal el Ma met the sheep. By now these were shepherdless and, harassed, they had evidently decided that their best option was to return to the quarry where they were corralled. Once again they blocked the pass. The Nahas now divided, some taking the eastern slopes and some the western, and then they galloped towards the piles of spears that remained. It was a practised manoeuvre in their best tradition; one after the other each leaned from his horse and seized a spear. In a few seconds the air became alive with lethal darts, and confronted by these the Riyal el Ma threw down their arms and fled, swarming on foot over the steep rocks of the ridges above. Few reached safety and many fell from the rocks they tried to scale.

Abu Hamesh came and found me. I had been hit on the head with a rifle butt and, concussed, was sitting on the ground. I looked up groggily. 'You barely came in time.'

'The right time as promised,' replied Abu Hamesh.

*

Soon the Sha'ar Pass became silent once more, empty except for the sheep which had regained their quarry and resumed their grazing, whilst the vultures quickly settled on their feast of carrion, soon joined by all the vultures of southern As'ir.

It was time to retrieve the horses from *um laj* and make our way to Abha. In doing so we were alone, for by the time we left the Nahas had mysteriously disappeared.

For the bewildered citizens of Abha the sudden departure of the enemy had left a strange hiatus which made them fearful that some new invader was about to appear. Consequently, as we arrived there was an unwonted silence and the streets were empty. It was a while before the starving citizens dared to show their faces, but when they found out what had happened they were completely overcome. Suddenly, the city was filled with jostling crowds and when they recognised me I was mobbed in the streets. Much celebration followed, but before long this was interrupted and new war cries were heard; many feared that the city was indeed about to be attacked once more. But in fact these cries came from the Nahas, who at this moment came galloping through the streets, firing their rifles in the air in an alarming fashion. They certainly looked spectacular: instead of rags they now wore expensive *firwahs* and *abbas* with multicoloured head-cloths that trailed in the wind, and their mares had splendid saddlecloths. As soon as they saw me they reined to a halt, drew into line and yelled their Naha greeting: '*Al hamdhu l'illah*. To our blood brother may God grant long life and strength and let him now be rich.'

Then there was a great clatter as the Nahas threw down their rifles until they formed a great pile in the square. 'No more shall Ullobi warriors be without arms, for here are guns,' they shouted.

Behind them came a line of mares, which they began to untie, followed by two splendid fawn *dhalals*. 'No more shall Ullobi's warriors fight their battles on foot, for here are horses and here are camels.'

This continued, under the direction of Abu Hamesh, until exactly half of everything they had looted was placed before us: rifles, daggers, ammunition belts and clothes of every description, in a pile which grew as more and more baggage animals arrived. Even this was not all, for following the camels a flock of sheep was driven into the square. 'No more shall the people of Abha starve,' they shouted. 'For today they shall feast with Nahas.'

With surprising swiftness the beasts were slaughtered and fires were lit for roasting them so that the people of Abha might celebrate their deliverance. It was not surprising that in no time at all the Nahas became very popular indeed.

After the feasting the saga of the Battle of Sha'ar Pass was told by Abu Hamesh himself in his own particular style. His version of history was colourful rather than accurate, and when he reached the great climax of the battle the people of Abha might be forgiven if they failed to grasp the exact timing of the arrival of the Nahas.

As he finished and others took up the tale I drew Abu Hamesh to one side, for he was determined to find what exactly had taken place at Riyal.

'Your Nahas look half starved,' I taunted him. 'Tell me truthfully,

Abu Hamesh, did you feast your Nahas well?'

'We feasted like warriors, God be our witness.' Abu Hamesh's expression gave nothing away.

'And where did you eat?'

'At well of *um laj* which is in the Jebel . . .'

'The well and the place I know, and I know that it was water that you drew from the well in order that you might drink the water. But what did you eat?'

'The choicest most delicate pieces, we ate them all and they were sweeter than lamb, tastier than dried camel meat, rarer even than the *fagah* truffle.'

'And what you ate, did it have a name?'

Abu Hamesh burst into noisy laughter, and his face shone with animal glee, revealing his remaining teeth. 'So it has truly proud one. Name is Riyal el Ma.'

# Chapter 26

FOLLOWING THESE CELEBRATIONS the first thing I did was to go to the Manadhir in search of some member of the Ahl Yazid so that I could discover exactly what had happened. The Riyal el Ma had, it seemed, made several attempts to dislodge the Sa'er, this lawless tribe of outcasts who had been my captors, but these had proved costly, and when they failed they left the Sa'er alone, in the belief that they would starve when food ran out. Little did the Riyal el Ma know that the Manadhir held limitless supplies and with its own deep well was equipped to survive a lengthy siege, as many invaders had found to their cost. The Sa'er, still at the Manadhir, presented an inconvenience, but I decided that it was a problem that would have to wait whilst more pressing matters were dealt with. In particular, I wanted to find out what had happened to your own family and the rest of the Ahl Yazid. I quickly discovered that Hassan ibn Aidh, after he had killed the Saudi governor, had tried to seize the Amirate and planned to fight the Saudis when they returned. Other members of the ibn Aidh evidently thought differently, and fearing to be involved in this mad enterprise, had gone into hiding; likewise the bin Mufarrih, in case they were accused of complicity in the murder.

The whereabouts of your own family was my first concern, for in your absence it was plainly my responsibility to protect them. It seemed that they had fled the city and gone into hiding but had covered their tracks lest the Riyal el Ma should find them; I was sure that they would have survived, otherwise it would have been known at Abha. The problem was that the citizens had become so cautious, and were so faithful to you, Tabarhla, that they would never have dared to reveal whatever they knew for fear that word might reach the Riyal el Ma, of whom they were still terrified.

I left Mubarrak and the Saudis the task of keeping order at Abha until a new governor arrived from Riyadh, and next day set about the task of finding your family. Their hiding place could not be Nejidah for it would have been too easy for the Riyal el Ma to discover them. I decided to search for my trusted friend ibn Musa, the baker, who better than any could find out what had become of them. When I found him the poor man could hardly contain himself: he couldn't believe that I had survived, and he declared, 'I swear that I have never ceased to grieve that I let them take you away before my eyes, oh woman of the um Bina!' He had known who I was in spite of my disguise.

I drew him aside so that we could not be heard. 'Ibn Musa, there is something I wish you to do. Find out what has happened to the family of the bin Tahir, for whilst Tabarhla remains in Riyadh I must protect them. They are not at the Maqabil, which has been stripped bare, and they will have not dared go to Nejidah.'

Ibn Musa beckoned to his son to take charge of the bakery and disappeared into the crowd. An hour passed, and more tribesmen arrived from the outlying villages to celebrate, a scene, I reflected, that must have taken place many times in the past when the city had been taken and retrieved. Late in the afternoon, ibn Musa came elbowing his way through the crowd. 'They are safe,' he whispered. 'I have sent to tell them that you are here. They are at the house of ibn Sawah, the blind *mut'awah* at Dhohyah. Abdullah is there too.'

It was now late afternoon and it was some time before I could find the mountain path that led to Dhohyah. After an hour's riding I came to a shepherd's hut and stopped there to ask directions. The shepherd recognised me, and throwing a *firwah* about his shoulders and shouting to his family who crowded behind, untied his horse and led me out into the dusk. We made our way up a path in the bed of a dried-up wadi, where the horses stumbled on the stones, and after a while reached the tiny oasis of Dhohyah, with its cluster of small farms. The *qasr* of ibn Sawah was in the court-yard of a farm whose livestock, mainly camels, made a great noise at our approach.

As soon as the family saw me the whole place exploded into life. From storage barns and other makeshift quarters they emerged in ones and twos, and every reed lamp was lit so that they could examine me. What struck me was how well they had survived the exile, for they were in much better shape than the half-starved citizens of Abha. Their excitement was intense, for they all assumed that since I had been freed you could not be far behind, and when it transpired that you were still in Riyadh their spirits fell. However, they persuaded themselves that you must indeed return soon, and I did not dissuade them. I eased their disappointment by telling them the news that the Riyal el Ma had been driven from Abha and they would soon be able to return home.

It was some time before the full story of their exile came out and it was possible to grasp what had happened. Your family had escaped from Abha at night and had reached Dhohyah after walking for several days. Once they got there Ayesha had approached ibn Sawah, the blind *mut'awah* who had married yourself and Sheikha Na'ema, and begged for *dakhala*, protection for herself and her family. This gentle man at once gave them refuge, offering Ayesha his own *qasr*, and set about seeking quarters in the adjoining farms, where in the end hiding places were found for all. Much deprivation followed, for food was scarce and their survival had depended upon Abdullah, who reached Dhohyah some days later after he had escaped from the Maqabil. Rice and corn were in short supply since the farm produced little except animal fodder, and in the first months the family had been reduced to eating almost every kind of animal that existed in the oasis, and on one occasion even lived for a week on locusts; they had eaten monitor lizards, jerboas and also a fox, which in normal times might have been considered profane. Eventually horses were obtained and Abdullah rode out in search of bustards, and weakened gazelles that could be run down. Facing the threat of starvation, all had made common cause, and the usual customs and division of the household into separate harems ceased so that by and large everyone lived and ate together, even battling with each other for the last bean in the stew pot.

I examined them closely. Of your wives, Sheikha Ayesha had changed the most and seemed to have resigned herself to what was effectively widowhood. Her spontaneity and enthusiasm had gone, and she had become aged, her bones aching from exposure. The others had rubbed unguents into her joints and wrapped them at night in herbs; even so, when she knelt to pray it caused her much pain and difficulty.

By contrast your other wives, freed from the constraints of the Maqabil, seemed to have survived very well, as had their sons Zahl and Bandar, both now five years old and inseparable companions. They had even contrived catapults to make their own contribution to the pot, although this proved not always popular with the local farmers. Sheikha Nura's way of life had changed the least, for somehow she still possessed slaves and spent some of the day in her own quarter on the upper floor of the house of ibn Sawah. In this setting she was surprisingly well groomed and immaculate in matters of dress, and she remained distant from the others. Sheikha Na'ema had reacted differently, for she seemed to have thrived on hardship and had a new found independence that seemed somewhat unconventional.

It was decided that since it would take time for the Maqabil to be made ready the family and I would go meanwhile to Nejidah, from where Abdullah could ride to Abha. So after a short time, when camels and litters had been obtained, the family set off for their summer quarter in the mountains.

Somewhat to my surprise, Sheikha Na'ema, dressed in a make-shift riding habit, rode alongside Abdullah and myself. During the course of the journey we discussed the affairs of Abha, and Abdullah made an important decision. He did not believe the guardianship of Abha should be left to a few Saudis, however popular and capable their leader. It would only be a short time before some sheikh of the Ahl Yazid returned to make trouble, and he decided that he must get there first and be in a position to outface anyone who might have ambitions of his own. I had to agree: what Abdullah must do, I suggested, was to hold and open *majlis* for as many of the Beni Mughei'd as could be gathered, and seek their agreement that he should act in your place until all the Saudis returned. It was decided that I should remain at Nejidah to manage the return of the family to the Maqabil when that proved possible.

My plan is then to return to Riyadh as soon as I can do so to make a further attempt to persuade ibn Saud to release you.

# Chapter 27

THESE TURNED OUT to be my father's last words to Tabarhla, for now I had read the last letter. This brought me back to reality with a jolt, for it showed that, as Father had said at the beginning, his purpose was to acquaint Tabarhla with the facts in order that he would be well prepared on his return to Abha, and this was an event which was assumed to be imminent. The fact that he had not received the letters was heartbreaking, and made worse by the evidence that he never saw them even when eventually he did return.

However, there remained a package that bore only Father's name in Arabic letters. As I opened it, even a cursory glance was enough to tell me that this was something different, and evidently not part of the history of Abha since it quickly progressed to other matters. It became clear that it was in the nature of a personal testimony such as might be used by a writer preparing his auto-biography. Perhaps this was his intention: here was my father for the first time recording thoughts about his past life, matters which he had excluded from the other record. For me this was what I wished to hear beyond anything else. It was his own testimony, in a word it was himself. The writing starts at the point where Abdullah had left to go to Abha.

*

When we reached the crossroads that led to Abha Abdullah left us, and as a result I found myself riding to Nejidah alone with

Sheikha Na'ema; a *nasara* escorting a sheikha, which, if it were known, would be considered most improper, and in some parts of Arabia an outrage or worse. This must have occurred to Sheikha Na'ema too, for she spoke not a word, and after a while slowed her horse and rode some distance in the rear. In this fashion it seemed that a degree of propriety had been restored, much to my relief.

However, before long Sheikha Na'ema halted her horse and remained where she was. I went on unaware of this, but when I realised what had happened I turned and retraced my steps, fearing that some misfortune must have befallen. I found her sitting motionless on her horse and glaring at me in a manner that distinctly unnerved me. A moment later a storm broke over my head. Her eyes were wild. She exploded in a torrent of words that came even faster than she could form them and at times were scarcely coherent.

'You deserted us,' she screamed. 'You didn't care what became of us. You didn't stop to care. If it hadn't been for me and Etza we would all have died. You had sworn, you and my husband, to protect us, then you deserted us. You left us to fight for ourselves, escape from Abha on our own and somehow find shelter with strangers.' She didn't pause for breath.

'You are out of your mind,' I protested. 'You know quite well what happened. The Wahhabi came and took us away to Riyadh.'

'If you had been real warriors you wouldn't have let them take you away. You would have fought them.'

'But, Sheikha Na'ema, you don't understand, we could do nothing. They were an army of ten thousand men. Sometimes you have to retreat, or even surrender. It's one of the rules of war. You live to fight another day, which is better than being killed.'

'What rules are these? I will tell you what rules they are. They are just part of a great big game that men play. The women don't count; they are left to look after themselves and pray.'

'But, Sheikha Na'ema, we were seized as hostages. I got away, returned to Abha, was put in a dungeon from which I escaped and finally came back. It's all part of fighting.'

'You fought, you fought very well, only you lost. Then you made friends with the Wahhabi so that at the end you have a wonderful story to tell each other. Battles, victories and all the rest, what are they? Just a great big game for men to play and make stories out of while women bake bread, bear sons, make a home.' I bowed my head as the tirade continued. I abandoned any attempt to reason with her and simply waited for whatever demon had taken possession of her to go away. When at length that happened she burst into tears.

I wanted to comfort her, reach out and touch her, but she would not have allowed it; how could she have? Eventually our journey was resumed in silence, but then as we reached Nejidah, Sheikha Na'ema turned and said, 'Teach me, teach Abdullah, teach all of us, so that we can fight with swords the way you do.' Her tone was so innocent that I thought she must be living in some realm of fantasy of her own.

It was a long time before I could view this episode in perspective, for it had unsettled me. I had to admit that part of what Na'ema said was true, for what reason was there that women should be passive hostages to fate, accept their lot and not learn how to defend themselves? Why should a young, strong woman be much different from a youth, and what reason was there that she should not be trained to use a sword just like a man? Certainly, I reflected, it would be a good idea to teach Abdullah and his friends proper swordsmanship in place of the primitive kind practised by the Beni Mughe'id. If Abdullah chose he could covertly teach Na'ema, but that would be his affair, although a woman warrior was not exactly something I could easily picture; certainly it would be impossible for me to teach her, that much was obvious. This decision came as a relief, yet my discomfiture was not to be so easily assuaged for Na'ema had touched a nerve. I wanted more than anything to return to my normal life in the city.

*

At Abha I found a frenzy of activity as the citizens resumed their normal lives, and the sight of Abdullah gave them heart. As the son of Tabarhla and also, as they now learned, the recent saviour of the Bin Tahir family, they assumed that he would take charge, although the true test of that would come when the Ahl Yazid returned. However, when that happened the sheikhs who came were elderly, long past fighting age and there because the ibn Aidh and the bin Mufarrih were so wary of each other that where one family went the other followed. When they found that Abdullah had taken charge it suited them quite well, for it saved argument between them, and they readily settled for this solution.

At the Maqabil Abdullah found that there was much to be done. As soon as his return was known many of the old servants and slaves reappeared, grateful to find that they could resume their old positions in the household, and at once set about making it ready for the return of the family. In a week they had finished and he was able to send fresh camel litters to bear the family from Nejidah. Then, as all thought fitting, the harems and the old hierarchies were soon re-established to the satisfaction of mistress and slave alike. Truly, it seemed that the old days had returned and that everything was just as it had been before.

As soon as I could do so I returned to my villa in Abha to enjoy the domestic comforts that I had missed for so long, and much to my relief I found that little had changed. I had my personal slave and two other servants who managed the affairs of the household, and for relaxation there was Muna, an unmarried daughter from one of the tribes. Actually she was the latest of a line of daughters provided as part of Abha's hospitality. So far as the Beni Mughe'id were concerned the maidens were my wives, and it was naturally accepted that if one ceased to please she was returned to her family in the customary way, as were any that became pregnant, so that the child could be reared in its own family. Neither eventuality was a matter of disgrace, for being a wife of Ullobi was widely regarded as an honour whilst for the returning daughter a new husband would quickly be found.

Bedu maidens were comely, although not all were as slim as might be wished and the best came from the leaner mountain tribes. These had been brought up to present themselves with much care, without excess adornment with henna, and all body hair immaculately removed; certainly no one could have faulted their willingness to please. Altogether it was a satisfactory arrangement, and probably unique for a *nasara*, although I was inclined to regard it as payment in kind for services rendered and therefore my natural due. It was one of the rewards of the life of adventure that I had chosen, and I had grown to have a great fondness for the Bedu customs and the simplicity of their daughters, brought up to ask no questions of life.

Sometimes I found myself comparing them with the girls I had known in England, whom I often recalled with fondness. When I was young what had seemed so permanent had always proved to be transient, just as it was now. I thought of Lavender, Lavender Dolittle, whom I had married, and Ivor the wonderful son she had borne me, but more often I thought of Emma, the gorgeous Emma Littleboy whom I had loved to distraction. If I had married Emma instead of Lavender I might have remained in England and settled down to the life of a regimental officer, and the call of the wild places of the earth might never have beckoned. Emma Willoughby . . . if only.

I recalled the day when Lavender had told me she was pregnant and the fear that passed from her to me. I felt helpless, and sought out my father and told him; then my mother had to be told and together they had confronted me. Lavender's honour was at stake, and her child must be born in wedlock, whatever the cost to myself. It was like the cup of hemlock that was offered to Socrates: I had no choice, I was bound to marry Lavender Dolittle. In private my parents believed that this was for the best anyway, although they did not say so. I would put down roots where my family lived and curb the natural instincts of a Willoughby to seek adventure in distant places or, which was worse, do what Willoughbys had always done, which was fighting.

So I had done the 'right thing'. This was then, but I wouldn't do it now. I would have gone to hell and taken the Willoughby's honour with me and married Emma. I wondered what had happened to her; it made me sick to think that she might have married some dull husband at Ewelme in Oxfordshire. If I had married her I might have stayed in England, if that was what she wanted. She was cleverer than I was, and she had been to an Oxford college. She was my natural mate, an equal, which Lavender never was. I couldn't understand what I had seen in Lavender in the first place; I knew from the beginning that I would leave her. It was the reason that I volunteered to join the task force General Allenby sent to the Hejaz where I had met Tom Lawrence, who became my friend. For a while I had the wild thought of returning to England to seek out Emma, then realised that the idea was ludicrous.

These thoughts were like a swarm of bees in my head and would not go away; after a while they made me feel that there was something missing from my life. Much as I loved the Bedu maidens what I most wanted was a wife, an equal. No such person existed in Arabia, but one drunken evening I had sat next to a slave dealer called Ferdhan bin Murzuk, and my companions had asked him if he could find me a wife. Everyone thought it a great joke. Ferdhan the marriage broker, they laughed – they were just making fun of Ferdhan. I had laughed too, but somehow it hadn't been a joke.

It came as a relief to return to Abha for I had been uncomfortable at Nejidah ever since Na'ema's outburst. Something had disturbed my peace of mind which I did not understand, and it would not go away. I sorely needed the distractions of the active life of Abha.

There was, for instance, the idea of a school of swordsmanship. Word of this had reached Abdullah, and he was keen and wanted to begin immediately. He pressed me on the subject, and as the news spread others wanted to join the venture. Certainly I had known for a long time that instruction was sorely needed, for the Beni Mughe'id still used their swords to hack and slash in the old

Bedu way. They must be shown how easy it was to parry such blows and use the point of the sword as the striker was left exposed.

On my return this project gradually came together, and in one of the courtyards of the Maqabil the School of Swords was established. Soon it abounded with eager pupils as the new style of fighting, first on foot and then on horseback, caught on; indeed, if a suitable enemy had presented itself at the gates of Abha at that moment no doubt it would all have been put into practice, though for once in Abha's history none happened to do so just then.

The citizen of Abha took close interest in these proceedings and excitement rose when it was announced that the School of Swords would carry out a demonstration of the new methods. A mock battle would be fought in front of the walls of Abha between two sides of twenty swordsmen each. The swords would be blunted and all the sword strokes would be carefully rehearsed, although these details would not be revealed to the audience.

As the demonstration started there was much betting as the citizens eagerly crowded the walls to watch and cheer their chosen side. However, all did not proceed quite as intended; before it had properly begun the mock battle was interrupted by another drama which altogether stole the show. The gates of Abha were opened and out, at a great pace, came a chariot drawn by warriors. It held a maiden who clutched the carved and decorated sides of the chariot for dear life, her unplaited tresses trailing in the wind. As it entered the mêlée it became the only focus of attention.

'*Markab, markab*,' yelled the crowd and at the sight of it their excitement knew no bounds, for it was their ancient war chariot that bore a maiden into the heart of the battle to encourage the warriors. It was said that such a maiden had even been known to shed her clothes to drive them to even greater heroics.

The sword fight was forgotten as the swordsmen themselves gathered about the *markab*, quite carried away like the rest of Abha. Older citizens would have remembered it in battle, for it was the very essence of the lore of the Beni Mughe'id, a ritual that stretched far back into history. In a real battle the maiden's screams must have been partly from terror, although she was quite safe for her person was sacrosanct and she was never harmed. In its present reincarnation the chosen maiden handled herself with becoming modesty, and lubricious old men remembering their youth and straining from the walls in the hope of seeing the full display, were on this occasion to be disappointed.

It was a long time before they would let the *markab* be drawn away and much longer before the citizens of Abha ceased to talk about it, for it had stirred their imagination. Enquiries followed, and before long a discovery was made: the revival of the *markab* had been the work of Sheikha Na'ema, just as some of us had guessed all along. After this her fame and popularity soared.

*

At this point Father's account came to an end since what remained of the package had been chewed into small pieces by mice. I turned to Etza in the hope that she might be able to add to the story.

'Of course,' she said, 'I knew about Na'ema and the *markab*, also that she contrived to join the School of Swords by dressing as a youth. I did not know about her outburst during the journey to Nejidah, which was odd because Na'ema always told me everything. She had done from the beginning.'

'Na'ema's outburst seems very strange,' I said. 'I mean, she scarcely knew my father. I don't understand why her anger was directed at him. It seems to have upset him and made him think about the past; it sounds in a way as though it was a moment of truth.'

'Indeed it was, which is why she kept it to herself. Your father had done nothing to warrant her anger. He was beyond her reach and it must have been her only way of touching him. This is something I would not have wanted to hear and she would have known this and kept it to herself. In the Galla we have a saying, that to awaken the Goddess of Fire is only for the brave, because she can light a flame in the human heart which cannot be quenched.' There was anger in Etza's voice, and sadness too.

'Why do you think it had such a strange effect on father?' I said, still confused.

'Somehow it confronted him with his past. He needed to escape his own demons that troubled his soul. He could not find in reality quite all that he hoped; there would be evidence in the stars were it otherwise and his did not move. As a matter of fact soon after this they faded.'

# Chapter 28

'TELL ME WHAT happened to Tabarhla in the end.'

'Eventually, he returned to Abha. It should have been a joyous affair and certainly it gave rise to celebration, but a heavy shadow was cast over it. He was not the man everyone remembered, for whilst his spirit was buoyant his body was shrivelled like a leaf in autumn and he had the appearance of an old man. It was plain that he was sick and it seems that whilst in Riyadh he had caught a fever – the dreaded one that does not go away but causes the body slowly to waste. On his return he shunned attention and as soon as he could do so returned to the Maqabil, where he was reunited with Sheihka Ayesha in her harem.

'At once she sought my help for, I knew about such fevers and as soon as I saw him I knew that what afflicted him was the *sil*; sometimes the sufferer declines slowly, sometimes otherwise, and at all stages there is coughing of blood. This does no harm, for it is the way the evil poisons leave the body and allow it to heal. Each day plenty of camel milk must be given, especially that from a young camel directly after its first calf is born. If this gives out the milk of goats and sheep can be taken instead, but at all costs the body must be kept nourished to prevent wasting. The only medicine that helps is tea made from the leaves of the *ramram* plant.

'As soon as Tabarhla's illness became known, the Maqabil was invaded by pedlars of remedies of every sort, and especially by cauterers. They declared that the burning must be first on the left wrist, and then on the right, if there wasn't improvement. If both these failed they would have to cauterise the underside of the tongue.

However, I was determined that the treatment should be what I had planned, because cautery does not work in cases of *sil*. Here I had the support of Sheikha Ayesha, who knew this too, because one of her sons had died of *sil* in spite of cautery. Before long Sheikh Tabarhla began to improve and stopped coughing blood, the fever lessened and he even began to gain weight. At this, the mood of the Maqabil lightened and there were celebrations as hope rose.

'He stayed in Sheikha Ayesha's harem and a new *majlis* was made there so when he grew stronger he could receive visits from the sheikhs of the Ahl Yazid. They came bearing gifts and strange mixtures that were sworn to cure. Abdullah came too, to seek advice since he was in charge of the day-to-day affairs at Abha.

'Sheikh Tabarhla was not allowed to receive visits from Nura and Na'ema, and I would not let him go to their harems because young women often sicken with the *sil* themselves. Winter was coming, which is a bad season, for *sil* sufferers need sunlight and in winter there is not enough strength in the sun. Besides, it means that husband and wife sleep under the same quilt, covering all of them and drawn over their heads, so the *sil* often spreads from one to the other.

'At all times I gave them hope and told them Sheikh Tabarhla would live for years. Everyone knew that in the end the *sil* carried away all that it touched, but this was something that was not spoken of in Sheikha Ayesha's harem.'

*

Etza's voice had shrunk to a whisper and to my great disappointment the history of Abha ended here. It seemed just to peter out. Etza lapsed into silence, her face was immobile and she stared in front of her as if she had seen a ghost.

'But what happened?' I cried. 'I want to know what happened to my father. When I first came here you made if clear that he was killed fighting, but I want to know exactly how that happened. It is what I came to Arabia to find out.'

'I have told you everything that I know. What came later I cannot say because I was not at Abha. I left when I married and came here to Ayinah where my husband was.'

'What happened to the others? What happened to Na'ema, and what happened at the Manadhir with the Sa'er?'

'I believe that Sheikh Tabarhla died after about a year and Sheikha Ayesha followed him to the grave within the year, as I expected that she would. She had been very close to him, and surely it was the will of God that they should die and be together. Abdullah became Amir and made his peace with the Saudis. Sheikha Nura remained at Abha but is no longer a sheikha and became an outcast from the family – I do not know why. I believe that the Sa'er were expelled from the Manadhir by some kind of ruse. I heard your father was killed in a skirmish, some quarrel that no one knew about. He was found afterwards near one of the gates, and given a proper burial. That is all that I know.'

'Then what happened to Na'ema? She must know more about my father. Is she still at Abha?'

'She is not at Abha. I do not know what happened to her.'

'But Etza, you were her slave. You loved her and she depended upon you, so how could you not know?'

'I did not see her after I left. As I said, I came to Ayinah, which was a very isolated place at that time. Abha was a world apart. As I have said, that is all I know.'

'Then I am determined to find out more. If you cannot tell me I must find Na'ema, because I believe that she will know what happened to my father.'

'As I said, Sheikha Na'ema left Abha a long time ago.'

'And you do not know where she went or, for that matter, why it was that she left?'

Etza shook her head.

'Surely,' I cried, 'you must have seen it in the stars which tell you everything. I've got to find her.'

She raised her hands in a gesture of resignation. 'It's foolish for you to search for her. She will be at peace, and the place is known only to God. It is far better that you should search not for Na'ema but for yourself. I have been observing you. You lack harmony and you neglect your own needs. For instance, why are you not married? In your heart you are one of us, so why do you not become a Muslim and discover peace? Let me find you a maiden who will please you and bear you sons, and then you will be surrounded by a family and you will cease from searching.'

'Etza, I truly thank you, but my mind is made up. I must find out everything. I will leave, and first I will search for Na'ema, because I believe that she can tell me the things that I wish to know. But I do not know how to find her unless you help me. Etza, I believe that you are hiding something from me.'

She looked away and it was a while before she spoke. 'If you are so determined, all I can tell you is this. In the stars I see a woman who lives by the sea. She lives on her own. Perhaps she is the one who can answer your questions.'

'Is this person Na'ema?'

Etza shook her head. 'That I cannot say.'

'But where is she, and which sea is it?'

'These are questions I cannot answer. All that I know I have said.'

I did not believe her, I could not. Yet why should she be so intent on making such mystery of Na'ema? It was just the same with my father – there must be something she did not wish me to know. I cajoled her, entreated, protested, but all was in vain. She closed up like an oyster in a storm and a great gulf seemed to open between us, perhaps the difference between our two cultures.

*

For all my anguish and frustration I had to admire her. She was so determined, so proud in her bearing, so statuesque in her person. I knew that she must have had the same effect on others that she had on me and I understood now why, even as a slave, she had been so indispensable. As I left Ayinah I was moved to tell her so.

'Handsome, charitable Etza,' I said, 'I shall remember you. A slave you may have been but in reality you are a princess, a true princess of Arabia.'

Her manner changed and a far-away look came into her eyes as she spoke. 'What you have said happens to be true. Indeed, I was born a princess, not of Arabia but of my own country. In Addis Ababa, where we lived, my father was the chief of the Galla, but the tribe that ruled there was the Amhara and it was they who provided the emperors. So they were rich and we were poor. One night my father had a dream in which the Prophet called out to him and commanded that before he died he must make the pilgrimage to Mecca. Then he would be blessed with riches in heaven, and would gain the right to call himself Haji, although the Prophet himself did not refer to this particular detail. So the decision was made, and in due course we set out for Mecca, the whole of our family, my father and mother, my brothers, my three sisters and myself. It proved to be an arduous and costly journey. We crossed the oceans and finally reached a port called Mukalla, where we joined a caravan bound for Mecca. By now much of my father's savings had been spent and we had to pay the heavy taxes levied on pilgrims by the Sheriff of Mecca. Worse was to come, for robbers descended upon our caravan and before we reached the holy city we were penniless. One by one my sisters were sold in a desperate attempt to obtain the means to continue, and finally I was the only one left. I was my father's favourite and he swore that he would never sell me even if we all starved, yet that is what happened. Before the family reached Mecca and could enter the *ka'bah* I too was sold to a slave dealer. I will not bore you with what happened after that, although I can tell you that those things never caused me to harden my heart. What you have said is correct: once, long ago, I was indeed a princess.'

She took from her neck a chain bearing an ancient and battered bronze medallion. 'If you do find Na'ema I wish you to give her this.' A tear welled in the corner of her eye. 'It belonged to someone that she knew and it will be precious to her.' For a moment I thought that at last the veil of secrecy might be cast aside, but I was mistaken.

Next day I made ready Dukhaala, left Ayinah and set my course for Jeddah and the coast of the Red Sea.

# Chapter 29

THE JOURNEY PROVIDED me with plenty of time to ponder the enigma of Etza. I was certain that for whatever reason she had concealed much more than she would reveal, and it was not just a whim. There was some solid reason that made her hold back, as though she had been forbidden, perhaps by Na'ema herself, to reveal what she knew. I could detect the fear lurking in her eyes, like that which had come into them whenever there had been mention of the Ihkwan. However this might be, I would have to find Na'ema if I was to reach the truth of the matter and finally discover what had really happened to my father. That his death had been more that just a casual mischance I was instinctively sure. He could have died a hero in the cause of Abha; equally well, he could have been regarded as a marked man by the Ihkwan who, if they knew of him as they must by this time, would have excoriated him as a *nasara*.

From the beginning of my journey I missed Etza terribly, her knowledge and understanding and the warmth of her companionship during so many months of our intimacy. I missed the colourfulness of her household at Ayinah as well. Without Etza Arabia once more became a vast empty continent where I journeyed alone, with no guidance from any other. I was all too aware that from now on I was my own *mahrah*, but so confident was I of my mission that I saw it not only as my duty but exactly what my father would have wished. He would have regarded it as a matter of family pride. Obviously, it was only by finding Na'ema that I would have any chance of following his trail, yet once more

I wondered if this was just a coincidence or whether there could have been some unfathomable connection between them.

The task I had set myself was indeed formidable. I had already decided that the woman who lived by the sea must be Na'ema. I asked myself what the circumstances could be that would make such a person as Na'ema disappear and live alone; I had not heard there were hermits in Arabia. I began to regret that I did not have a degree in psychology and wished I could understand what makes a hermit – perhaps it was some horrendous event, a mental trauma or some consuming religious passion. I had heard of Bedouin who had become outcasts, murderers for instance, but it was always said they did not survive excluded from the tribe, whereas the stars clearly showed that, whatever else, Na'ema was alive. I realised that I would need to develop an insight into her mind: she must have been physically and psychologically strong, but then again, what could induce the wife of an amir to become a hermit? And how did the sea come into it? I recalled what I had been told, that she had once been stolen by pirates, so perhaps the sea was part of her upbringing and familiar to her.

In order to survive, water must be key, and this might offer a clue. I resolved to discover more of the geography of the Red Sea and the coastline of the Hejaz and the As'ir. I would cable the Naval Bureau to find out what they knew about the coastal tribes in the thousand miles between Aqaba and Yemen and the places where water was to be found. As soon as I reached Jeddah I did so, and in due course received a salutary answer: there were no settled tribes anywhere on the Red Sea coast because there was little water and the Bedouin hereabouts were nomadic. The reply added that the Bureau was relieved to hear from me for they had feared that I must have disappeared or be dead. There were from time to time naval vessels in the Red Sea and they repeated their offer of help if I needed it. They added that there were no ports between Yenbo and Jeddah and the Yemen except small ones at Jaizan and Hali, which were unsuitable for naval use, which I already knew, having sailed the coast with Vartak. The Bedouin found pasture after the winter rains and a single crop of millet was sometimes grown before they moved on. There was some local fishing and fish were plentiful, as were oysters and clams on the shore. This information came from frigate captains who had patrolled the coast in support of Colonel Lawrence in the desert war.

It was not a promising start, yet as time went by I began to have an instinctive confidence in Na'ema herself and a belief that she would somehow survive even in such an inhospitable setting as the Bureau described, just as she had done at Dhohyah. I tried to imagine what I would have done in her situation: by some means I would have to find a supply of water and if there were no wells or wadis then a catchment might be contrived. Also, I would learn to fish.

I decided to test my ideas by surveying as much of the coast as I could reach from Jeddah. I loaded my saddle-bags and set off northwards in the direction of Yenbo, riding several hundred miles and making camp each night. The conditions in late October allowed me to ride for much of the day, but the coast I explored was a succession of featureless sand dunes and what villages existed were inland and thus malarious. This coast was bleak and waterless, as the Bureau had said, and I saw very few Bedouin nomads. I was relieved to return to Jeddah.

However, I did make one discovery. I noticed that at all the settlements I passed there were green flags to be seen, showing that Saudis had passed that way. I was convinced that any hermit would attract the interest of roving Wahhabi *ulemas*, especially if the hermit was a woman. Consequently, it was obvious that it would be better to concentrate my efforts further south, which would be out of their range.

I decided to move my base to the town of Qunfidah, which was where my Arabian travels had begun the year before, and this caused me to reflect on how much had happened to me since then. From Qunfidah I explored the coast northwards and then southwards but even there all I found was the same succession of empty sand dunes without vegetation; certainly no place where anyone could survive.

After two months of searching this inhospitable coast my frustration mounted, yet my instinctive faith that Na'ema had survived did not lessen. As I reflected on the stories that Etza had told me about her – as well as what she had declined to tell me – I was increasingly convinced that somewhere on the coast of As'ir I would find her. Unfortunately, from Etza's account one vital piece of information was missing, which was Na'ema's origins. It was known that in the latter part of her childhood she had been stolen by pirates but nothing else – Na'ema, no doubt for psychological reasons, had no memory of this terrifying event. She knew that with other slaves she had been sold to a slave dealer and taken to Abha and that was all. Etza, who must have suffered a similar fate herself, would not have sought the details for the last thing she would have wished was to disturb this precious remnant of Na'ema's memory. It was enough that she had been stolen from the Red Sea coast, and from the manner of her speech this must have been the As'ir.

All of this resonated with the woman who lived by the sea, whom Etza had seen in the stars. It might be that by some natural instinct she had returned to the place of her birth, and I was more convinced than ever that I was right to follow this theory. I would continue my search however long it took, even if I had to return to do so winter after winter.

There was, however, something of significance that caught my attention: in searching south of Qunfidah I came across the dried-up bed of a wadi, known as the wadi Yiba, which I recalled had been marked on one of Bridgewater's maps, together with another further south which I had failed to find, although this might appear when the rains came. It made me think that there might be others that were unmarked where the mountain spine lay closer to the sea by the Yemen border, though this would be hard to reach on account of the distance from Qunfidah – nearly two hundred miles.

But then I had a break. I found a packet steamer that would transport me, with horse, either to Hali or Hodeida. Hodeida was on the border with Yemen, and that would have to wait for later, but Hali was a better prospect. It was where I had lodged whilst waiting for Vartak and his *Alhambra* and it would allow me to search Bridgewater's wadis. I booked my passage and was pleased that finally I passed myself off as an Arab, with no question asked. I must have been mistaken for a returning pilgrim, which was what from my frayed appearance I must have looked like.

At Hali I found the lodging that I had used earlier and explored the town. Once again, I noticed the barriers of driven stakes offshore which had puzzled me earlier, and which I now decided would certainly have been used as a defence against marauders from the sea. If Na'ema had been stolen, could it have been from here, or somewhere like it? I decided that Hali was a good base from which to continue my search.

*

I carried enough food and water for an expedition of four or five days, and I explored the coast north of Hali until I reached the part of it I had already examined when riding from Qunfidah. After this I searched southwards towards the Yemen, but in both directions the coastal dunes were wild and deserted and I saw no one, not even a single Bedu. However, on the return journey from my second trip, there were grey clouds overhead, and although rainfall was unusual in these parts before December, there was a sharp downpour. In a matter of minutes patches of green appeared as the landscape stirred, which Dukhaala scented, and her mood became alert.

Migrating swallows from Caucasia descended on the coast in their thousands, settling on every resting place, their tiny bodies shrunken after their flight across continents. Soon other migrants arrived: terns, fulmars, oyster-catchers and other wading birds, whose vast flocks spread across the wet sands, soon to be followed by peregrines, there to pick off the stragglers. Some, like the swallows, moved on, but most remained, and I realised that for the seabirds these were their winter feeding grounds: plainly the seashore must have plenty of marine life, as the frigate captains had reported.

I studied the coast with an eye to survival. There was plenty of sea food to be picked up at low tide and if any of the birds bred here, especially the fulmars, there could be eggs and also fledglings which could be snared, salted and stored. My search clearly had to take account of these rhythms of nature, so I slowed my pace and walked Dukhaala, finding at once that I could pick out more detail in the landscape. I found that where birds roosted there were rocks half hidden behind the dunes, which I had missed, and realised that I should discover more by moving slowly – just as the Arab proverb points out.

I returned to Hali and with about ten miles to go I did finally see a human being, or thought that I did; it seemed to be a solitary Bedu, and my heart leaped as this was the chance to get local information. But when I reached the place several minutes later the figure had disappeared and I could find no sign of anyone. At Hali I tried to summarise what I had discovered thus far: there was certainly enough food, for the shore held a feast in waiting, and providing that water could be found it would not be difficult to survive. I asked the townsfolk if they collected clams or other shore food, but surprisingly it seemed that they did not. Their diet was the fish that they salted and the rice it enabled them to buy; the seafood was waiting for hermits.

My thoughts turned to Na'ema again, and I tried to put myself in her place. Where would she have chosen to live and what sort of dwelling place could she have found? The answer must be that it was somewhere that she had known when she was growing up, and if that was somewhere like Hali then it would be not a great distance from it. There was no point in my searching further the coast to the north where there were only sand dunes and no wild life. I decided to concentrate on the area south of Hali where the seabirds were.

I started by exploring the sand dunes that lay inland from the coast to look for any sign of habitation. I did not find any but there were hidden rock formations that by a stretch of imagination could provide some shelter, and I decided that these would need to be searched carefully. I resolved to explore the whole area at walking pace, which also suited Dukhaala, who foraged to find vegetation where I thought none existed.

A month passed and then the winter rains came in earnest. Water ran everywhere and I made a discovery: the wadi that Bridgewater had marked, the one I had not been able to find earlier, came to life, and its water ran as far as the sea. No doubt it was what the migrating birds were waiting for, but for me it had another significance for it was where I had seen the solitary Bedu. I made enquiries at Hali and learned that it was called the Wadi Hali, because by some mysterious underground route it fed the wells at Hali which held water for the whole season. No one knew of any well at the point I had discovered where it entered the sea, which was about ten miles south of Hali itself. They told me that the Wadi Hali and the Wadi Yiba were the only source of water in over a hundred miles of coast. It made me wonder whether there was not some way in which the water I now saw running to waste could be stored.

I went back to the place I had seen the Bedu to look for footprints, but soon realised that I would have needed to be a tracker, for all my own prints were quickly obscured by the wind. However, some days later I saw a figure in the distance at the same place as I had seen it before and hurried to the spot, but once again found no one. However, this time the sighting was certain and proved that there must be Bedu in the area. I returned to Hali and made enquiries but was told that none had been seen; furthermore, if there had been a solitary Bedu in the neighbourhood it would be known since a careful look-out was kept for nomads who rustled sheep and goats. The people of Hali prided themselves on their isolation and since this was their chief security they were extremely watchful.

This was strange, because I had definitely seen someone walking along the shore, and I decided that it must be significant that it was the same place. I determined that somehow I must contrive a hiding place where I could lie in wait until the tide revealed the oyster beds and the clams when the mystery figure was most likely to appear. Certainly the person I had seen seemed to be collecting something.

The next day I went to the same place and hobbled Dukhaala on fresh pasture some distance away, then with branches of thorn bush made a bird watcher's hide at a place in the dunes from which I could observe the shore. I began my first vigil but before long became restless and realised that this was against my nature; I would never make a detective because I didn't have the patience. It was like being in solitary confinement. To pass the time I set myself to recall fragments of poetry which I repeated over and over, remembering more as I did so. I discovered that after an hour or two in the hide it was all too easy to fall asleep – which was sure to happen at the very moment I needed to be awake.

I went to my hiding place each day and for the next week saw no one, but finally my patience was rewarded. Somewhere in the middle distance I abruptly became aware of the figure of a woman dressed in black, walking slowly along the tide's edge with her back towards me. From time to time she stooped to pick something up, presumably the clams. My pulse quickened; was it possible that I was looking at Na'ema? Then as suddenly as the figure had appeared it vanished, and I was left to doubt the evidence of my own senses. One minute she was there and the next she was not, and I could not understand how I could have failed to see where she went. I left my hiding place and went to the spot to look for footprints. They were distinct where the sand was wet but beyond that I could not follow them. There was no sign of any habitation behind the shore where as elsewhere the landscape appeared bleak and featureless, except for the dunes and a few rocks behind. I collected Dukhaala and rode back to Hali, trying to make sense of the new encounter. I began to think of the jinn which all Arabs believe in implicitly.

# Chapter 30

YET MY OPTIMISM persisted, and I made up my mind that the figure was Na'ema, that my calculations had been correct. It fitted the picture of her that I had formed and somehow it seemed right, yet I knew that if I showed myself it would scare her away, whoever she was, and then I would never know. I decided that the next step was to start collecting clams myself and leave some on the sand close to my hiding place so that I might obtain a better view if she picked them up. I collected a bagful and spread them on the wet sand at the tide's edge where I could observe what happened, then returned to my vigil and passed my time reciting poems. In due course I was rewarded, for a black figure appeared, found the clams and picked them up, which allowed me to see how she came and went. It was a matter of agility, for while she was collecting the clams she moved slowly, even with frailty, but when she had what she needed she darted away like a startled animal and disappeared into the rocks.

Next day I repeated the procedure and watched as the same thing happened. Then I started to leave the clams in small heaps as a hint that there were two of us on this shore; all were collected as though there were a natural bounty of the tide. Either she must have believed that it was a wonderful season for clams, or was it, as I now dared to think, that I too was being watched, as we never seemed to coincide at the tide line?

After the same thing had happened several times I decided that the charade had gone far enough. It was obvious that she was aware of my presence and must regard me as an intruder: it was the moment for a signal of some sort which might be interpreted as a sign that I was not a threat. I found a matchbox in one of my saddle-bags and left it on top of a heap of clams. I thought this must lead to a contact, make or break, and the next day I left another, this time filled with matches to make it even more obvious. Both were collected without any indication that my presence had been registered and the matchboxes might just as well have been clams.

I decided to play my ace: I found Etza's chain with the medallion and next day left it on top of another heap. I watched her as she picked it up and this time her response was dramatic, for suddenly she dropped to her knees and knelt, clutching the medallion, staring at it fixedly. She presented the picture of someone overcome by emotion who had seen a vision; for all the world she looked like a nun at prayer.

I emerged from my hiding place so that I could easily be seen, but there was still no sign that she even registered that I was there. I returned to the pasture, relieved Dukhaala of her hobbles and rode slowly towards the kneeling figure. All the time she remained motionless, holding the medallion in front of her. I could see the stain from the wet sand creeping up the hem of her garment and for a moment she might have been that same Naomi of the Old Testament; she was like a widow, stricken anew by grief. Her face was frightened, as though she was haunted by this contemplation of an object from her past. Yet there was no picture or engraving on the medallion, only two large dents.

As I reached her, I felt that I was an interloper, intruding on some strange personal drama. '*Salaam aleikhum*' was all I could think of saying. She did not reply; indeed, she still gave no sign of being aware of my presence, which left me wondering what to do next. I decided that I could not disturb her in this state of trance, and more than that, I had no right to be there. I departed, but when I had gone a little way turned and looked back. She was standing now and had drawn her shawl across her face so that all I could see was a pair of black eyes staring at me. She did not speak but her eyes said everything: 'How dare you?'

'I am looking for Sheikha Na'ema, who lived at Abha.'

She did not answer or move, but just stood there glowering at me. For several minutes I waited uncertainly, then turned again and rode back to Hali, haunted by the vision of this distraught woman and the eyes that pursued me.

*

For the next two days I remained at Hali, which was not what I had intended, but on the return journey Dukhaala cast a shoe. It flew off, looking like a discus, for the shoes cover the whole hoof in these parts. After this misfortune it took two days to find a farrier who could make a new set of shoes, and I was afraid that this delay would imperil such contact as I had managed to make, and even cause Na'ema to vanish.

As soon as I could, I returned to the same stretch of shore in the hope that if I stayed there long enough I might find her, although I was filled with uncertainty. I was still trying to make sense of her strange behaviour, and feared that it was all too likely she might repeat her old pattern and have disappeared. She might not even return at all.

The day passed in a fruitless search. Dusk came, the moon rose and shone luminously on the sea, and the wild calls of the night echoed across the water as the seabirds settled in their roosting places. I sat motionless on my horse, filled with a sense of the majesty of nature, the sea, the sand dunes and the rocks behind me, which as darkness came merged into a single form that loomed like a distant mountain range, the silver moonlight making snow-capped peaks. All that I could hear was the slow breaking of the waves on the shore. I felt humble, grateful to be in such a place so different from the Arabia I knew, and so beautiful. It was exactly where I would have chosen had I been a hermit myself. I would have broken the rock and built a house and lived off the bounty of nature like Robinson Crusoe.

It grew cold and I began to shiver. I was about to leave when I caught sight of the faint glow of marsh gas beyond the sand dunes, the will-o'-the- wisp, a sure omen of good fortune. As I searched the darkness before me I saw it again, not a luminous glow this time but a flicker of light, which surprised me because it was in the same place as before.

Abruptly, I came to my senses. It was not the will-o'-the-wisp but the light of a flickering candle and I suddenly remembered the matchboxes. Then the full force of this discovery struck me: I must be looking at Na'ema's hiding place.

The light, which was very faint, seemed to come from within the rocks themselves, and I went towards them in the darkness, after tying Dukhaala's halter to a stump. I crept nearer on foot and searched in the hope that I might find a cave, but by moonlight I could see that there was no way into the rock mass. I marked the spot by taking rough bearings so that I could examine it again by daylight.

Next morning I returned and checked the bearings I had taken, but in the light of day everything looked different, and though I examined the whole area I could see there was no chance of finding a cave, for the rock face was solid and unbroken. I placed a gift there, this time something more substantial, which was the foreleg of a lamb I had bought for the purpose from a shepherd at Hali. It was a mystery, yet I was certain that I had found the place where Na'ema lived; I decided that the best strategy was to wear her down, for after all she now knew I was there. Since I had started by leaving gifts of food I decided to continue doing so.

For the next two days I remained at Hali to write up my reports and then on my next visit, to my great excitement, I found that there had been a response: written in the wet sand, as by a sharp stick, were the words, 'Who are you?'

I wrote a reply, 'I am Ivor, the son of Ullobi.' I walked a short distance, then had second thoughts and decided that I had to be bolder. I returned and wrote underneath, 'I carry a message from Etza.' I decided that since she knew that I had found her hiding place, or at least the rocks where it must be, she must realise that she could not avoid meeting me, and after all the trouble I had gone to so far I was quite prepared to wait and let natural curiosity play its part. I would leave it to Na'ema to work out how and when the meeting should happen.

I returned once more to Hali but that night I awoke in a sweat. I realised that I might be wrong. Perhaps it was not Na'ema at all but someone else, some deranged woman who would think I was stalking her. It was certainly true that so far there was nothing that identified her as Na'ema except my imagination, and the medallion might not have any special significance for it could just be yet another device to ward off the evil eye. I might have invaded a stranger's sanctuary. I decided that I should make no more assumptions, for if Na'ema had survived as a hermit so could others. It might be true, as they said, that outcasts did not live for long, but these were men and therefore dependent on the tribe. No one ever spoke of women outcasts; yet why should they not exist – there were plenty of reasons why a woman might flee, fear of being stoned to death for some misdemeanour for instance, and if this were so why should not some survive? They were more adaptable and resourceful than men and would not be concerned with the tie of brotherhood with the tribe as men are. Because it was not recorded that did not mean it did not happen – perhaps there was a whole legion of women hermits. It did not have to be Na'ema at all. If it was someone else she would have every right to be suspicious of me and to disguise her movements. My presence would present a threat, yet if by chance I came to be accepted, such a person might become psychologically dependent upon me, and then if I disappeared that could be very hurtful. I slept little that night.

However, with daylight my confidence returned and once more I convinced myself that it was Na'ema. I rode off as usual and went to my hiding place, but there another surprise awaited me for I found that my hide had been completely dismantled, in fact not so much dismantled as smashed to pieces, and on the sand in front a message was written. I bent down to read it for this time the Arabic writing was indistinct. It was a vulgar word for 'depart'.

But then nearby I found another one which seemed to contradict it. This said, 'Come at dawn.' Starved of human contact, it seemed that her natural curiosity was getting the better of her as I had hoped.

I read the messages a second and then a third time, walking from one to the other in a state of mounting excitement. Now I felt sure that this must be Na'ema, and that whatever happened I had won.

*

At the first glimmer of light next day I set out once more on the journey that had become so familiar. As I approached I could see her in the distance on the shore line, and if I had thought of her as old and frail I had to change my mind for what I observed was a youthful figure striding up and down impatiently. The contrast of this with the figure that I had seen kneeling on the sand was so striking that, strange though it may seem, I was overawed, even frightened. It could not possibly be anyone but Na'ema.

I dismounted and walked towards her, holding Dukhaala's halter. Her rags of clothes were black and covered her completely, including most of her face; all I could see was a pair of eyes which glared at me as she silently took me in. There was no question who would be the first to break the silence for it was all too clear that it was she who was granting me the audience. Finally she spoke. 'Yes, I am Na'ema.' She spat the words at me and there was anger and disdain in her voice.

'I know,' I said. For a moment she stood there staring at me and the tension was tangible; then she turned and with the tiniest of gestures motioned me to follow. We walked across the sand dunes until we reached the rocks and she waved an arm to indicate where I should tie my horse. I saw that there was an iron ring attached to the rock-face and when I looked more closely I could see that there were others, enough to tie a whole troop of horses.

The rocks grew denser and larger and the passage between them was so narrow that I could barely squeeze myself through. Finally she stopped before a rock that was in the shape of a huge dolmen, upright and smooth and supporting horizontal stones above. She placed both hands on the rock, pushed and the stone moved; it was evidently partly hollow, and when she pushed again it turned on a perfect fulcrum and opened to reveal a black void beyond. I could make out steps leading downwards cut into the rock, and these we descended into the bowels of the earth; my eyes were slow to adjust to the darkness.

I sensed at once that I was in the presence of great antiquity. I struggled to comprehend it and felt as the discoverers of the tomb of Tutankh Hamoun must have felt. Or rather, it was exactly as I imagined the inside of a pyramid would be, yet unlike the pyramids this one was inhabited by a living person. If executioners affronted by my presence had jumped from the walls I would not have been amazed.

We reached a chamber, the size of an ordinary living room, carved from the solid rock by some unimaginable labour in the remote past, and as my eyes adjusted I was aware that there was a tiny amount of daylight which came through horizontal slits where flat stones had been laid on top of each other, separated by small spaces. On the side walls shelves had been cut and upon one of these she gestured me to sit whilst she settled cross-legged on the floor. She appeared very slightly to relax, although there was no slave bearing a tray of cardamoms in this *majlis*.

In the semi-darkness I looked at the cave about me. It was certainly spartan but it was also a very organised space, evidently an ancient fort which in earlier times would have been part of the defences of Hali, an outpost holding perhaps a dozen men who could keep watch for intruders from the sea. It could also have been a refuge for the Sheikh and his family if Hali was overrun, or in some other time of need, which was how it was being used now. If so, I judged that it must have been a secret retreat known only to the family that had ruled Hali, which in turn led me to wonder if Na'ema herself had been part of such a family.

She picked up a string of beads and toyed with them as she spoke. 'For a start I must tell you that I am extremely angry. I find it hard to believe that Etza could have revealed the secret of my dwelling place. She was sworn on oath to disclose it to no one, in any circumstances whatsoever, and now she has betrayed me.'

'Etza did no such thing,' I replied. 'Finding you was entirely my own doing. Etza refused to say even whether you were alive or dead. All she said after telling me the story of Abha was that in the stars she had seen a woman who lived by the sea, she did not know where or who this was. It was I who decided that this person might be yourself. I had a difficult puzzle to solve and I worked it out for myself. Since I believed that you came from the coast of the Red Sea I decided to look for you there, and for months I have searched from Jeddah to Yemen to find you. The reason for this is that you are my last hope of finding out what happened to my father. That is why I came to Abha, managed to discover Etza and have finally come here.'

'What else did Etza tell you?'

'A lot of history; but she did not tell me what happened to my father, only that he was dead.'

Na'ema rose and paced up and down. 'This is a private, most secret place. It is a wonder that you have found it since I did not believe that it could be found by anyone. It has not been easy for me to allow you to enter my sanctuary, but I see that it is intended and God's will is ever inscrutable. It must be that God has a purpose in revealing me to you, though I cannot guess what this may be.'

As the sun rose it shafted through the slits between the rocks and lit up the corners of the cave; I could see that there was another chamber leading off it, where a goat was tethered, sniffing at grain scattered on the floor. I thought of the pasture where I usually left Dukhaala and felt guilty in case I had stolen the goat's grazing. Through the rock slits there was a clear view of the shore, a full half of the compass, and one could even make out the promontory of Hali in the distance. I realised that she must have seen every move that I had made, even as I picked up the clams and placed them in piles for her, and then watched me building my hide. It was small wonder that she was so suspicious and so angry.

Na'ema spoke again, but now the fire had gone out of her. 'I wish you to repeat to me everything that Etza told you. However, I tire easily.' She pointed to her head. 'My concentration is poor and it is only at the start of the day that I can think clearly and remember. I need to consider what you have told me. Tomorrow or the next day, if you so wish, you may return and talk to me about Etza. Now I wish you to depart.'

She rose and led me to the stairway, once more seeming the frail person that I had first encountered on the shore, and I noticed for the first time that she had a disability which affected her left arm, possibly the result of a wound she had received in her warrior days. We reached the dolmen, it turned once more and I went out into the brightness of day.

*

The elation that I felt at my discovery soon gave way to further perplexity. Why should one of the sheikhas of Abha hide herself in such a place, be fearful lest someone could betray her and renounce all contact with the world and exchange with other women, the natural pastime of all women that ever lived? It was clear that she was not some religious eccentric, and in spite of her haughtiness and uncertain temper she was like anyone else. I even questioned why she had decided to admit me to her world. Was it that she was just curious, or was she perhaps more vulnerable than she seemed? She had been a resolute warrior as everyone said and what I saw now looked like a personal choice. She was certainly not starving and evidently had all the means of survival. Indeed, I wondered if she was truly isolated or might still have some link with Hali. Could it be through an erstwhile slave perhaps, or might she even venture there herself? Then again, why had Etza been so reticent about her at the end of her story, and even more so about my father? I began to wonder whether it was possible that there was some connection between the two.

On my next visit the day was dull. Soon the blessed rain was falling, and as though to greet it Dukhaala constantly threw up her head, shook herself and snorted. When I reached the cave the dolmen stood open and I made my way down the steps into the intimidating darkness.

The cave seemed oddly different, more homely in its atmosphere, and in the absence of sunlight a reed lamp was burning. It was made of bronze and hung from the wall on a heavy chain with a round bulb for the oil and a sea-serpent projecting at the bottom, holding the reed in its mouth, a little masterpiece of Arabian antiquity. In the dim light I could make out several features that I had not observed before. There was a fireplace, not at the moment in use, with slabs of dried camel dung for fuel piled on one side, and in a recess there was, surprisingly, a small well with a bucket hanging from the tiny wellhead. It was a much more elaborate dwelling than I had realised.

Not only the cave but Na'ema also seemed different, for her manner had changed: all her suspicion of me had gone and I noticed that she now wore round her neck Etza's chain with the bronze *zarar*. We exchanged greetings as if we were old acquaintances, and I sat down on one of the benches that was now graced with cushions, which was just as well if I was to act the part of historian. As soon as we started it became clear that she had made up her mind exactly how the telling of the story should proceed, and any hope I had of giving a shortened version of Etza's tale was quickly dashed. At first she hung upon every word like a child but then she started to interrupt and correct me, giving her own version of events, cross-questioning me and arguing when she disagreed. The story was treated with the gravity of a saga, where every detail is debated each time it is told, and evidently it had become her obsession.

She had also decided to have it one piece at a time, perhaps on account of her limited concentration, and so after half an hour I was bidden to stop. She needed time to remember and to reflect on what I had said. A certain glow of happiness now radiated from her and I realised that she was reliving her own part in the story as I told it; she probably planned to ensure that it would last as long as possible, and the size of the task I had undertaken began to dawn on me. The fact that I was now effectively a prisoner of this new arrangement was plainly a matter of no consequence to Na'ema at all.

Two months went by, and we had reached the depths of winter, which in Arabia can be extremely cold even on the Red Sea coast, but the cave itself was never cold; it was homely and always a place of welcome. I paid visits several times a week, though not every day since her habit of virtually re-enacting each part of the story seemed to tire her, as indeed it tired me. In general it seemed to give her much pleasure, but there were also times when it clearly caused her pain. Sometimes her reaction was so intense that I thought this must be a kind of catharsis, which left me wondering whether this was simply in her nature, or whether it was the experiences themselves which triggered such a response. On one occasion this was quite alarming: I was referring to the infamous massacre at Taif and had reached the point where the Ikhwan released their mob on its luckless inhabitants. The *ulemas* started to accost the women-folk, who were seized and beaten for the smallest infringement in matter of dress or prayer times, which grew more and more violent until in the end they started killing them.

This provoked Na'ema to fury and then she burst into tears.

'It was the same at Abha,' she sobbed. 'It was always the Bedouin women in rags who got beaten. They were not quick to grasp the danger and if they were too slow they took the brunt of the Ikhwan fury. And then . . . then . . . a most terrible thing. They seized a woman who they claimed had been caught in adultery. They made a pretence of a trial but it was obvious they would find her guilty. They dug a hole in the ground and buried her up to the waist. They tore off her clothes until she was naked and then they . . . they stoned her . . . I cannot describe . . . what happens to a woman's body . . . she . . . breaks up . . . pieces of her flew into the air.'

Na'ema became incoherent and started screaming and crying at the same time. The terror of the moment seemed to enter her as she relived the scene. I had to stop and then I was seized with guilt – I felt that I was the involuntary voyeur of another's agony of mind. I stood there hoping for the storm to pass but it did not, and after a while I decided that I must go, for I did not think it became me to remain.

# Chapter 31

I WAS KEEN to reach the point where my father entered the story, yet this goal proved strangely elusive: she would barely talk about him and seemed reluctant even to mention his name, although I was relating events in which he had taken part which she must surely have known.

My disappointment gradually turned to anger and we had an argument. 'It seems to me,' I said, 'that you always leave Ullobi out of the story and I wish to know why. Surely he played such an important part in what happened at Abha and everyone must know about him.'

She became evasive. 'These are matters that Etza has already told you about and there is nothing that I can add.'

'But Etza did not tell me what happened and how it was that he died. This is what I have come to Arabia to find out and I believed that you would be able to tell me what happened.'

'I do not know what happened.'

'I think it very strange that Etza could not tell me either.'

'Etza left Abha at the same time that I did. She went to Ayinah to be married. I had given her freedom long since and she was free to do so. I have not seen her since that time and it is a great regret to me that our ways have parted.'

'Tell me what made you, the wife of an amir, leave Abha and come here.'

'I had reasons. At that time I did not wish to remain at Abha.'

'Even though Sheikh Tabarhla had just returned from Riyadh?'

'I was not allowed to see him, much, because he was ill and

Ayesha would not let me go into her harem for fear that I would catch his fever.'

'You still have not told me why you came here.'

'As I have said, I did not wish to remain at Abha. I have my reasons but they are private ones. All that I know about your father is that he was killed in a fight, and nothing more except that it was at Abha. I believe it was by the Western Gate.' She fingered the *zarar* nervously.

'Etza said that you learned to use a sword.'

'Abdullah taught me because I made him do so.'

'When I first went to Abha there was talk in the market of a sheikha who was a warrior and fought in battles.'

'I never fought in a battle but there were skirmishes.'

'Did Ullobi fight in them?'

'I don't remember.'

'How was it that a sheikha was allowed to fight?'

'It would not have been allowed but I dressed as a youth. I had learned to ride when I was young. I would go with my brothers to the fort and play at battles. Only our family were allowed to use it because my father was ruler.'

Here she stopped and once more I was left none the wiser. She did not know more or would not tell and nothing I said would persuade her otherwise; it seemed that at the mention of my father's name she changed the direction of our conversation just as Etza had done.

I abandoned the attempt altogether. In my frustration and anger I spent days brooding on the fact that my mission had failed. I did not return to the cave and decided to leave Hali, but still for days I hesitated. I simply could not bring myself to let matters remain as they were. For my own peace of mind I had to know the truth; somehow I had to find a course that was subtler, perhaps even devious. It was obvious that I could not force my way into this secret defended citadel.

I became miserable, and my mind was preoccupied by images of Na'ema. She was in her cave milking the goat or cooking by the light of the reed-lamp on her fire of dried camel dung, or scavenging the shore, pulling oysters from the oyster beds or picking up the clams. She would be alone now once more. It made me wonder how she endured the loneliness and even whether she might have some contact at Hali after all. I tried to imagine how she passed her time and what bed she made for sleeping at night. I wondered if she watched the shore line through the tiny slits, if she was waiting for me and would come out and greet me on the sand; after all I was the only companion she had found and had now lost. I thought that perhaps I had come to be a little in love with Na'ema. I craved to return and finally I could not stop myself. We would begin again from where we left off.

Next morning I rose early and fetched Dukhaala. The winter solstice was two months past and with the stirring of spring the dawn was filled with bird calls as I rode. The tiny wadi which marked the cave still held water where it entered the sea and I was sure that Na'ema would come out to greet me. Then we would quickly end our quarrel and all would be as it had been.

To my chagrin there was no sign of her and I made my way to the cave, uncertain now how I might be received. The dolmen was closed but I pushed it as she had done until it opened, and I descended the stone stairway, fearful even that she might not be there. At once I was aware that something had changed. Na'ema was not in her normal place.

It was a minute before I could make out in the darkness that she was lying motionless on the floor of the cave. I gathered her up and placed her on the bench which was her usual seat. She seemed to recover although she did not speak. I noticed when I lifted her that she was lighter than I had expected and her left arm was swollen and now hung limply at her side.

At this point a strange thing happened, which in this context – an Arab woman in the presence of a man, and a foreigner at that – I doubt had ever happened before. With her good hand she took mine and placed it against her breast on the left side where the arm was swollen.

At first I took this to be some strange symbolic act of friend-ship, but that could not be so because it is an inviolable rule in Arabia that a woman's breast is forbidden territory to any but her husband and baby. Then I realised that she must be trying to show me something and when I recovered from the shock I realised that what I had touched was not normal at all but hard, something that felt more like a cricket ball. I am not a doctor but at that moment I wished that I had been so that I might understand what it was that she must be trying to show me.

For a moment my imagination was clutching at straws but then an image floated into my consciousness. What I had touched was the same as something I had once seen in a painting which had somehow etched itself on my memory. It is a painting called *The Baker's Daughter*.

It was painted in 1527 and is by Raphael. Its subject is a young woman, bare-breasted, sitting and viewed obliquely from the left. With her right forefinger she is pointing to the breast which is nearest to the viewer, and where her finger touches the skin there is a bluish shadow and a hint of fullness, or perhaps swelling. Her left arm rests on a cushion and like Na'ema's it is slightly swollen, the whole of the arm and also the hand. Authorities differ in their interpretation of the subject of this strange painting. Some say that for once Raphael failed to be the master of anatomy he usually was, and had lost his proper sense of perspective, but another view is that he was painting exactly what he was looking at, indeed what the subject is showing him.

The baker's daughter was Raphael's mistress. Her gaze is frank and she looks directly at the viewer; some have seen a certain haughtiness, others an expression of resignation and even nobility. There is no evidence of what Raphael intended in making such an unusual painting, but it is known that the baker's daughter entered the hospice of a convent in Rome in August of that year, 1527, and her death is recorded in the same month.

For me it was a fearful moment of recognition; I prayed that it was my imagination which had run away with me but in my heart

I knew that it was not. Na'ema was showing me just what Raphael painted in his mistress' breast, something threatening.

*

As was the case with the baker's daughter, Na'ema also was at peace with herself and stoical in the face of mortal danger. I offered to search Hali for a healer, for there were no doctors in this corner of Arabia, but this she refused. She made it plain that all she wished was that I should know how matters stood so that I should not be caught unawares, and she asked me to give her a proper burial when the time came. She showed me a shroud of coarsely woven linen in which she would be buried; it was not yet finished and if I had wondered how she spent her days, at least I now had part of the answer, for the fabric had been woven on her own primitive loom set up in a corner of the cave. I wondered, in a practical way, how it would be possible to tend and dress a woman's body after death, and we did not mention this detail, for in Arabia it is the rule that only another woman may perform this funeral act. However, she was quite clear how she should be buried: as the sand covering the rocks was too shallow for a grave to be dug, she was to lie in the cave itself. At some time in the distant past a hollow had been hewn in one of the walls for this purpose and fashioned into a shelf-like tomb, wide enough to receive a body, and now fresh stones had been placed in readiness beside it so that when she died her body could be sealed in.

It was inevitable that our relationship changed entirely; it became about human companionship in face of adversity and Abha's history was no more our focus. Often there were long silences and when she became tired she drifted into sleep; but on such occasions I was no longer bidden to depart, rather she demanded that I should remain. Etza's story was left unfinished, although perhaps for the most part it was now complete, but there was one detail that I was determined that Na'ema should explain. This was the bronze medallion on the chain with which I'd been entrusted by Etza and which had evoked such an extraordinary display of emotion when I left it on the shore for Na'ema to find.

This was evidently not a question she had expected and for a moment she hesitated. 'It is because the *zarar* protected each of my husbands. Each would have died if he had not been wearing it and it was handed down by one to the other.' She took the chain from her neck and pointed to the medallion. 'You can see the marks where bullets have struck it and been deflected. There are two, one for each husband.'

I was incredulous. 'You are saying that you had two husbands? I never heard that.'

'You could not have known because no one knew. My second husband was my own secret. It was known only to God and myself, for others would not have understood. I am pleased that it should be so but more than this I cannot tell you. I am happy as well as humbled, because it is a miracle that God in His wisdom guided Etza to find it, for she is the only one who understands all that it means to me.'

Quite simply, I did not believe her story. I could not see how it could be true, especially if the marriage was known only to God: it must be a fantasy. However, her manner was so guarded and she was so nervous as she spoke that I knew it would be hopeless to press her. Once again the book of her life snapped shut, and I was left with one more puzzle than I had before.

# Chapter 32

THERE WAS A sudden spring thunderstorm and I swear that a bolt of lightning actually passed through our cave. In the drama that followed the central part was played by the goat, which reared up in terror, tore away from the rope that secured it and dashed about the cave. However, to my utter astonishment the goat was not alone, for in pursuit of it came a small girl who darted out of the corner where the goat had been tethered and must have been hiding behind it.

She caught the goat and tied it up again, but the secret of her existence was revealed, which so far as Na'ema was concerned was quite clearly not what she had intended. The girl looked about twelve years old, and she had black hair and vivid blue eyes, at once noticeable because this was such an unusual feature in these parts, and she had about her a certain boldness of manner. I had the uneasy realisation that she must have been witness to everything that had happened in the cave all the time I had been there, and I cursed myself for my failure to observe what had been around me. It was clear that I had not been meant to see her, and as this sank in I began to be angry that I should have been deceived in such a way.

Na'ema was plainly as confounded as I was myself, and her expression turned to anguish as she perceived my anger.

'I could not tell you,' she faltered. 'I'm sorry, but I didn't think you would understand.' Her voice trailed off to a whisper. 'It must be God's will that He should make this happen. I see now that He wishes that she should be revealed to you. I didn't know His purpose, I didn't understand, I'm sorry.'

'I'm afraid that I don't understand either. Until you explain it.'

'She's my daughter, Isis.'

I noticed that Na'ema spoke only to me but said not a word to Isis, who now seated herself on the floor in the middle of the cave, carefully reordered her mop of black hair, straightened her shift and smiled. Plainly she was enjoying the accident of her liberation and showed no sign of wanting to return to her lair; in fact it was all too clear that the genie, having escaped, would not easily be returned to its bottle.

Next a strange thing happened. Na'ema rose, picked up a stick and with it wrote in Arabic letters in the sand on the floor of the cave. Isis glanced at them, took the stick from her and wrote some words of her own, looking at her mother as she did so. It was all done so naturally that this odd behaviour did not seem to be so.

Na'ema sat down beside me. 'I must explain that Isis cannot hear and cannot speak. She was born deaf and dumb. We communicate by signs, but now I have taught her to read and write so that we can talk to each other by writing in the sand.'

'I'm lost for words,' I replied. 'But it seems to me that since Isis has entered our lives you had better tell me how she comes to be here.'

At this moment I had a flash of intuition: I could see what had happened and could imagine the whole chapter of history that was Isis, for there was something about her, especially the colour of her eyes, which was familiar. I knew that I had stumbled upon the truth, but I wanted to hear it from Na'ema herself. However, so great was her confusion at this moment that I saw it might be best to offer her a little help.

'Isis is the daughter of your second marriage, is she not, and your second husband was Ullobi, my father?'

She did not answer, but instead tears began to fill her eyes and fall down her cheeks. I glanced at Isis but her expression had not changed, and it was clear that so far as she was concerned she wasn't going to let her mother's tears spoil her outing. For a while we sat in silence, broken only by Na'ema's sobbing. Finally I said, 'I do not wish to be inquisitive or intrude on what are private matters, but I think it may be best if you tell me all that happened. The time will come when you will enter another world, and I don't believe that any cause will be served by your leaving behind a mystery. Perhaps you also owe it to Isis to tell me since she can't explain her existence herself.'

'I didn't dare to tell you before. It was wrong of me. I was confused because I did not understand it was His purpose.'

'Truth, Na'ema, is what it is called. What you call God's purpose I call truth. I am *nasara* and to me the truth is sacred too.'

Na'ema hesitated. 'It is very hard for me ... I will tell ... what happened ... I will tell you all the truth. It was ... at the time of the battle at the *majlis* ... soon after that Isis was born.'

She paused again, then took a colossal breath and the story came pouring forth, accompanied by a flood of emotion pent up over the years. It was partly incoherent and she spoke so rapidly that it was hard for me to follow, but by degrees I was able to piece together what had happened.

*

The continued occupation of the Manadhir by the wild tribe called the Sa'er had by this time become the city's besetting problem. Not only were the citizens exposed to capricious sniping from the walls, but it was a running sore in the pride of the Beni Mughe'id. However, expelling the Sa'er from that fortress was a matter that was easier said than done.

Eventually, as might have been guessed, it was Ullobi who devised the ruse by which it should be done, risky though it might be. A messenger was to be sent to the Sa'er offering them the contents of Abha's treasury in return for their vacating the Manadhir and leaving Abha. Naturally, the Sa'er had already searched and ransacked the castle but had failed to find the treasury, which was so securely hidden that it could be retrieved only by means that were known to the Amir and his closest family. After protracted negotiations a truce was agreed and hostages were exchanged as a guarantee of good faith by both parties – a somewhat uneasy arrangement in view of the reputation of the Sa'er. Unknown to the Sa'er, the hostages sent by the Beni Mughe'id were in fact Ullobi and Abdullah, neither of whom was known to them, who would reveal the place where the treasury was hidden. This, as it happened, was in the principal *majlis* itself, but what the Sa'er did not know was that also hidden there were the means for the *majlis'* defence.

In the case of the legend of Odysseus the enemy in occupation consisted of the importunate suitors of his faithful wife Penelope, and the hidden weapon was the long bow hanging on the wall, which only Odysseus himself was strong enough to bend and string. The weapon in the *majlis* of the Manadhir was altogether different: it was a tapestry.

This covered the entire wall at the back of the dais and where it reached the floor it concealed the boxes in which Abha's treasury was stored. The tapestry itself was woven with scenes of hunting and figures from Arabian sagas who bore swords and other weapons, which for better effect had real handles. However, concealed behind them in the tapestry were real swords and daggers which could be withdrawn for use. In addition to the weapons the *majlis* had other means of defence, for the roof of the main chamber was made of palm trunks kept in place by ropes which also appeared in the tapestry design. This had been so designed that if the ropes were cut the trunks would fall in sequence across the floor of the chamber.

After the exchange of hostages had been completed the portcullis of the Manadhir was raised and Ullobi and Abdullah were admitted. However, a small *ghazzu* armed with rifles was hidden nearby and this included Na'ema herself. Ullobi and Abdullah were led to the dais where, flanked by two enormous negros, sat Marshaq, the leader of the Sa'er, and they were released from their bonds so that they could reveal the treasury.

Just above the floor of the dais was a wooden panel which ran the entire length of the rear wall and was concealed by the tapestry hanging above. This was held in place by springs at either end, and at a given signal these were released by Ullobi and Abdullah. The panel fell forward, striking the floor of the dais with a resounding thud, and boxes piled high with silver riyals came into view.

It was too much for the Sa'er. They surged forward and gleeful shouting filled the *majlis* whilst Marshaq himself fell on his knees, seized handfuls of riyals, and let them run through his fingers. Meanwhile the two slaves beside him were so engrossed in what was happening that they turned their backs to watch. It was long enough for Ullobi and Abdullah, who seized the swords in the tapestry, wrenched them free and fell upon the necks of the slaves before they could react. At this, with lightning speed, Marshaq leaped from the dais just before he too was cut down.

Uproar filled the *majlis* and a number of the Sa'er drew their swords and advanced on the dais, but before they could reach it Ullobi and Abdullah had severed the ropes hidden in the tapestry which held the roof beams. There was a rumble and a palm trunk as thick as a man's waist crashed lengthwise in front of the dais. It pinned down the advancing Sa'er and left them struggling beneath a cloud of white dust. Ullobi and Abdullah seized the moment to grab spears from the tapestry, which they now threw into the mass of the Sa'er, their bamboo shafts breaking upon impact. Before they could recover, the next beam fell, and after that in orderly sequence the others, some bearing sacks of flour that exploded as they hit the floor. This had been designed as a barricade to protect the dais, and the warriors holding it had the rest of the *majlis* at their mercy; however, a misfortune occurred: one of the beams jammed and Ullobi seized one of the releasing ropes and swung across the *majlis* chamber to kick it free. It was a momentary chance for the Sa'er, and one threw a *huardhi* which struck Ullobi in the side just as he had freed the beam and was swinging back to the dais. He pulled out the knife, made light of the wound and continued to fight. The beams now continued to fall, but soon the

Sa'er had had enough and flung open the portcullis in an attempt to escape.

Outside they ran into the *ghazzu*, who, with the help of the rifles left by the Nahas, shot them as they emerged. The only lucky ones were the hostages, who were later released as had been promised. In celebration the *ghazzu* ran through the streets of Abha with Abdullah in the lead, but not with Ullobi.

*

Na'ema described what happened next. 'I was with the *ghazzu* and suddenly realised that Ullobi was not there. I went back to the chamber and found him lying on the dais. He was unconscious. I knew he had been wounded but had no idea it was so serious, and I panicked. Between us we carried him to the Maqabil for I knew I must get him to Etza to dress the wound and decide what to do. I took him to my own harem.

'The wound was much worse than it appeared for when the bleeding stopped water trickled out and we realised that the knife had struck one of his kidneys. It was then that Etza used her knowledge and her great experience, for every time the wound closed she opened it again and as she did so more urine came away. This continued for days, but eventually it began to dry up and when the urine stopped altogether Etza applied her herbs and let the wound heal. Then there was much happiness in the harem for we knew that Ullobi would live to fight again.

'Then something bad happened because I found myself not wanting him to get better, or at least not too quickly. As the wound healed Etza let him walk and I helped him do exercises to regain his strength. Then I had a strange feeling, because I touched him and must have trembled; Etza saw this and promptly sent me away. I wanted to sleep on the floor at the end of his couch in case he needed anything but Etza wouldn't let me and slept there herself.

'As he recovered his strength the time came when he could walk, but I tried to stop him. It had reached the point where he was the centre of my life, for I had a new purpose and could not bear to lose it. I persuaded myself that he needed me and I lavished attention upon him, which he seemed to like.

'When I was alone I cried and did not know why I cried but now I realise that it was because I was in love. I tried to deny it because I knew that I should not be. I told myself that it was wrong and stupid and I hid it from Etza, but she saw it and we had a bitter argument. She said she would care for Ullobi and my help wasn't needed any more. After this she was watching me all the time and would never leave us alone together. She arranged everything so we should not be.

'But there came a day when she was not there, which he must have been waiting for. He caught my arms and pulled me down on to the couch beside him. I could not believe what was happening but I did not resist him as I should have done. It was very wrong of me but there was nothing I could do, and I did not dare look into his eyes for I knew that if I had I would have done anything he asked. At this moment we could hear Etza returning and he let go of me. I was angry with Etza and the next time she had to go to the market I made up things that I didn't really need just to keep her there longer. I had lost all control of myself and didn't feel any shame.

'Then I could not restrain him for as his strength returned he was hungry, craving for me. He was so strong I could not resist him. He simply took me and I had to give him what he wanted. Soon it was he who did not want to get better and he began to make out that he was ill again, but what was terrible was that I encouraged him. I couldn't help myself and whenever Etza wasn't there it always happened, but she must have guessed it. She made him walk and then run and drove him out of the harem. He went back to his own house.

'I was bereft and wanted to kill myself. Something had awoken inside me that I did not know was there, which was so strong: I couldn't bear to lose him. He was there all the time in my mind, and finally I did a wicked, terrible thing. I went to his villa and found him. It was only a few times, but then he got angry with me. He said it would be the death of us both and I must not come back. He was very hard with me and said love was an illusion anyway, and I would grow out of it. He said I had a duty, and even if my husband was not there my duty was to my son. I was angry with him and told him I knew that he loved me. I told him it was his son I wanted to bear. I wanted to look into his blue eyes and watch him grow up and be a warrior too.

'I left but I soon returned. I had to see him. It seemed as if a fire had taken hold of me and was burning inside me and nothing could quench it. I said we should flee from Abha and start a new life in another place. It would be far away in the north and we would make a house together and I would have not just one son but many. We would live for each other and our love would never cease.

'Ullobi had a far-away look on his face, and I could see I was persuading him to share my dream. He seized my fingers and pressed them to his eyes, which were wet with tears. He did not tell me to go any more but stopped resisting, and when he clutched me to him I knew I had captured his heart. We swore to each other that what we had found we would never lose, then tears flowed and our lovemaking started again.

'In my new freedom I was as strong as he was. Afterwards it was like a dream we had shared, and we just lay there; time did not move. He poured out his soul to me; his fount of love had been empty and now was full. For me it was just the same and was what my life had been created for. Now I would be happy in eternity even if it should come soon. This madness of the heart, it was as though we were ruled by a force outside our own beings.

'Eventually Etza made me come to my senses, and after a while our lives seemed to return to normal, or at least outwardly. But the damage had been done. All the time Ullobi had been in my harem Nura's spies were watching us, and they followed every movement I made. She knew that I was pregnant even before I knew myself.'

# Chapter 33

'TIMES WERE UNEASY at Abha, for since Sheikh Tabarhla was confined to Sheikha Ayesha's harem there was in effect no Amir. The Ahl Yazid accepted Abdullah acting in his place, and he dispensed justice at the daily *majlis*, which was now held at the Manadhir once more. They did not object, when Abdullah was absent dealing with outlying tribes, that Ullobi should do so instead. Both the Ahl Yazid and the people loved Ullobi and never questioned his judgements, even if there was blood money to be paid.

'But trouble lay ahead. White turbans began to be seen at Abha and the market and the caravanserai emptied as people locked themselves in their houses, mindful of the punishments the Ikhwan would inflict on them. Little did we guess that the arrival of the *ulemas* was the work of Nura, who had sent them word that Ullobi presided at the *majlis* – in other words, that a *nasara* was ruling at Abha.

'The Ikhwan laid a trap. At first their *ulemas* withdrew from Abha to make the people believe that danger had passed, for they well knew their effect on citizens everywhere. Then they bribed a small tribe from the mountains whom they knew to be enemies of the Beni Mughe'id, since the two tribes stole camels from each other, and paid them to carry out a cattle raid. They waited until Abdullah was not there and placed a force of Ihkwan warriors out of view. They knew that Ullobi would react and would ride out to retrieve the stolen camels.

'On this occasion I managed to conceal myself in his *ghazzu* as I often did. It was easy, because the warriors thought it amusing that a woman should dress up and fight as a man, for they were young and didn't have the same outlook as the older ones. We decided that such cattle thieves were not worth bullets and planned to use our swords on them. Ullobi guessed that I was there for he knew my habit of joining the *ghazzu*.

'The tribe had stolen the camels near the Bab el Shastri, and we were surprised at their daring for never before had they come so close to Abha. We easily retrieved the camels and for good measure took some of theirs, but suddenly we were confronted by twenty or thirty *mutair*, the Ihkwan's most dependable warriors. At that moment we were in the hands of God and God was angry at what I had done. He decided I must pay a price for my sin.

'Ullobi was unflustered. He looked around and rode to where I was. "We'll deal with this little lot," he said, "but you must go because if the Ihkwan find you they will stone you. Go quickly and ride anywhere. When I have finished I will follow your tracks and see you are safe."

'I saw that the Beni Mughe'id were much outnumbered, although I knew the *ghazzu* would fight to the death. Nonetheless, I feared it might be the last time I saw Ullobi. If he was going to die I wanted to die with him and I hesitated. He screamed at me in fury. "Go now. In the name of God, go!"

'It was my horse that decided it, for she had a sixth sense of danger and knew what was best. We galloped until dusk and then halfway through the night. By dawn we must have gone fifty or a hundred miles. I had bitter regrets at leaving but I was pregnant and told myself that it must be God's will that the child I would bear be saved. Finally, I reached Hali, which I remembered was where I was born and grew up, and came to this cave, which had belonged to my father, who was ruler. I had known it in my childhood because for me and my brothers it was our very own secret place. Here I gave birth to Isis and with my teeth I cut the cord that bound her to me, but God was angry with me as I knew He should be, and His vengeance was not yet finished. The very moment that Isis was born He struck her deaf and dumb. This was to be my punishment and it is what Isis has to endure in my place whilst I, her mother, look into her eyes and never forget the reason why she is afflicted so. It is Ullobi who sustains me, he has been with me every minute night and day that I have been here.'

'I do not understand why it is that you have to lead such solitary life. Surely the people of Hali would have rejoiced when they knew you had returned after so many years.'

'They would have forgotten me. Even if they had remembered I would not have dared to show myself because of the Ihkwan. As everyone knows, they have a long arm and after Nura told them what she knew they would never have stopped until they found me. They would have sworn to kill me. At Abha the people would know that I was not killed and must have escaped. They may have wondered what became of me but in any case they would have preferred to remain in ignorance of where I might be, in case someone might betray me.'

'I can assure you that when I asked them about you at Abha the people would say nothing at all, only that there had been a warrior sheikha called Na'ema. They did relate the story of the *markab*; in fact they wouldn't stop talking about it. I asked them about my father but again they would say nothing. I could never understand why this was, but now I realise that they were pretending ignorance in order to protect you.'

'Bless them for their good sense. The Beni Mughe'id were intensely loyal and whatever they knew about either of us they would have hidden. Besides, to the people of Abha you were a stranger. You may have told them that you were the son of Ullobi but you do not look like him and they might have thought you were a spy. They know very well that the Ihkwan never give up and would not cease until they had hunted me down. Indeed, soon after I came here, two of their *ulemas* rode out from Hali searching the coastline. They had the impudence to wear the green sashes of the Wahhabis, which was never allowed after the Ihkwan massacred the people of Taif. This was ordered by ibn Saud himself.'

I returned to the present. 'But although you live in such isolation you have means to survive?'

'At Hali in the old days we always lived off the sea. It was our way of life and so I am used to it, and there are other means.'

'There don't seem to be any fishing boats at Hali.'

'There aren't because no one would dare to go out fishing for fear of the pirates. In the spring and autumn there are great shoals of fish which are driven into the shallows by larger fish hunting them and all the people come out to catch them in nets that stretch for miles. Then they salt them and dry them and store them so that they last the season. They are called *chanad*, and I still find them if I go to the market. I go dressed as a Bedu woman but not more often than I have to. I prefer to collect the clams and oysters on the shore, and we search for the sea birds' eggs and sometimes catch the chicks before they fly. My father always had oil and rice and fuel stored here, and riyals too, because he was worried that our castle was so close to the edge of the sea that it might be raided by Somalis, which I am afraid is what happened. Everything was a secret and only the family knew about the cave. As you can see God may have given us the sea but He also sent us pirates.'

'Surely the loneliness must be very hard to bear.'

'It is, but I have learned to bear it. I have Isis. First we used signs but now I have taught her words and we can talk to each other by writing in the sand. We have our spinning wheel and I have taught her to spin goat hair and we weave the cloth for our garments. I have the Quran which we always kept here, and I read it and teach it to Isis by writing it on the sand, and now she knows much of it by heart. Then I have Ullobi, my true husband, who sacrificed everything for me. I live for him and feel his presence always, so I am never alone.'

'Tell me why Etza sent you the medallion. I'm sure she wanted me to find you so that I could give it to you, although she would not say so. It seemed to me it must carry some message.'

'Certainly it did carry a message. It told me that after Ullobi died Etza found him and buried him. That's what I needed to know more than any other thing. Now I am sure that Ullobi had a proper burial and has his own resting place I know that we shall meet again in paradise and be together always. The *zarar* is the most precious object I could imagine and I never believed that I would possess it. I shall carry it always and it shall be about my neck when I die. This is something that Isis understands, she who carries my burden of sin all her days.'

'It is a burden that she seems to carry very lightly. She's always smiling.'

'It's true. She lives for the day and is blessed with happiness. She is the light of my life. And I depend upon her, for it is she who goes to Hali to buy what we need when I do not dare to go myself. Isis is the best bargainer that ever was and she has the market sellers in the palm of her hand because she uses her deafness as a weapon. When they say a price she pretends that she doesn't understand, picks up her stick and starts to walk away, which flusters them.'

'Her stick?'

'Her stick is her way of speaking, and she uses it for bargaining. The stall-holder knows that she's deaf so he has to write his price in the sand, then she writes hers. After that she is so stubborn it can go on all day. But the merchants in the market love her dearly and the last thing that they want is for her to walk away. They know that she is not from Hali but don't know where she does come from. They believe, and I'm being quite serious, that she is a messenger from God. They obey her because they think that they don't have any choice, and this gives her great power, which she is fully aware of and uses ruthlessly. She has been going to Hali since she was six years old, and now she's eleven. She appears older than her years because responsibilities have made her grow up quickly, and so has the hardship of our life. I have told her of my sickness and when the time comes she will know what to do.'

'Will she remain here in the cave?'

'God will take care of her. Many times He has promised me that He will provide for her. Now that I have told you these things it brings me much relief. God has spoken. He has made me tell you everything that happened. The guilt of my sin, which has been a great burden for me to bear, is lifted for the first time.'

She smiled, the only time I had seen her do so. It was a smile that lingered on her face, full of a beatitude that emerged from her soul. She had found her redemption at last. I was persuaded that my own voyage of discovery had after all been of a certain value, and that my search for truth had served a purpose of its own, even if rather different from what I had expected.

*

As I rode back to Hali I felt elated at this final revelation of all the secrets which had been so carefully hidden from me until this moment. But soon the glow of success evaporated as I became increasingly aware that the three of us stood at the edge of an abyss. Even great resourcefulness would not be able to sustain the solitary survivor, whatever holy dispensations had been offered. It was obvious now that no plan had been made for the care of Isis; indeed, so feckless are the Arab peoples in such matters that I realise it would have been foolish to expect any. No doubt Na'ema had earned the solace she gained from her unquestioning faith, but I found myself preoccupied by the problem of Isis and in particular what would happen when Na'ema died. In these parts there is vociferous keening by the womenfolk which lasts for three days and renders them distracted and incommunicable. It is a ritual, and no doubt this release of emotion is what allows them to resume normal life, which they do immediately the days of mourning have passed; but clearly this could not happen in this case because there was no normal life for Isis to return to. I was at hand to help, but I feared that I might be the unwitting cause of some interference at this vital moment.

*

Next day, I arrived after the sun had risen. The dolmen stood open and the cave was filled with morning light. Na'ema was sitting upright on the stone bench that was her bed just as she had been when I had left the day before, motionless now but for her eyes which followed me as I went down the steps and crossed the floor of the cave. She was quite changed from the Na'ema I had last seen and evidently was resigned to her impending death. Her seraphic smile remained.

When she spoke her voice was weak and words came haltingly. 'I prayed that you would come. I feared that it might be too late. I wanted you to know that in His great mercy God has granted me forgiveness. I have had a vision of His splendour and when I journey to His Kingdom I shall be embraced by His love. He will love me for what I am. I am full of wonder that you have searched and found me and brought me this happiness.' Here she stopped and the next minutes passed in silence.

When she spoke again she rambled incoherently, about her past life, her death and how it would lead her to Ullobi. Her voice grew weaker until only her lips were moving. Her eyes were open very wide, but not in fear, and seemed no longer to focus on anything. I stood in awe at what I was seeing, then bent and kissed Na'ema's forehead. After a time her breathing became laboured and was the only sound to be heard in the cave. Finally it faded and no sound broke the eerie stillness.

# Chapter 34

AN HOUR PASSED. I remained rooted to the spot, transfixed by Na'ema's staring eyes. During that time I was not my own person but in some strange way I was hers.

I was restored to my normal senses by the sound of footsteps as Isis came down the stairway, leading the goat. It was the moment I had dreaded and was now least prepared for, but I need not have worried. Isis took in the situation at a glance and hesitated, her face showing no emotion, then continued until she reached the bottom of the stairway. For a while she stood there and silence filled the cave, broken only by the sound of the goat's chewing. It was not what I had expected.

But then I realised that I had quite forgotten that Isis was dumb, and whatever her anguish she could not express it. In any case, nothing happened as I had expected, for in that moment she became the complete mistress of the situation. With a tiny gesture towards the dolmen she handed me the goat's rope.

I knew exactly what she intended. I took the rope and led the goat up the steps and to the pasture where I had left Dukhaala, and waited whilst Isis performed her task. Clearly such a ritual would not be hurried, and I allowed the rest of the morning to pass before I decided to return to the cave with the goat. Na'ema lay on her stone bed, now bare of its covers, in the straw-coloured linen shroud that she had woven for this moment, with the *zarar* about her neck. Her eyes were not closed, and Isis sat at her side, tenderly painting her hands and feet in fanciful designs of dots of red and black henna, so absorbed in this task that she did not appear to notice I was there. Another hour passed whilst Isis continued her handiwork, until she was satisfied that Na'ema was suitably prepared for entry into her new life.

When all had been done, she rose and picked up one of the stones from the collection that had been prepared in readiness for this event, and offered it to me. I lifted Na'ema and placed her in the hollow of the wall that had been excavated as a sepulchre, and laid her on her side so that she faced Mecca. I drew up the *zarar* and placed it against her cheek, then picked up the stones one by one and built a wall which sealed Na'ema into her tomb, all the while watched by Isis, impassive and motionless.

When all was done we stood back and surveyed the scene. It was our last salute to Na'ema as she began her final journey. The cave seemed to close about her and in that moment it was no longer a cave but a mighty pyramid, sealing and enfolding Na'ema for ever, where none might find or disturb her. Together we climbed the stairway, and Isis tied up the goat outside whilst I closed the dolmen, moving it until it was tightly closed. Then I heaped against it the largest stones I could find. By the time it was finished, it was impossible to tell that an entrance had been there and Na'ema had a tomb as secret as any Pharaoh's. A great grief descended upon us, but then I received a precious gift, for Isis smiled. It was as though in our shared hardship she was smiling encouragement to me. I was amazed, and remain incredulous to this day that one so young could have been so much the mistress of a situation which must have been the most terrifying of her life.

\*

For the first time I felt weak, my mind drained by the events of the day, but now another moment of truth was at hand, and this concerned Isis. It was hard to see how there could not be a parting of our ways. I was sure that at Hali she must have friends whom she had made in the market and who would look after her, and at this moment it seemed most natural that her future lay at Hali since it was the only place she knew. She would not be an abandoned waif there, for they believed that she was a messenger from God. Besides, in Arabia generosity towards orphans is part of the religion, commanded by the Quran, and therefore it is limitless because it is believed that such bounty will be rewarded in heaven.

At first this was reassuring, but then I had to remind myself that it was only speculation, and the more important matter was what Isis wanted for herself. It must have been a subject of much discussion between Isis and her mother, even if I myself had not given it enough thought. Yet why had Na'ema not instructed me, she who had planned every detail of her death?

We left the cave and walked to the pasture where Dukhaala was grazing, and I made a slow business of adjusting her halter and sorting out my saddle-bags in order to put off the fateful moment of parting. All the time I was watched by a pair of blue eyes until my heart strings were stretched to the point where I could hear them sing. Was it for such a moment as this that I had come to Arabia, this place of destiny for me, where in all that had happened I had found so many of my own bearings in life? Now I beheld someone who at this moment was searching for hers, just as once I had for mine, and she was even my own flesh and blood. I was suddenly aware that it was not just Na'ema that I had searched for and found, but, had I known it, someone who was equally precious. At that moment I knew in my heart that I could not leave her.

I picked up my riding stick and wrote a sentence in the sand: 'You are my sister. I will care for you as my sister.' I did so on impulse, without knowing what I properly meant, or having any idea of what this would mean in practical terms. Isis examined what I had written and several minutes passed. I looked at her face but it bore no expression that I could determine, and at that moment the future seemed to hang in the balance, as though at the very point of parturition. But then my expectancy turned to anguish, for Isis turned and slowly started to make her way back to the cave. It was her home and the only one that she had ever known, and even though it was sealed I should have realised that she would not leave it. I watched as her figure diminished until finally she reached the dolmen, where she paused. But there was something that we had both forgotten in the tension of the moment, which was the goat. Isis untied its rope, then turned and led it back to where I waited, astride Dukhaala's back. Deftly she tied the goat to Dukhaala's tail, then came and took my hand. I lifted her, or she jumped, and perhaps in some way Dukhaala herself assisted, for she landed behind me on Dukhaala's rump and I felt two small arms encircle my waist.

*

My mission in Arabia was complete. With this event an era seemed to have passed and by the next day another had begun to dawn. It was the beginning of spring, which at Hali, provided that no sand-laden winds were sweeping through it, held blessings that no other place on the Red Sea shared; no doubt this accounted for its popularity both with its tribe and its pirates. The change in the season could be sensed as wild creatures stirred in the warm air, and in the market, too, where there were camels and donkeys laden with lucerne and other greenery.

I had made the decision to return to my original base, the port of Jeddah, and for this we would need provisions. The market at Hali was a *khamis mishait*, which is to say that it was held on a Thursday, and for this privilege the town paid its dues, nowadays to the Saudi Amir in Riyadh. It was Thursday in theory only, for in practice the merchants discreetly opened their shops and stalls on every day of the week except Friday. Usually, when I had travelled alone, I had bought only necessities, but now that there were two of us some catering was required. I shrank from the prospect but then I had the bright idea of leaving everything to Isis. So I set her down in the market, gave her my purse, which contained not all the money that I possessed but a sizeable part of it, and signed to her to buy food for our three-day journey. Rather more days if we took the goat. However, Isis evidently had her own ideas about the goat, for as she dismounted she untied it from Dukhaala's tail and disappeared into the market, trailing the goat behind her.

I now had a mission of my own. A telegraph had recently been installed at Hali which enabled me to communicate with Cairo directly, and so I cabled the Locust Bureau. I explained that my survey of the As'ir was complete and that I would present my findings in person on my return, together with the file of my predecessor, Bridgewater. For their encouragement I added that I had found no locust swarms in the northern parts of Yemen, which I had succeeded in surveying in spite of much difficulty. I explained that I intended to return to England and so was resigning my post. I cabled The Naval Bureau separately, reminding them of their offer of assistance if I needed it, and said this was now the case. I told them that I was on my way to Jeddah and intended to go to Cairo and then return to England, and needed transport for two persons and a horse, provided a suitable vessel could be diverted to Jeddah. I gave the code number of the telegraph station there in case they did not have it, and said a silent prayer.

After this I returned to the market, where I found Isis was waiting for me, and noted with relief that she was no longer leading the goat. For that matter she was not carrying anything at all, but a little way behind her came a negro porter bearing a great weight of goods which looked to be sufficient for weeks rather than days. Somehow, these were put into the saddle-bags, and when all had been stowed the burly negro bowed and then embraced Isis. It was evident that he was bidding her farewell from the whole market, and as he turned to leave there were tears in his eyes.

I wondered if so many purchases might have been expensive, but at this point Isis reached into the recesses of her *thaub* and drew out the purse I had given her, which remained untouched. Next, she produced another purse, and one by one counted out twenty riyals, then placed her hands on the top of her head in imitation of the horns of a goat. Either the goat was more valuable than I had thought or else this was further evidence of Isis' powers of bartering, or of being the messenger of God.

The next day we set off for Jeddah to await the response from the Naval Bureau. The workings of the Royal Navy would, I knew, be reliable although they might be slow; however, I had great faith in them and well knew that I had merited their services. I found lodgings for us both at the old British arsenal and an alarming number of days went by before finally there came a reply: 'HM Corvette Perseus, Cdr. Norrington, returning from China station will refuel at Jeddah in approx six weeks. Will call at Port Said, Malta, Gibraltar and Plymouth. Have requested the Captain to give you every assistance.' I blessed the Naval Bureau – how could I have doubted them? But then, as Isis reminded me, all the praise be to God.

My thoughts turned to England, where it would be April or May and the time of bluebells. I would go home to greening Oxfordshire and to our house at Crowmarsh Battle. The arrival of Isis would be sure to cause no little confusion in the Willoughby household, but I figured that my grandfather Sir Hugh, if still alive, would be my ally, and even if Lady Parthenope expressed some surprise I knew that in the end she could be depended upon to follow where Sir Hugh led.

Just how my mother Lavender would receive this unexpected addition to our family was a matter of conjecture, but then I remembered that she had always prayed for a daughter, and now after all she would have one; besides, she was ever my father's fond spouse even if a neglected one. The rector at Benson church could be expected to express stern views on the irregularities of his one-time parishioner and would no doubt draw useful material for his Sunday sermon from this latter-day story of Naomi and her daughter. The ladies of the sisterhood, who would be gathered afterwards as accustomed, would certainly want to have their say. They would declare to each other that they had always said that something like this would happen, although some, recalling their girlhood, might be anxious to discover what had become of the gallant lieutenant from Crowmarsh Battle.

However, when at length the scandal had been savoured in all its particulars, and they had surveyed Isis herself, I knew their hearts would soften, and then, I was sure, the sisterhood of Benson would know just what should be done.

*

*I knew that one day you would come, my son, and I am grieved I am not there. I know that you will be disappointed. I want you to greet Lavender for me and care for her, for I fear that I did not serve her well. It was the same when you were young: I was not there. But a man must follow his destiny.*

*From the first moment, I knew that mine was Arabia.*

*In the main I lie content, yet there is a matter which disturbs my peace. You see, I think I fathered a son, or perhaps a daughter. I do not know which, for it happened at a time when I could not be there.*

*Now that you know my secret, my son, I want you to find and look after this person, who is dear to me. I pray that this may find you in good health.*

# Afterword

THE PROVINCE CALLED As'ir is the part of south-western Arabia, bordered by the Hejaz to the north, where Mecca lies, and Yemen to the south. Its fertile coastal plain beside the Red Sea is known as the Tihama, while its centre is in the mountains and on the eastern side *wadis* carry the run-off from the winter rains into the central desert. The tribal areas, or *dirahs*, tend to be small and sharply delineated, especially in the mountain regions. At the time of the story As'ir was largely hidden from the world and there is no record left by travellers, nor did any of the famous explorers of Arabia penetrate this province. However, it was known in Roman times, especially to the younger Pliny who wrote of Arabia Felix contrasting it with Arabia Desert, the central sands.

Abha itself always had importance since it lay on the caravan route that connected the Hejaz and Mecca with the southern ports of Arabia whence the pilgrims and the spices came. Its ruling family was called the bin Tahir, meaning the sons of Tahir, who provided the Amirs in the three generations described in my story: Zeid bin Tahir, the family's venerable tyrant; his son Tabarhla with his three wives, Ayesha, Na'ema and Nura; and the eventual successor, Ayesha's son Abdullah. The bin Tahir would have been typical of their time although they are not historical. Their tribal rule lasted until the fall of Abha in 1921 to Abdulaziz ibn Saud, the rising asheukh or overlord of the Saudi tribe whose city is Riyadh in the Nejd, one of the eastern provinces of Arabia.

The achievements of this great warrior who eventually became king of what he renamed Saudi Arabia are legendary although outside the compass of this book. His was the first unification of Arabia in the history of the peninsula and began from virtually nothing. A tribe called the Rashid from Hali had captured Riyadh ten years earlier and the ibn Saud family had been driven into exile in Kuwait. In the year 1901 a younger son, Abdulaziz ibn Saud, then aged twenty-one, vowed to retrieve Riyadh or perish in the attempt. Together with forty followers, he secreted this tiny force over winter in the deserted Empty Quarter or Rub el Khali, and in the spring emerged by stealth to storm Riyadh and kill the Rashid governor with his entire garrison. The story of this endeavour is one of the greatest feats of arms in recorded history.

During the thirty years that followed, Abdulaziz ibn Saud successfully defended Riyadh and steadily forced into submission each of the great tribes of Arabia in turn, including the Ateiba and the Ajman led by Faisal al Dawish, Arabia's most famous warrior of the day. In all, ibn Saud fought more than thirty major battles and never suffered a defeat. The principal Sheikh of each tribe was pardoned, made to swear fealty, restored to his position and, finally, for good measure, Abdulaziz, having divorced one of his four wives in advance, usually married one of the daughters of the Sheikh. Such was his success that by 1931 he had eliminated every rival and at this point, with control of the pilgrimage, he took the title of Sultan of Nejd and Sheriff of Mecca, later advancing himself to King of Arabia, the first king that Arabia ever had. Only the Gulf States and Yemen retained their independence. The Hashemites, who ten years earlier had been supported in the Desert War against the Turks by the British under Lawrence of Arabia, were banished.

Abdulaziz ibn Saud deserves his place as one of the great men of history, an Alfred the Great of his time. He lived to the age of seventy-three and bore countless offspring. He gave the first concession to drill for oil, then became deeply saddened by the changes that followed as the huge and sudden wealth brought with it the destruction of the old Arab customs, as well as its unique and wonderful tribal culture. As'ir itself is now a backwater of history and Abha is a base of the Saudi Air Force.

A word needs to be said about the Ihkwan who played a vital role in the earlier part of ibn Saud's rise to power. The family of ibn Saud were the hereditary Imams of Wahhabism, a puritan form of Sunni Islamic faith that arose in the eighteenth century. In consequence Abdulaziz was able to form settlements of warriors which became his fighting force and which were known as the Ihkwan. Eventually their overbearing fanaticism led them to terrorise much of Arabia, and amongst other excesses they were responsible for the massacre of the inhabitants of Taif, a city near Mecca. From that time the Ihkwan spread like a forest fire. They crossed the border into Mesopotamia (Iraq), at that time a British Protectorate, where they were bombed into submission by the RAF after much diplomacy between ibn Saud and the British Resident at Basra. The Saudis themselves, who might otherwise have been driven out of Arabia by Faisal al Dawish the paramount chief of the Mutair, were saved, although Wahhabi fundamentalism never completely disappeared. Some idea of its strength may be gauged by the fact that at its height sixty-seven Ihkwan settlements had been formed in central Arabia by the Ateiba and the Mutair alone. It is surprising that so important a passage of history is not better known in the West.

A NOTE ON THE TYPE

The text of this book is set in Adobe Caslon, named after
the English punch-cutter and type-founder William
Caslon I (1692–1766). Caslon's rather old-fashioned types
were modelled on seventeenth-century Dutch designs, but
found wide acceptance throughout the English-speaking
world for much of the eighteenth century until being
replaced by newer types towards the end of the century.
Used in 1776 to print the Declaration of Independence,
they were revived in the nineteenth century, and have been
popular ever since, particularly amongst fine printers. There
are several digital versions, of which Carol Twombly's
Adobe Caslon is one.